Modern Critical Views

Maya Angelou
Asian-American Writers
Jane Austen
James Baldwin
Samuel Beckett
William Blake
The Brontës
Robert Browning
Albert Camus
Lewis Carroll
Willa Cather
Geoffrey Chaucer
Anton Chekhov
Kate Chopin
Samuel Taylor Coleridge
Joseph Conrad
Stephen Crane
Dante
Charles Dickens
Emily Dickinson
John Donne & the
    17th-Century Poets
Fyodor Dostoevsky
T. S. Eliot
Ralph Ellison
Ralph Waldo Emerson
William Faulkner
F. Scott Fitzgerald
Sigmund Freud
Robert Frost
George Gordon, Lord Byron
Thomas Hardy
Nathaniel Hawthorne
Ernest Hemingway
Hispanic-American Writers
Homer
Langston Hughes
Zora Neale Hurston
Henrik Ibsen
Henry James
James Joyce
Franz Kafka
John Keats

Stephen King
Jamaica Kincaid
D. H. Lawrence
Sinclair Lewis
Gabriel García Márquez
Carson McCullers
Herman Melville
Arthur Miller
Marianne Moore
Toni Morrison
Iris Murdoch
Native-American Writers
Joyce Carol Oates
Flannery O'Connor
Eugene O'Neill
George Orwell
Sylvia Plath
Edgar Allan Poe
Contemporary Poets
J. D. Salinger
William Shakespeare–
    Comedies
William Shakespeare–
    Histories & Poems
William Shakespeare–
    Tragedies
George Bernard Shaw
Mary Wollstonecraft Shelley
Percy Bysshe Shelley
Sophocles
John Steinbeck
Henry David Thoreau
Mark Twain
John Updike
Alice Walker
Eudora Welty
Edith Wharton
Walt Whitman
Tennessee Williams
Virginia Woolf
William Wordsworth
Richard Wright
William Butler Yeats

Modern Critical Views

HISPANIC-AMERICAN WRITERS

Edited and with an introduction by
Harold Bloom
Sterling Professor of the Humanities
Yale University

CHELSEA HOUSE PUBLISHERS
Philadelphia

© 1998 by Chelsea House Publishers, a division of
Main Line Book Co.

Introduction © 1998 by Harold Bloom

Printed and bound in the United States of America

10 9 8 7 6 5 4 3 2

∞ The paper used in this publication meets the minimum
requirements of the American National Standard for
Permanence of Paper for Printed Library Materials,
Z39.48-1984

Library of Congress Cataloging-in-Publication Data

Hispanic American writers / edited and with an introduction
    by Harold Bloom.
        p.   cm.—(Modern critical views)
    Includes bibliographical references and index.
    ISBN 0-7910-4786-5 (hc)
    1. American literature—Hispanic American authors—
History and criticism.   2. Hispanic Americans in literature.
I. Bloom, Harold.   II. Series.
PS153.H56H56 1998
810.9'868—dc21   97-53071
                                                          CIP

Contents

Editor's Note

My Introduction considers the problem of poetic influence in regard to Chicano poetry's relationship to Mexican poetry, centering upon Américo Paredes' study *With His Pistol in His Hand: A Border Ballad and Its Hero* (1958, 1971).

Jane Rogers begins the sequence of critical essays with her brief consideration of Rudolfo A. Anaya's *Bless Me, Ultima*, where she explores the myth of *la llorona*, the lonely goddess of the river valley. Ron Arias' *The Road to Tamazunchale* is praised by Eliud Martínez as contributing to a new sense of contemporary reality in the Chicano novel.

Oscar Zeta Acosta's novels are viewed as narratives of social protest by Norman D. Smith, while Luther S. Luedtke analyzes José Antonio Villarreal's novel, *Pocho* (1959) as an inaugural work of Chicano fiction.

Nasario García meditates upon three categories of time in Orlando Romero's *Nambé—Year One*, after which Eduardo Seda Bonilla reflects upon Puerto Rican dilemmas in Pedro Juan Soto's *Hot Land, Cold Season*.

Vernon E. Lattin also reflects upon ideas of time, in his study of Nash Candelaria's *Memories of the Alhambra*, while Marta E. Sánchez describes Bernice Zamora's poetry of sexual conflict.

Rudolfo A. Anaya's *Tortuga* is seen by Edward Elías as a hopeful narrative of rebirth, after which Tomás Rivera studies the humanistic essays of Richard Rodriguez.

The fiction of Fray Angelico Chavez is defended by Genaro M. Padilla, while Marvin A. Lewis analyzes the narrative technique of Aristeo Brito's *El diablo en Texas*.

Tomás Rivera's stories receive a temporal study by Alfonso Rodríguez, after which Zora Neale Huston's sense of community is contrasted to that of Rolando Hinojosa by Heiner Bus.

Rudolfo Anaya receives further consideration as a mythic writer by

Enrique Lamadrid, while Erlinda Gonzales-Berry proposes works by Vicente Bernal and Felipe Maximiliano Chacón as being appropriate for a new canon.

Alvina E. Quintana finds the ethnographic impulse in Ana Castillo, after which Monika Kaup concludes this volume with an appraisal of the aesthetic *praxis* of Gloria Anzaldúa.

Introduction

Chicano poetry, more even than the Mexican-American novel, is still in a very early phase, and merits considerable encouragement. Unfortunately, in the current cultural climate of the United States, Hispanic American writers are subject to many of the same hazards that afflict the better African American and other "multicultural" literary endeavors. Overpraise, generally allied to ideological enterprises, emanates endlessly from our resentful academics and journalists alike. Perhaps two generations will have to pass before Chicano literature (or Puerto Rican writing in English) will be judged by authentic cognitive and aesthetic standards. Myself Bloom Brontosaurus, the academic dinosaur, I am well aware that I can no more intrude traditional canonical considerations than I can intervene helpfully in any of our current multicultural contexts. This Introduction therfore in no way contests or quarrels with the critical judgments reprinted in this volume. Rather, I wish only to raise the problem of influence and its anxieties in regard to the Mexican and Chicano *corrida*, the border ballad. As my primary text I will take Américo Paredes' *With His Pistol in His Hand: A Border Ballad and Its Hero* (1958, 1971). Paredes tells us that:

> *Corrida*, the Mexicans call their narrative folk songs, especially those of epic themes, taking the name from *correr*, which means "to run" or "to flow" for the *corrida* tells a story simply and swiftly without embellishments.

Paredes and his work, both as scholar and as poet, have been praised by José E. Limón, in his *Mexican Ballads, Chicano Poems: History and Influence in Mexican-American Social Poetry* (1992). Very much an academic of our moment, Limón's critical heroes in this book—besides Paredes himself—are the Marxists Raymond Williams and Fredric Jameson. The critical villian is the aesthete Harold Bloom, whose books on poetic influence are severely

1

chastised by Limón for their palpable ignorance of "the sociopolitical realm." Having acknowledged that I am Limón's devil to Paredes' angel, I shall not venture to defend myself, but instead shall question both Paredes and Limón as to their shared argument, which is that the influence of the *corrida* produced a strong poetry in English in the work of Paredes himself and in that of political Chicano poetry of the 1960's and 70's composed by Jose Montoya, Rudolfo Gonzales, and Juan Gomez-Quinones.

Paredes, in his study of the Mexican border ballad, emphasizes the continuous strength of an oral tradition that goes back to the border conflicts of the 1860's. Limón, after comparing Paredes' own poetry to the *corrida* argues that *With His Pistol in His Hand*, Paredes' study of the *corrida*, is actually a "strong sociological poem," rewriting the ballads in a true Return of the Dead. By the same logic, Limón's *Mexican Ballads, Chicano Poems* is a strong misreading of Paredes, a process that could continue indefinitely. In such a continuity, poetry perpetually dims and politics grows more and more intense. The Chicano movement, admirable from the perspective of any striving for social justice, is no more an inevitable source of poetic strength than is any other protest against injustice. The English-language ballads that Limón quotes are very sincere but, as Oscar Wilde observed, all bad poetry is sincere. I refrain from quoting any excerpts or texts praised by Limón, because they cannot bear quotation. The heroic *corrida* of the oral tradition frequently had a rough vigor; its imitations are strident, and poetically self-defeating. If Chicano poetry is to survive its own Mexican heritage, then the poets will have to go beyond the constraints and repetitions of politics. Ideology at best can produce period-pieces, not poems.

JANE ROGERS

The Function of the La Llorona Motif in
Anaya's Bless Me, Ultima

In *The Odyssey*, Circe warns the homeward-bound Odysseus of the menace of the Sirens, who, surrounded by the mouldering skeletons of men, lure and bewitch the unaware man with the music of their song. Yet just beyond their lovely voices—which Odysseus escapes by having himself lashed to the mast of his ship—lurks peril, a choice between annihilation on the sheer cliffs of the Wandering Rocks or a meeting with the double menace of Scylla and Charybdis, the former hideously fishing for a passerby with her twelve dangling feet, the latter but a bow's shot distance away threatening to suck men down into the deep waters near the foot of a luxurious fig tree. Certain death is the fate of the man who succumbs to the sweet lure of the sirens. The peril of life, and yet the promise of home, is the alternative.

A similar theme is developed by Rudolfo Anaya's use of the *la llorona* motif in *Bless Me, Ultima*. In the novel, Antonio, symbolically both Christ and Odysseus, moves from the security and from the sweet-smelling warmth of his mother's bosom and kitchen out into life and experience. As he weighs his options—priesthood and the confinement represented by the farms of the Lunas', or the Márezes' freedom on the pagan sea of the llano —and as he grows from innocence to knowledge and experience, the *la llorona* motif figures both on a literal mythological level and as an integral part of Antonio's life.

As "literal" myth, *la llorona* is the wailing woman of the river. Hers is the "tormented cry of a lonely goddess" that fills the valley in one of Antonio's

From *Contemporary Chicano Fiction: A Critical Survey.* © 1986 by *Bilingual Press/Editorial Bilingüe.*

dreams. *La llorona* is "the old witch who cries along the river banks and seeks the blood of boys and men to drink." This myth is closely related to Cico's story of the mermaid. The mermaid is the powerful presence in the bottomless Hidden Lakes. Her strange music is a "low, lonely murmuring . . . like something a sad girl would sing" (p. 109). Cico relates that all that had kept him from plunging into the bottomless lake when he heard the sound was the Golden Carp, whose appearance caused the music to stop. Not that the singing was evil, he relates, but "it called for me to join it. One more step and I'da stepped over the ledge and drowned in the waters of the lake—" (p. 109). Cico continues with the story of the shepherd taken by the mermaid. A "man from Méjico," working on a neighboring ranch, not having heard the story about the lakes, had taken his sheep to water there. Hearing the singing, he ran back to town and swore he had seen a mermaid.

> He said it was a woman, resting on the water and singing a lonely song. She was half woman and half fish—He said the song made him want to wade out to the middle of the lake to help her, but his fear had made him run. He told everyone the story, but no one believed him. He ended up getting drunk in town and swearing he would prove his story by going back to the lakes and bringing back the mer-woman. He never returned. A week later the flock was found near the lakes. He had vanished—. (p. 109)

As an integral part of Antonio's life, the *la llorona* motif emerges in his experiences with nature. *La llorona* is the ambivalent presence of the river, which Antonio fears and yet with which he senses a sharing of his own soul and a mystic peace. *La llorona* speaks in the owl's cry and in the dove's cou-rou. Even the dust devils of the llano bear *la llorona*'s signature, embracing Antonio in swirling dust as the gushing wind, which imprints evil on his soul, seems to call his name:

Antonioooooooooooooooo . . . (p. 52)

But more significantly for Antonio, the *la llorona* motif emerges in his relationship with his mother and in the imagery of the women in the novel. It is the primary image associated with the mother, Maria. Her frequent extended calls of "Antonioooooooo," like that of the whirlwind, reflect the wailing call of the *llorona* of Tony's dream:

La llorona seeks the soul of Antonioooooooooo . . . (p. 24)

In the same dream, Tony hears his "mother moan and cry because with each turning of the sun her son [is] growing old . . ." (p. 24). On his first day of school Antonio awakens with a sick feeling in his stomach, both excited and sad because for the first time he will be away from the protection of his mother. As he enters the kitchen his mother smiles, then sweeps him into her arms sobbing, "My baby will be gone today" (p. 50). At Ultima's stern but gentle persistence, Antonio is separated from his mother, yet as he leaves, following the sisters Deborah and Theresa up the goat path, he hears his mother "cry" his name. Maria, as she prays around the Virgin's altar for Antonio and his three older brothers, is *la llorona*. On the return of Andrew, Eugene, and Leon from the war, Maria alternately sobs and prays until Gabriel complains, "Maria . . . but we have prayed all night!" (p. 58). Mother and Virgin both assume the mournful aspect of *la llorona* in one of Antonio's dreams just prior to the three brothers' return:

> Virgen de Guadalupe, I heard my mother cry, return my sons to me.
> Your sons will return safely, a gentle voice answered.
> Mother of God, make my fourth son a priest.
> And I saw the virgin draped in the gown of night standing on the bright, horned moon of autumn, and she was in mourning for the fourth son. (p 43)

Similarly, the *la llorona* motif is echoed in the tolling of the church bells and in the imagery of the mourning, lonely women as they are called to mass on the morning following Lupito's death. "Crying the knell of Lupito," the bell "tolled and drew to it the widows in black, the lonely, faithful women who came to pray for their men" (p. 32).

La llorona emerges in the patterns of imagery that surround the episode at Rosie's on the day of the Christmas pageant and of Narciso's death. The "single red light bulb" which shines at the porch door over the "snow-laden gate of the picket fence" is "like a beacon inviting weary travelers in from the storm." Light shines through the drawn shades, and from "somewhere in the house a faint melody" seeps out and is "lost in the wind." Antonio knows he must get home before the storm worsens, yet he is compelled to linger "at the gate of the evil women." The music and laughter intrigue him. His ears "explode with a ringing noise," and he is paralyzed to flight (p. 155). Instead, he must remain to learn that he himself has lost his innocence. The cry of the sirens prevails over Andrew, too, as the red-painted woman calls him from the back of the house:

Androoooooo. . . . (p 156)

When Andrew is summoned by Narciso, it is the giggling girl, her voice "sweet with allurement," that holds Andrew back. He fails to assume the responsibility that would have meant help for Narciso. Instead he succumbs to the allure of the siren.

Wherever it emerges in the novel, the *la llorona* motif harbors ambivalence. *La llorona* invites with music and warmth, and she offers security. Yet, like the mermaid in the hidden lakes, *la llorona* threatens death. For Antonio, his mother offers warmth, fragrance, security. But his own maturity demands that he deny it. To succumb would mean the death of his own manhood and—like the fate of William Blake's Thel, unwilling to accept the consequences of the generative life of experience—withdrawal to an original state of primal innocence. Yet this world holds an even darker fate because it becomes at once prison and paradise, a state of natural innocence and a state of ignorance. This is the choice Antonio must make. He moves from the fragrance and the warmth and the security of his mother's kitchen, from the reassurance of her call, out into the world of experience, the world of school and his companions.

Antonio is introduced into the inferno of school life by Red, who leads him on the first day into the dark, cavernous building, its radiators snapping with steam and its "strange, unfamiliar smells and sounds that seemed to gurgle from its belly" (p. 53). Antonio races the Kid and Time across the bridge to and from school as the years pass and he matures chronologically. With the tutoring of Samuel he learns of the Golden Carp which is to provide apocalyptical knowledge and understanding, an illumination which burdens him with doubt and responsibility. Cico leads Antonio to Narciso's magic garden where he tastes of the fruit—the golden carrot—and to El Rito Creek where he at last experiences the Golden Carp, the "sudden illumination of beauty and understanding," an understanding he anticipated but later failed to find in the ritual of the Holy Communion. Coincident with his vision of the carp, Antonio doubts his own Christian God when he suddenly realizes that Ultima's power had succeeded in curing his Uncle Lucas where the Christian God had failed.

Antonio sees the powers of good and evil contend in Ultima, who serves as his guide through life, and in the dark, diabolic Tenorio. He experiences the deaths of Lupito, of Narciso, and of the angelic and heretical Florence. He sees his brother Andrew deny his responsibility at the summons of the girl at Rosie's, of *la llorona*. Andrew remains to indulge in pleasure, yet the knowledge that he has failed in his responsibility to Narciso drives him, finally, away into the death, the world of lost wanderings, of his other brothers, Eugene and Leon.

The experience at Rosie's is equally ambivalent for Antonio. He is at once lured and repulsed. It marks for him the beginning of a ritual death as he becomes abruptly aware of his own loss of innocence.

> I had seen evil, and so l carried the evil within me. . . . I had somehow lost my innocence and let sin enter into my soul, and the knowledge of God, the saving grace, was far away. (p. 158)

The illness which follows is a "long night" as Ultima sits by, "powerless in the face of death."

> A long, dark night came upon me in which I sought the face of God, but I could not find Him. Even the Virgin and my Saint Anthony would not look at my face.
> . . . In front of the dark doors of Purgatory my bleached bones were laid to rest. (p. 167)

But, unlike Andrew's death, Antonio's experience at Rosie's becomes one that leads to death and ultimate rebirth. Antonio recovers from his illness, and though the events of the spring, of catechism and first communion, do not provide the enlightenment he finds with the carp, Antonio is a new man. His life has changed; he feels older. He faces directly the question of the existence of evil, and he is ready to accept his father's explanation that "most of the things we call evil are not evil at all; it is just that we don't understand those things and so we call them evil. And we fear evil only because we do not understand it" (p. 236). Antonio learns to accept the greater reality of life, that he is both Márez and Luna, that he does not have to choose one but can be both. He accepts his father's explanation that the understanding he failed to find in the Holy Communion will come with life. He comes to realize that one's dreams are "usually for a lost childhood" (p. 237). More importantly, he learns from Ultima that "the tragic consequences of life can be overcome by the magical strength that resides in the human heart" (p. 237).

Antonio spends the summer working on the farms with his uncles in El Puerto. Finally, as he struggles to get back to Guadalupe and his family to warn Ultima of Tenorio's threat when his second daughter dies, Antonio encounters *la llorona* once more:

> With darkness upon me I had to leave the brush and run up in the hills, just along the tree line. . . . Over my shoulder the moon

rose from the east and lighted my way. Once I ran into a flat piece of bottom land, and what seemed solid earth by the light of the moon was a marshy quagmire. The wet quicksand sucked me down and I was almost to my waist before I squirmed loose. Exhausted and trembling I crawled onto solid ground. As I rested I felt the gloom of night settle on the river. The dark *presence* of the river was like a shroud, enveloping me, calling to me. The drone of the grillos and the sigh of the wind in the trees whispered the call of the soul of the river.

Then I heard an owl cry its welcome to the night, and I was reminded again of my purpose. The owl's cry reawakened Tenorio's threat . . . (p. 243–44).

Free of the call of *la llorona*, of the "dark *presence* of the river" which called to him, Antonio runs "with new resolution." He runs "to save Ultima" and "to preserve those moments when beauty mingled with sadness and flowed through [his] soul like the stream of time." Antonio leaves the river and runs across the llano feeling a new lightness, "like the wind" as his strides "carried [him] homeward" (p. 244). No longer does he feel the pain in his side, the thorns of the cactus or the needles of yucca that pierced his legs and feet. Yet Antonio knows his childhood is over as the report of Tenorio's rifle shatters it "into a thousand fragments" (p. 245).

Antonio has come home to himself. He has eluded the death call of *la llorona*, and as he buries the owl, Ultima's spirit, he takes on the responsibility of the future in which he knows he must "build [his] own dream out of those things which were so much a part of [his] childhood" (p. 248). Antonio has avoided annihilation on the sheer cliffs of the Wandering Rocks—the fate of his brothers—and he has moved through the narrow strait and evaded the menace of Scylla and Charybdis as he comes to face the reality of his manhood.

ELIUD MARTINEZ

Ron Arias' The Road To Tamazunchale: *A Chicano Novel of the New Reality*

Quiero decir que yo estoy convencido de que, si yo soy mexicano y vivo en México y escribo en México, mi obra será de
México, lo mismo si me refiero a una anécdota de mis coterrá-
neos del Bahío que si trato de enfocar, sinceramente, desde yo
mismo, los efectos de la revolución francesa o mi admiración por
el milagro griego.

–José Rojas Garciadueñas, "El mexicanismo y nuestra literatura."

The critical reception of *The Road To Tamazunchale* has to date been
uniformly enthusiastic. In addition to its having been nominated for the
National Book Award, the novel has been justly praised for its magic realism;
its lean, crisp prose style; its blending of fantasy, magic and reality; its affini-
ties with contemporary Spanish American fiction; its careful craftsmanship;
its mock-heroic parody and humor; its faithful rendering of spoken conversational idioms; and for its humane and compassionate treatment of Death,
the novel's central theme. The author has also been rightly praised for
his simple, joyful, storytelling gifts—in the most praiseworthy sense—and
for his commitment to art and truth which transcends but does not preclude
social commentary on facets of the Chicano experience.

Equally deserving of praise is the novel's contemporaneity, which
reviewers comment upon but do not emphasize. Ron Arias' *The Road To
Tamazunchale* brings contemporary Chicano fiction into an association with

From *Contemporary Chicano Fiction: A Critical Survey.* © 1986 by *Bilingual Press/Editorial Bilingüe.*

international literature and the arts that it has never before enjoyed. The purpose of this paper is to examine some of the outstanding contemporary qualities of this novel.

The *Road To Tamazunchale*, first of all, obeys a conception of fictional reality which Robbe-Grillet, Carlos Fuentes, and others call "the new reality." This term, which subsumes "magic realism," calls to mind the art of Pirandello and Genet; Buñuel, Fellini, Bergman and Antonioni; Borges, Robbe-Grillet, Rulfo, Cortázar, Fuentes, and countless others. The new reality, then, is a contemporary conception of artistic reality which has its origins in Modernism. It provides the esthetics for much of what is considered Post-Modern—that is, contemporary—art, including the novel, theatre, film and painting. The esthetic ideas, doctrines and techniques of the new reality cut across schools and movements such as surrealism, expressionism, the theatre of the absurd, the "new novel" (French and Spanish American), and so on.

In the novel the new reality represents a continuation and culmination of the modern novelist's preference for depicting interior reality and states of consciousness as opposed to exterior reality. Much of the action of *The Road To Tamazunchale* takes place in the imagination and dreams of Fausto, the novel's protagonist. "Are you awake?" is a constant refrain in the novel. Fausto is about eighty years old and he knows that he is dying. In fact, as the reader learns at the very beginning of the novel, Fausto, since his retirement six years earlier, has been leading what might be called a death in life.

> For six years he had shuffled to the window, to the bathroom,
> down to the kitchen, through gloomy rooms, resting, listening to
> the radio, reading, turning thin, impatient, waiting for the end.
> Six years ago she had convinced him to stop work. (p. 14)

Chapter One also describes Fausto's symbolic "change of skin," of which his niece Carmela remains unaware. "She must be blind, she didn't even notice. . . . Next time I'll give her my heart, and she'll say . . . Tío, don't play games. Put it back" (p. 13). This change of skin and the symbolic sound of a flute, heard only by Fausto and associated throughout the novel with the theme of Death, propel the novel forward. Both symbolize the old man's determination to make his remaining days meaningful; his first impulse is to take a voyage to Cuzco, Peru (p. 15).

The new reality is also characterized by an emphasis on play and make-believe. The lovable Fausto therefore is able to journey back and forth in time; as he stumbles up the stairs to his bedroom in his Los Angeles home, he arrives in Peru, where buses, taxis, airplane terminals, concrete, train tracks and telephone poles co-exist with colonial viceroys, archbishops, and a procession of foot soldiers, arquebusiers and lancers. The ripoff of a pack of cigarettes at the local black market leads Fausto to compose "an elegant, detailed report to the viceroy" (p. 16). Another example of make-believe is described in a later part of the novel. Fausto says to one of the wetbacks in the group which (he dreams?) he is smuggling into the United States: "When we get to where we're going, all of you must pretend you're dead" (p. 70). And toward the end of the novel when a young priest comes to give the dying Fausto his last rites Fausto blesses him. "He's a strange man," says the perplexed priest to Carmela. "He likes to play games" (p. 95) is her reply. In this novel, death is the most serious game of all, and Fausto plays it with great frequency.

One of the most delightfully humorous episodes in the novel describes Fausto's encounter with two girls at a bus stop. Wearing his dead wife's pink nightgown as a cape and carrying a hoe which he believes to be a staff, Fausto boards the same bus that the girls take. Both girls are described as dark, one of them with dyed blonde hair. When the suspicious bus driver is rude to Fausto, Mario, an "apprentice wizard," a goateed teenager, intervenes and befriends Fausto. As Fausto takes a seat, Mario waved and

> . . . gave him the thumbs-up sign. "Good try," he said as Fausto sat down. "But I'll tell you what's wrong."
> "What?"
> The boy slid over to Fausto's side and tugged at the cape.
> "This."
> "My cape?"
> "Yeah, it don't look too cool. I mean it's not the thing to wear when you're trying to score . . . . They don't dig capes no more. That went out two years ago. (p. 25)

An extremely important convention in the arts of the twentieth century which emphasizes make-believe is the story within a story. This convention is followed in the theatre and film as well as in the novel. A work of art becomes, as in Hermann Hesse's *Steppenwolf*, a "magic theatre," a spectacle in which the imagination is allowed complete liberation. In a work of the new reality, vision, fantasy, hallucination and dream are celebrated. Everything imaginable, even the impossible, is possible.

In this connection, *The Road To Tamazunchale* contains a play within the novel that is extremely important for an understanding of the novel's esthetics. It is a device which allows Arias to comment upon the esthetics of his novel and to make that commentary an integral part of the work itself. All of Chapter Eleven (pp. 84–90) is important for this reason, and it is intended in addition to prepare the reader for the impossible events depicted in Chapter Thirteen, the last chapter of the novel.

Several possible titles and settings for Arias' play within the novel are discussed by the characters. Tiburcio, one of them, proposes "Vida y muerte." After some discussion he also adds that "the title should have some mystery to it, maybe something about a man with a mask" (p. 83). The play is to be performed to entertain the heavy-hearted group of wetbacks smuggled by Fausto into Los Angeles. It takes place in an abandoned theatre, and as it turns out, the title of the play is "The Road To Tamazunchale." This is important for reasons that will be taken up later.

This chapter contains a great number of expressionistic details: to begin with, an abandoned theatre. There are improvised props, such as the simulated bus; makeshift costumes; theatrical make-up; ambiguous dialogue; and a carnival or circus atmosphere—popcorn, candied apples, footlights, whistling, laughter, applause and bewilderment. Tiburcio, like the barker at the circus, announces the play. Everyone is in a playful, make-believe frame of mind.

At the end of the play illusion and reality meet and overlap. Like at the end of Fellini's film 8 1/2 or in a "happening," the child plays the role of Fausto, gestures to the audience, and invites them to join the actors. The play, therefore, discards in an expressionistic way the convention which separates performers from audience and projects beyond the physical limitations of the stage to incorporate the spectators. Chapter Eleven closes with Fausto in his own bed, asleep and dying, clapping and clapping his hands, much to the bewilderment of Carmela and Mario (pp. 90–91). Arias makes a cinematic transition at this point in the novel. He links the two chapters and establishes a subtle artistic continuity between them by shifting the scene or the situation and having Fausto clap his hands in both. The theatrical or make-believe nature of the play within the novel and the fictional nature of the novel itself are made apparent for the attentive reader by this overlapping of illusion (in this case, dream) and reality. There are other examples of the story within a story principle in *The Road To Tamazunchale*.

Illusion and reality overlap in other ways in Arias' handling of some of his characters. In passing from modern to contemporary, the arts of the novel, theatre and film are characterized by a noteworthy development, the emergence of what I call *the new breed of character*. Antecedents for the new breed of character may be found in a number of symbolist, dada, expressionistic and surrealistic works. They are exemplified in a great number of contemporary works—films, novels, plays. Ron Arias' use of the new breed of character constitutes another praiseworthy aspect of his contemporaneity as a novelist.

Characters of the new breed are illusory, contradictory and ambiguous. When they are compared with traditional characters their complexity becomes even more pronounced. Pure fictional creations, as Robbe-Grillet has pointed out in *For a New Novel*, are true in proportion to their falseness. And they are subject to the most extravagant mutations in the mind of the creator and to the whims and fancies of the characters themselves. *The Road To Tamazunchale* offers generous evidence of the new breed of character.

Characters of the new breed, for example, are frequently fictions in the minds of other characters. Ana, for example, one of several Vergil-type guides for Fausto in the novel, appears to him in his imaginary voyage to Cuzco. She ambiguously fuses with Carmela in Fausto's mind, and whether she is a prostitute who brings warmth once again to the loins of the aging Fausto remains unclear (pp. 18–21). The Buñuelian shepherd from Peru, Marcelino Huanca, with his flock of alpacas offers another example of the new breed of character. The music from his magical flute is a recurrent leitmotif throughout the novel. It keeps Fausto's imminent death present in the reader's mind, for Marcelino is a Bergmanesque messenger from the other world. One of the most humorous and surrealistic episodes in *The Road To Tamazunchale* takes place on the Los Angeles Freeway; it is reminiscent of Buñuel:

> "What's that?" Mario said, jumping up.
>
> Fausto hurried to the sidewalk. "Vente, don't be afraid," he told Mario, then stepped off the curb into the mass of bobbing, furry heads. The shepherd, lagging behind, seemed confused by the traffic lights and horns. At the intersection leading to the freeway on-ramp the frightened alpacas blocked a row of funeral cars, headlights on. Fausto, shouting and waving his hoe, stumbled up the ramp and tried to turn the herd from disaster. Mario ran after him, catching a glimpse of the motorcycle escort racing to the head of the funeral procession. (pp. 28–29)

In this episode Marcelino exists for both Fausto and Mario, but not for the policeman. In other parts of the novel Marcelino seems to exist only for Fausto (p. 35), and the flute music is heard only by him, as at the very beginning and other parts of the novel. In another part Fausto introduces Marcelino to Carmela and her boyfriend Jess (p. 47).

Alive or dead, moreover, the new breed of character wends in and out of the narrative, appears and vanishes and reappears like Rulfo's characters in *Pedro Páramo*. Fausto's dead wife, Evangelina, for example, appears to Fausto in several parts of the novel, once inside the van in which he and Mario have hitched a ride (pp. 72–73), and another time in his bedroom in a hallucination brought on by fever (pp. 80–81). Another excellent new reality fictional device, the logical development of an absurd premise, is used in combination with the new breed of character in Chapter Seven (pp. 57–62).

Chapter Seven develops around the discovery of an anonymous dead wetback by several of the novel's characters. The cause of his death is never established, and even though there is no water anyplace near, the wetback's death is attributed to drowning. David is the name which Mrs. Rentería, a spinster, finally decides on. This name, whether deliberate on Arias' part or not, is most suitable in view of the wetback's Michelangelesque beauty:

> Everyone was silent. David was certainly the best looking young man they had ever seen, at least naked as he now lay. No one seemed to have the slightest shame before this perfect shape of a man; it was as if a statue had been placed among them . . . Some of the men envied the wide chest, the angular jaw, and the hair, thick and wavy; the women for the most part gazed at the full, parted lips, the sunbaked arms, the long, strong legs and of course the dark, soft mound with its finger of life flopped over, head to the sky. (p. 58)

The spinster adopts the beautiful corpse. She bathes and shaves David, cuts his hair and powders his face, manicures his hands, and displays him. Everyone comes several times to shake the dead man's manicured hand and to admire his beauty, until he begins to decompose and smell. In the end David is not buried: "A body so perfect should not be buried," Fausto tells Marcelino (p. 62), and so the shepherd, using ancient Inca knowledge, restores David's decomposing beauty. And David, in perfect condition, is taken to a place near a river, "where others can find him" (p. 62).

In this chapter magic and fantasy overlap. One is reminded of Borges' "The Circular Ruins" and of a statement made by the narrator of "The Garden of Forking Paths." This statement offers a good commentary on the new breed of character: "This book—says the narrator—is an indeterminate heap of contradictory drafts. I examined it once: in the third chapter the hero dies, in the fourth he is alive." In Arias' novel Fausto dies in Chapter Twelve; in Chapter Thirteen he is "alive" again.

The new breed of character, in addition, is aware of his existence as a character. As such he or she consciously plays one or several fictional roles. In the play within the novel, Smaldino, a character, dresses as Smaldino; Mrs. Rentería, another character, plays the role of Mrs. Rentería; and "someone, probably Robert, Smaldino's eldest son, hobbled out from the side, a hoe in one hand and wearing a shabby pith helmet, a moth-eaten cape and baggy trousers. Black, crayon wrinkles were drawn above and below the eyes and at both sides of the mouth" (p. 85). Robert plays the part of Fausto.

In the novel of the new reality the intrusion of "real life" into a fictional work ruins the artistic effect: "Get him off the stage," says one of the characters to another character in the play within the novel, referring to a third character. "He's ruining everything" (p. 86). Earlier in the novel, when Fausto and Marcelino walk into a Hollywood film in progress, as far as Fausto is concerned they are back in colonial times, in Colombia or Trinidad or Santa Marta (p. 52). But as they walk across the set a filmmaker cries out: "Get those guys out! . . . What kind of costumes are those anyway?" (ibid). And when an actress mistakes them for actors playing the role of beggars, Fausto is offended:

> "Madame, do we look like beggars?"
> "Well, I'm a whore."
> "Madame, we are visitors."
> "I also play a flower girl. I did that yesterday."
> "I hoped we would get treated with respect."
> "Don't get touchy. One day a beggar, another day a soldier.
> And don't call me madame. I'm just a whore." (p. 53)

But in a novel of the new reality, as the above examples show, the intrusion of dream and fantasy into real life, the overlapping of illusion and reality, is both desirable and artistically sound. In many parts of *The Road To Tamazunchale*, as one can see, Arias skillfully blurs the boundaries between art and reality. His characters suddenly appear, disappear and reappear in the minds and perceptions of other characters.

It was noted above that whether or not the drowned wetback's name had been deliberately selected by Arias to suggest classical beauty, the name itself invites the kind of interpretation set forth. In *The Road To Tamazunchale* certain names are extremely important. This is certainly true of the novel's title and of the play within the novel. The latter tends to multiply the novel's levels of reality. First of all, the name itself is real, as the author points out in his *Postscript* (p. 108); Tamazunchale is a former

Huastec capital and its precise location on the map is fixed. It is briefly described in *Frances Toor's New Guide to Mexico*. It is pronounced like "Thomas and Charlie" (p. 106). But Tamazunchale makes an extraordinary visual and psychological impact upon the reader, from whom this information is withheld until the very end of the novel; one had never heard of it until Arias' novel came along. And Arias artistically exploits that quality of the unknown which inheres in the unfamiliar name.

The title of Arias' novel has some mystery to it, as Tiburcio had wanted for the play within the novel. The title does not say *A Road*, but *The Road* to Tamazunchale. Tiburcio, in his introduction of the play, stresses that coming from or going to Tamazunchale, whether they know it or not, it's the same road. Thus, there is *only one* way to get there!

Consider, secondly, the characters' discussions of the name. Tiburcio explains the reason for the title of the play:

> You see, whenever things go bad, whenever we don't like someone, whoever it is . . . we simply send them to Tamazunchale. We've never really seen this place, but it sounds better than saying *the other*, if you know what I mean. (p. 84, my emphasis)

And the person who plays the part of Carmela says to the person who plays the part of Fausto:

> There's a boy who sits next to me in school, and he's always using *that word*. The other day the teacher heard him, and he had to stand in the corner for an hour. The teacher really got mad because he even wrote it on the wall. But that's nothing, I see it in the bathroom all the time. (p. 89, my emphasis)

But the character who plays Fausto expresses a different view:

> "Mijita . . . everyone should go to Tamazunchale."
> "What's it like?"
> "Like any other place. Oh, a few things are different . . . if you want them to be." (p. 89)

In Tamazunchale, he says, she can be anything she wants to be, a flower, the sun, the moon, the stars, a song of a million sounds or a little girl. She will be able to see all her friends there. When she asks whether they are going to die, he replies that no one dies in Tamazunchale. Some people pretend to die and others, he admits, do die and are buried. But then "they usually see how stupid it is to die, so they come out of the earth and do something else." In Tamazunchale there is complete freedom to be everything and everyone, even to be nothing (pp. 89–90).

In these commentaries, taken in connection with Fausto's "voyage" toward death, the name *Tamazunchale* acquires a serious vagueness and a deadly strangeness. Tamazunchale becomes a metaphor for the other world, to which there is only one road, only one way to go—by dying! Since no one has ever come back from there, no one knows what it is like. The novel as a whole, its central theme of death and dying, the strange events depicted in the last chapter, Fausto's final arrival in Tamazunchale where the impossible is possible, all this strongly supports the interpretation that Arias has used the name as a metaphor for the world beyond. According to the views of the characters Tamazunchale can be hell or limbo or purgatory or paradise. It is one and all of them because the novel itself admits them all as possibilities.

For Fausto, then, Life is a one-way journey toward Death. His journey is a quest for knowledge and beauty. The events through which Fausto passes and how he passes through them offer a commentary on Death. In a dying person, while he sleeps, while he drifts in and out of consciousness, life flickers off and on. In the process of dying the body remains while the soul wanders in and out, like consciousness, until the person dies. Then the soul remains outside.

The Road To Tamazunchale raises but does not answer the question concerning the state of souls after death. Where does the soul go? Is the grave the final "home" of the soul as well as of the body? At the end of this novel Fausto goes to Tamazunchale. For Fausto, Tamazunchale is Paradise. Hence, the last chapter communicates an exuberant joy and closes with a message of hope.

Tamazunchale names the afterlife without specifying its geography; it points to it symbolically. Another very important name is that of the main protagonist. *Fausto* is charged with significations. Even if the author never intended any reference to these significations, Fausto's discontent with his death in life, his aspiration to transcend earthly knowledge and physical limitations—these invoke Fausto's legendary namesake. In the same way, because Fausto Tejada is a dreamer and an adventurer, because he wears a "helmet" and a "cape" and carries a "staff," because he is a mock-hero who fights imaginary battles, not with windmills but with shadows, Fausto reminds one, in addition, of the knight-errant of the sorrowful countenance. Noticeable, too, in *The Road To Tamazunchale* is the number of guides—Ana, Carmela, Mario the apprentice-wizard, Marcelino Huanca (Fausto himself is a guide for the wetbacks)—who lead Fausto through his imaginary and real experiences. In the end, Fausto is himself the guide in Tamazunchale.

In a large sense, as one can see, the novel deals with universal themes that bring the Chicano experience into focus. The language of Arias' characters, particularly that of the disarming Mario, conveys an aspect of that experience, its linguistic reality. Arias has captured the special flavor, the rhythm and idioms of Chicano popular and conversational speech. The sprinkling of Spanish throughout the novel is always natural, never forced. There is a sense of shared cultural values among the characters. For example, Mexican superstition, folk medicine and the Catholic religion amalgamate in the characters' attitudes toward death. Arias even gently pokes fun at the drinking that takes place at a funeral and at the attitude toward Mexico that Evangelina expresses. The atmosphere of Los Angeles, the largest Mexican city outside of Mexico, is also felt in this novel.

Even the little episode describing Fausto's encounter with the two girls at the bus stop—they are both dark but one has dyed blonde hair—even this little episode makes a significant commentary on a facet of the Chicano experience in the United States. Very significant is "the wetback problem," a theme that runs through the novel. Illegal immigration is a vital and sometimes explosive issue today. The Indian heritage of Chicanos and the identification with Spanish American ethnic and cultural values are also mentioned. In the case of the former, mirrors are important in Chicano novels. Fausto

> washed himself in the bathroom. Puro indio, he thought, looking at the hairless face in the mirror. You're more indio than a Tarahumara, his wife used to say. (p. 15)

These and other facets of the Chicano experience are given artistic expression in the novel.

The Road To Tamazunchale, as a Chicano novel, has liberated itself from dogmas, as Tomás Rivera says in the Foreword to the novel. Chicano writers, in Rivera's words, "need to represent and make concrete every angle and side of the Chicano. Our intent in literature, then, has to be totally human." Ron Arias responds successfully to that need.

In terms of craftsmanship and artistry, no Chicano novel before *The Road To Tamazunchale* has tapped the artistic resources of the modern and contemporary novel (and the arts) in a comparable way, deliberately and intuitively. Arias' understanding and command of new reality forms and techniques is daring and commendable. His handling of the new breed of character is most deserving of praise. Other traits of the novelist are equally commendable: the skillful way that he develops episodes logically from absurd premises, the imaginative use of the play within the novel, his employment of cinematic transitions, the blurring of illusion and reality in a number of unusual and ambiguous episodes, his structural handling of time, the effective depiction of numerous processions—processions of *alpacas*, of funeral cars, of torchlights, of foot soldiers, of actors, of wetbacks—, the expressionistic rendering of certain scenes, the defamiliariza-tion of real places, and in general the admirable compression of a wealth of detail into 107 pages, among others.

The Road To Tamazunchale, moreover, contains surrealistic and "nonsense" images. It includes a Borges-type inventory of books, among which are books not yet written, "an early cosmography of the known and unknown worlds," "a neglected, indexed history of historiography," and "an anthology of uninvented myths" (p. 101). There are, admittedly, noticeable imperfections in the last chapter, in the handling of imagery related to the new breed of character. In Arias' handling of this extraordinary and complex literary device, however, such imperfections are to be expected in the case of a first novel, successful in so many respects, as this study tries to demonstrate. These imperfections are due to the attempt, I believe, to employ the humorous imagery of English nonsense verse in prose fiction without the forcefulness of rhyme, and they need not be adversely criticized.

The Road To Tamazunchale, then, is a carefully crafted work which exhibits and places in the service of Chicano literature a large number of artistic resources. For this reason it is a pace-setter and marks a new direc-tion for Chicano literature. Given the generous evidence which the novel affords it seems safe to say that *The Road To Tamazunchale* points toward the conviction that all literatures, all cultures and all the arts cross-fertilize one another. This conviction, I believe, is what is fundamental to artistic contemporaneity. Properly appreciated, *The Road To Tamazunchale* will undoubtedly influence the future course of Chicano literature and literary criticism. This international novel is a significant contribution to American literature by a Chicano.

Finally, it does not seem out of place to call attention to the fact that Ron Arias' writing of *The Road To Tamazunchale* was a direct and highly personal response to the deaths of his mother, father and grandmother within the period of a single year. And even as this novel was going through its second printing Death visited again; Jonathan Arias, the novelist's six year old son, was struck and killed by an automobile.

This is no ordinary novel, then. The *Road To Tamazunchale* is a safety valve, a novel of necessity. And one is left with a number of unanswerable questions, to which Arias has responded creatively and personally, with an incomparable largeness of compassion and a quiet, soft-spoken strength. Surely the words of another compassionate man speak comfortingly to the author for those of us who know him. In the fourth letter to a young poet, Rainer Maria Rilke says:

> Here where an immense country lies about me, over which the winds pass coming from the seas, here I feel that no human being can answer for you those questions and feelings that deep within them have a life of their own; for even the best err in words when they are meant to mean most delicate and almost inexpressible things.

NORMAN D. SMITH

Buffalos and Cockroaches: Acosta's Siege at Aztlán

"Mexico is such poor country, and I could never understand how, after the Revolution, they could produce all that beautiful art. But now I see it in our own strikes, it's a very small revolution, but we see this art beginning to come forth. When people discover themselves like this, they begin to appreciate some of the other things in life."

The complex question, "Is Chicano art literature or propaganda," is entertaining. However, these either/or critics generally affirm that propaganda and social protest are prevalent in Chicano artistic expression. And art is the vehicle conveying the message. But César Chávez's observation that revolution produces both social change and art synthesizes an aesthetic point of view helpful in the explication of Chicano writings. Chávez's notion that the adrenalin spent in the heat of struggle produces art concurs with the aesthetic statement found in Oscar Zeta Acosta's novels, *The Autobiography of a Brown Buffalo* (1972) and *The Revolt of the Cockroach People* (1973).

The narrator of Acosta's autobiographical fictions views his writing as a "dump" on his buddies, a dislike of the truth, and "death as a world of art." A point-blank telegraphic style enables him to conjure up a pastiche of images that repulse each other while they interlock: fragments of historical struggles are reflected in the Chicano's immediate revolution for cultural, social, and economic identity in an environment controlled largely by an unspecific, unyielding Anglo-Saxon establishment.

From *Latin American Literary Review.* © 1977 by the *Latin American Literary Review.*

In a rapid series of short sentences Acosta's images indicate that his hero-victim of *The Autobiography of a Brown Buffalo* cannot identify with his environment. Shedding the last vestiges of his innocent youth, Oscar asks, "Christ, what happened to the culture of the fifties." He says, "I speak as a historian, a recorder of events with a sour stomach. I have no love for memories of the past. Ginsberg and those coffee houses with hungry-looking guitar players never did mean shit to me. *They* never took their drinking seriously. And the fact of the matter is they got what was coming to them. It's their tough luck if they ran out and got on the road with bums like Kerouac, then came back a few years later with their hair longer and fucking marijuana up their asses, shouting Love and Peace and Pot. And still as broke as ever." Hypocritically, Oscar Buffalo Brown, becomes a spaced-out "fucking buffalo on the lam. *Dropping out with Timothy Leary*." Acosta has his protagonist running not from the law but from the limbo of living—merely surviving—between the Anglo culture and counter culture and his half-forgotten Mexican birthright. He is what Enrique Hank Lopez calls "a schizo-cultural Mexican or a Cultured schizoid American." Acosta sums up his anti-hero's cultural equivocation in the sequel novel, *The Revolt of the Cockroach People*. Gilbert recognizes the Buffalo as a type and says, "The *vato's* a flower child!"

The tumultuous conflict that gives *The Autobiography* its form is marked by Buffalo Brown's inability to reconcile his Anglo conditioning with his being "an innocent, brown-eyed child of the sun . . . a peach-picker's boy from the West Side. Riverbank." Sick—psychosomatically suffering from bleeding ulcers—Buffalo Brown, Oscar Zeta Acosta, protagonist, departs on a spiritual quest searching for both personal identity and a place within two countries, Mexico and the United States, where he might belong. His picaresque and episodic adventure has been interpreted:

> Acosta, in *The Brown Buffalo*, runs away from the hapless world of an Oakland welfare-lawyer, a so-called "lily-livered Legal Aid communist," and takes a left turn toward malaise. Oscar then roams throughout the west, from the Oakland-San Francisco Bay Area, to Aspen, Sun Valley, El Paso, etc., always, though haphazardly, in search of meaning and an identity, a place in the sun he finally does find in Ciudad Juarez. But not before paying his obligatory fee, struggling through and enduring a harrowing psychedelic American nightmare, typical of the late 60's, mixing drugs, booze, drifters, and numbness. Acosta's quest takes over six months, from his escape in July 1, 1967, to January, 1968. It is then that he finds solace, a budding desire to both affirm his Chicano identity and to write.

The protagonist views himself as a man of the future, a popular culture advocate. The historian who has "no love for the past" insanely tries to break out of his asylum; he says:

> It is all madness, I think to myself. Five years of madness in this hideout. No wonder I'm cracking up. I take the green death into my hands and see my reflection on waves on the mirror behind the bar. I am the son of Lorca, I remind myself. The only poet of this century worth reading. Did he suffer with those black eyes? That smooth, long greaser hair; did it make him hurt?
>
> Who are these strange people, these foreigners that don't understand me? Friends all, yet they bring me memories of pain and long suffering. I definitely must run. I've got to go hide, to seek my fortune in the desert, in the mountains. Anywhere but here.

Oscar, "thirty-three, the same age as Jesus when he died," dissipates, debauches himself, moving toward his own crucifixion. His Christ-like resurrection is foreshadowed in the pit of *gabacho* deprivation.

Ketchum, Idaho: Spaced out on the bennies and booze, high on Hemingway, the Brown Buffalo takes on the guise of Henry Hawk, a Blackfoot and Samoan Chief. With Karen Wilmington's family and friends, he drinks spiked Koolaid and eats a Frito covered with guacamole and peyote—placed for effect on the American flag. It is as much to say that Mexico and Mexicans are little more than Acapulco beach boys and grass. The irony is that Henry Hawk outgringos the gringos, saying of the guacamole: "Foul scum, green turd with arsenic is what it tasted like. But I am a macho who eats hot chili for a penny a bite, remember?" Acosta carefully develops obvious contradictions for his hero. The macho who eats hot chili is a reference to his Mexican cultural heritage when as a boy in Riverbank he took his father's dare. In retrospect, Oscar says of his childhood, "The sole purpose of childhood was to train boys how to be men. Not men of the future, but *now*. The peyote-guacamole experience violates Oscar. In this sense *Brown Buffalo* may be likened to Hemingway's Nick Adams tales of maturation. The violence that Oscar Zeta Acosta experiences is the catharsis which will bring him into manhood.

The catharsis, however, is more than merely allowing Buffalo Brown to come of age. His suffering, his loss of dignity, and his self vilification is a means of survival, survival as a mythical son of Malinche. Mexican novelist Carlos Fuentes poetically restates the original betrayal:

Your father will never recognize you, my dark-skinned son; he will never see you as an heir, but rather as a slave; you will have to make your way as an orphan, with the help only of the thorny fingers of your outcast mother. Get drunk, son of sadness, fornicate, sing, dance, dress in all the colors of the earth, my orphan son of the earth, so that the earth may be reborn in the clay of your hungry body; turn our land into a great secret celebration, underground and invisible . . . a fiesta; you shall have no other communion in your loneliness; no other riches in your poverty; no other voice in your silence, except those of the great fiestas of death, dreaming, rebellion, and love; dreaming, loving, rebelling and dying will all be the same for you—the delirious fiesta in which you rebel in order to love and you love in order to dream and you will dream in order to die; cover your body well with earth, son of mine, until the earth becomes your mask, and the masters are unable to recognize, behind it, your dreams, your love, your revolt or your death. Cover yourself with dust, my son, so that even when you are dead, you will seem alive and they will fear you, picaro, thief, drunk, rapist, rebel armed with firecrackers and razors and shrill shrieks, threatening even in your stubborn, silent submission. You will know how to wait and wait, as our ancestors awaited the arrival of the god Quetzalcoatl, the god who fled in fright from his own face, so that your own face, easily frightened, my son, would have the feathers of mist and jade, with a mask of dust and weeping. Someday, my son, your wait will be rewarded, and the god of good and happiness will reappear behind a church or a pyramid on the mirage of the vast Mexican plateau; but he will only appear to you if from now on you prepare to reincarnate him, you yourself, my little hijito de la chingada; you must be the feathered, the winged earth, the clay bird, the screwed and doubly screwed son of Mexico and Spain: you are my only legacy, the legacy of Malintzin, the goddess; Marina, the whore; of Malinche, the mother.

Acosta's Buffalo Brown, bumbler that he is, is similar to Ixca Cienfuegos, Fuentes' sad inheritor of Aztec myth and Mexican history in *La Región más Transparente* (*Where the Air is Clear*). Teodula Moctezuma, the omniscient priestess, passes her metaphysics on to Ixca, the journalist-observer in the shadows. Unlike Cienfuegos, Oscar's innocence must be defiled before he is allowed to visualize the truth of his quest. This truth, as interpreted by

Octavio Paz, is: "In every man there is the possibility of being—or to be more exact, of his becoming once again—another man."

After Oscar leaves Alpine and continues on his terrestrial *trip* to what he believes to be the land of his ancestral inheritance, El Paso and Juárez, he finds rejection and symbolic death. The Brown Buffalo agonizes. Again the challenge! Just when I'd thought I'd become a Mexican in a bed of whores some pimply faced old man with a white brooch under a cracked, long nose questions my identity once again." Insulting the hotel clerk he is thrown in jail. It is significant that Acosta appears before a female judge, a Malinche figure. She satirically asks in parting, "Why don't you go home and learn the language of your father." The barb of her directive is, of course, Oscar's father allowed his children to speak only English, the language of his adopted country. And home? Oscar says in a telephone conversation to his brother: "I've checked it all out and have failed to find the answer to my search. One sonofabitch tells me that I'm not a Mexican and the other says I'm not an American. I got no roots anywhere."

Flash—in the pathos of failure—Buffalo Brown sees what the gods have in store for him. He reincarnates himself Quetzalcoatl and buffalo, a new man to lead a new people. Naively, he rehearses a speech, daydreaming that he rallies the Brown Berets to create a new nation. He states his identity as another man: "I am neither a Mexican nor an American. I am neither a Catholic nor a Protestant. I am a Chicano by ancestry and a Brown Buffalo by choice." In the resolution his encarnation of Zeta, "the world-famous Chicano Lawyer who helped to start the last revolution" is incomplete; however, his commitment as revolutionary and as a writer of *truth* redirects him . . . giving him a transcendental view of the larger struggle of Chicanos.

In the mainstream of American fictional heroes, Zeta of *The Revolt of the Cockroach People* compares with Preacher Casey of John Steinbeck's *Grapes of Wrath* and medical student/journalist Luis Cervantes of Mexican novelist Mariano Azuela's *Los de Abajo* (*The Underdogs*). Like Preacher Casey, Acosta develops a proletariat orientation—mixing ideology with broads. "Who in the shit ever said that revolution has to be a drag?", Buffalo asks. And diametrically, he, like Luis Cervantes, is in the revolution to get the story, the money for personal aggrandizement. This conflict of interests keeps Acosta from becoming a romantic hero of epic proportions. The protagonist, then, becomes the Revolution itself. Revolution is bigger than the little people whose sordid lives have little to do with the momentum of the soul-lifting ramifications of the revolutionary spirit. Therefore, Acosta *dumps* on his buddies, developing a string of character types involved in the revolution. The *truth* of the matter is that the majority possess all of the weaknesses of people who have been deprived success and alienated racially, economically, and socially. In the struggle for social change—revolution and death—Acosta's characters achieve a dignified status. Or as he says, "Some of the men look at me strangely. They know that I'm no wimp, but here I am, running around the world, talking of writing and revolution and women and death. But my commitment to death is different, larger than theirs." Seeking death—not suicide—anticipating death—"determined to go out in a blaze of glory when the time arrives"—Acosta accepts death as the catalyst needed to produce revolution and art: "find your death before you can find your life."

Zeta's buddies, Pelón, Gilbert, and Black Eagle, are much like the deceased—murdered—Robert Fernández. They are *vatos locos*. As a type: "He wears a white T-shirt and a blue beanie, the traditional garb . . . the Chicano street freak who lives on a steady diet of pills, dope, and wine . . . You learn about life from the toughest guy in the neighborhood. You smoke your first joint in the alley at the age of ten; you take your first hit of *carga* before you get laid; and you learn to make your mark on the wall before you learn to write. Your friends know you to be a *vato loco*, a crazy guy, and they call you '*oso*,' or '*vato*,' or '*man*.'" Reared on the violence in barrios like Tooner Flats, "a neighborhood of shacks and clotheslines and dirty back yards," the militant Chicanos bring to their revolution a knowledge of hard, dirty fighting, jails, and death. An army of *vatos locos* organizes against a common enemy, and like the Buffalo's transformation, they quit rumbling with each other and rally to *la causa*. Setting the rhetoric of the revolution aside, Acosta's truth and art depend upon the integrity of his cockroach descriptions. He calls them, "a new breed of savages . . .the Cockroach People. . . the little beasts that everyone steps on." The primordial roach, symbol of Pancho Villa's marching song *La Cucaracha*, Acosta's characters are offensive, expendable, and nearly indestructible.

One of the interesting features of Acosta's descriptions—of his style— is the manner in which he sets the tone and mood of an episode by striving for a cinematic quality. Setting descriptions are minimal. The focus is on character action designed to affect film literate readers. Stereotyped settings, such as the one of Robert Fernández's second autopsy, provides a visual construct that doesn't compete with the action. For example: "In front of us, the casket is on a cart with small wheels. On a clean table we have scales and a bottle of clear liquid. There are razor-sharp tools, tweezers, clips, scissors, hacksaws, needles and plenty of yellow gloves. The white flourescent light shines down upon us." The mind's eye becomes the camera, and in this particular shot reads like a shooting script for a proposed film production.

The Bogart movie fantasies in *The Autobiography of a Brown Buffalo* and Oscar's confession, "I am the world's only living *T.V. Guide*," hint that a knowledge of filmmaking may enhance one's appreciation of Acosta's work.

Certainly the affectively grotesque autopsy may be visualized as a montage. An illustrating definition: "Among commercial filmmakers, montage is a term often used to describe a sequence using rapid superimpositions, jump-cuts, and dissolves in order to create a kind of kaleidoscopic effect to leave audiences with a particular emotional experience." The autopsy sequence begins with the narrative voice solemn with respect for the dead. "The body is intact, dressed in fine linen. Clearly, Robert was a bull of a man. He had big arms and a thick neck now gone purple." Concluding this paragraph, the author's tone becomes flippant and the atmosphere becomes grotesquely comic and absurd. He writes: "The chest has been sewn together. Now the orderly unstitches it. Snip, snip, snip. Holding open the rib cage, he carefully pulls out plastic packages from inside the chest cavity. I hold my breath."

A jumbled visual record follows: "Cut here. Slice there. Here. There. Cut, cut, cut! Slice, slice, slice! And into a jar. Soon we have a whole row of jars with little pieces of meat." And:

> The face is a mask. The mouth is where the brain . . . The nose is at the back of the neck. The hair is in the ears. The brown nose is hanging where the neck . . . Get your goddamn hand out of there.
>
> My hand?
>
> That is the doctor's hand. It is inside the fucking face.
>
> I mean the head.
>
> His hand is inside. It is pulling at something. What did he find in there. What is it?

. . . .

> God! With hammer and chisel in hand, the Chinese doctor goes to town.
>
> Chomp, chomp, chomp. . . Hack, hack, chuck, chuck, chud, chomp!
>
> Ah! Got it!
>
> Out it comes. Long, gizzard-looking. Twelve inches of red muscle and nerve dropping sawdust. Yes, we'll dissect this old buzzard, too.
>
> How about those ribs? You want some bar-b-que ribs, mister?
>
> Sure, *ese*. Cut those fucking ribs up. Chomp 'em up right now!

Superimposed on Robert Fernández's butchery is the reminder that this was once a man: "I see the tattoo on his right arm . . . God Almighty! A red heart with blue arrows of love and with the word 'Mother.' And I see the little black cross between the thumb and the trigger finger. A regular *vato loco*. A real *pachuco, ese*."

The emotional experience triggered by this montage vivifies Acosta's view of death. Death gives life. Robert's autopsy both arouses indignation over the events that caused his death and makes a Chicano proletariat martyr of Fernández. With Robert's death Acosta foreshadows the death of Ronald Zanzibar. The police and the court cover-up of the Fernández murder mirrors the corruption of the legal system that vindicated Sergeant Tom Wilson who killed Zanzibar with a bazooka. Because there is no justice for the Chicano, the dead must be desecrated to enlighten the public. Concluding the autopsy, Zeta prays "Forgive me Robert, for the sake of the living brown . . . I am no worse off than you. For the rest of my born days, I will suffer the knowledge of your death and your second death and your ashes to my ashes, your dust to my dust . . . Goodbye, *ese*. Viva la Raza!"

As revolutionary types Acosta's zealous *vatos* are a disorganized *palomilla:* "The *palomilla* . . . is essentially a peer group or association of Chicano males who interact, informally, with some frequency. The associations are highly personal and voluntary in character . . . . The principal group activity . . . was purely recreation in company of other men." Their *pelado* antics are humorous, and events before and after revolutionary death struggles are comically dissipating: i.e., the orgy that followed the Safeway bombing. The relationship of caricatures like Pelón and Gilbert to the revolutionary cadre, Ronald Zanzibar, César Chávez, and Rodolfo "Corky" Gonzales, is the dignity they share risking their lives as "soldiers of Aztlán." Zeta sums up by twice quoting the aphorism read in César Chávez's chapel:

> LA VIDA NO ES LA QUE VIVIMOS
> LA VIDA ES EL HONOR Y EL RECUERDO
> POR ESO MAS VALE MORIR
> CON EL PUEBLO VIVO
> Y NO VIVIR
> CON EL PUEBLO MUERTO
>
> (Life is not as it seems.
> Life is pride and personal history.
> Thus it is better that one die
> and that the people should live,

rather than one live
and the people die.)
Lopitos
Acapulco, Guererro, 1960.

Calculated to arouse empathy and benevolence, Acosta's tone becomes chau-
vinistic and patriotic, underscored by a vision of Aztlán.

With the respect that a son reserves for his spiritual father, Acosta
describes César Chávez: "I know that for twenty-five days now, César has not
tasted a morsel of solid food. He has starved himself like Ghandi. He believes
that physical resistance to oppression only produces lesser men. Self-defense
by design only creates violent characters. A revolution accompanied by brute
force generates but another bruted society. By way of example of his followers,
he gives up flesh and strength to their cause. The height of manhood, César
believes, is to give of one's self." As César and Corky Gonzales "are number
one and two in the Nation of Aztlán," Acosta does not "fun" with them as character types. Corky Gonzales is pictured:

> Corky has on his usual red shirt and black pants. He comes in
> cagey like the top professional boxer he used to be. He knows the
> men are here to run him through some tough questions. He
> knows he is still considered an *outsider* to the *vatos* on the street.
> Tonight, here in L.A., he knows the mistrust one Chicano has for
> another. He understands the fear in the room toward a leader
> from another barrio, suspicion of a strange leader because . . .
> because Santa Anna sold us out to the gringos . . . because Juárez
> did nothing about it . . . because Montezuma was a fag and a
> mystic who had the fear of the Lord for Cortez or for Malinche
> . . . because anybody who has so little is afraid to lose what he just
> barely has got.

Juxtaposing portraits of *vatos*, spiritual and militant leaders, and martyrs gives
Acosta's work a sense of immediacy in the dynamic present. Historical reference to Villa and Zapata, journalism and film accounts of the Moratorium,
and futuristic promises of a continuing revolution generically establishes that
The Autobiography of a Brown Buffalo and *The Revolt of the Cockroach People* is
a literary compilation documentary.

It is possible to view these two novels as a film script rebutting the shot
record of the film Sheriff Peter Peaches entered as evidence in the trial of the
Tooner Flats Seven. Peaches' film is a distortion of what happened in Laguna

Park. The establishing shot pictures Laguna Park as a happy, clean place for picnics, sports activities, and cultural awareness programs. The film cuts violently to helmeted policemen with riot weapons. Acosta narrates:

> And now you see people suddenly coming out. Now you see a cop lunge for a kid with long black hair.
> Cut to the sidewalk.
> A kid is winging at a cop. He has a red headband. The cops are pushing the people on the sidewalk. The people are being struck with clubs.

The Sheriff's film depicts contrasting scenes, purposefully emphasizing that the police and the sheriff's department were preserving both order and the good life.

As a script for a potential documentary film *The Revolt of the Cockroach People* fits what appear to be unrelated scenes, episodes, and eye-witness reports together creatively reconstructing the truth of the Moratorium riots, of Rubén Salazar's assassination, and, of the Chicano's right to the mythical homeland of the Aztecs, Aztlán. Had Salazar lived—called Ronald Zanzibar in the novel—Acosta probably would not have had to assemble this document. Zanzibar was murdered, he writes, because "He talked too much. And specifically because they knew he had photographs of what really happened that day back at the park. He had those films with him at the moment he was killed. They were never recovered." A non-fiction reference to Acosta's accusation has been restated by Albert Herrera: "Attorney Oscar Acosta charged that the deputies, knowing Rubén Salazar to be inside the tavern and fearing him as a spokesman for the Mexican American community, committed 'political murder, plain and simple.'" After the death of columnist and T.V. news reporter Rubén Salazar there was no one left objective enough to tell the truth. Except Acosta. He says:

> The book offer has made me enemies. That I would think to make money off the struggle for freedom of the Cockroaches has made some people whisper traitor, *vendido, tío taco,* uncle tom and a capitalist pig to boot . . .
> I have explained it a thousand times. I have no desire to make a martyr out of Zanzibar. I know he has been murdered . . . . But now there is no Zanzibar to tell our story, no way for us to use the media to get us back our land. . . . we need writers, just like we need lawyers. Why not me? I *want* to write.

Why not Acosta? The argument, for the defense was clear and eloquent; however, the Chicanos and causes he had been defending put him in the unique position of knowing too much. Perhaps this was the reason Acosta chose to give some of the characters pseudonyms based on real people. To tell the truth of the violence precipitated by both gringos and Chicanos, he could hardly avoid being labeled a *vendido* or sell out. However, since the truth had to be told, Acosta "was qualified and had a grasp of the situation." A Moses figure, Zeta was a tool for the revolution, a reluctant lawyer. Unable to participate, except for two conciliation bombings, he was always on the periphery of revolution and the Chicano promised land, Aztlán. As the Chicano lawyer he enjoyed special treatment—an untouchable status that kept him from being fully trusted by his clients. As Zeta says, "They just need me." But when the truce was signed, he is given the opportunity to write his "memoirs": "my swan song about all my friends and our many problems."

Revolution lifted the oppressed up—somewhat—and gave Oscar Zeta Acosta his identity as a man and writer. It produced the revolutionist and his art. *The Autobiography of a Brown Buffalo* belongs to the north from Mexico migrant genre of Chicano fiction celebrated by such able writers as José Antonio Villarreal, Tomás Rivera, Edmund Villaseñor, Raymond Barrio, Ernesto Galarza and others. What makes *Brown Buffalo* a novelty is Acosta's experiments with the time and point of view. Neither of his novels are narrated chronologically. Time is implied, and the reader sorts and separates stream-of-consciousness recountings. Like James P. Joyce, J. P. Donleavy, and Vladimir Nabokov, Acosta provides the reader with specific reference points whereby violent impression, afterthoughts, drug reveries, and daydreams may be associated. The impressions of Acosta's montages, particularly in *The Revolt of the Cockroach People*, give far more insight into the frustrations of the oppressed than could a straightforward narrative of the Chicano search for identity and ensuing revolt against the gringo establishment. Ultimately, *The Autobiography of a Brown Buffalo* and *The Revolt of the Cockroach People* possess an artistic integrity debunking "holy cows" of religion, of romantic revolutionary ideology, and of the supposedly innate nobility of the majority committed to *La Causa*. The nobility of La Raza is collective; but individually, Acosta's *vatos locos* are in his own words "a bunch of goddamn outlaws."

LUTHER S. LUEDTKE

Pocho *and the American Dream*

More than twenty years have passed since José Antonio Villarreal became the first man of Mexican parents to produce a novel about the experience of his people in the United States. In that time have appeared Raymond Barrio's *The Plum Plum Pickers* (1969), Richard Vásquez' *Chicano* (1970), Tomás Rivera's "*. . . y no se lo tragó la tierra*" (1971), Rudolfo Anaya's *Bless Me, Ultima* (1972), Oscar Zeta Acosta's *The Autobiography of a Brown Buffalo* (1972) and *The Revolt of the Cockroach People* (1973), Rolando Hinojosa-Smith's *Estampas del Valle* (1973), Ron Arias' *The Road to Tamazunchale* (1975), and a wealth of stories, poems, *actos* and anthologies. Scholars interested in the origins of Chicano literature have begun cataloging newspapers, journals, diaries, ballads and other literary prototypes of the Southwest, even while poets and critics concerned for the future of Chicano literature still are issuing its aesthetic manifestoes. In the midst of the burgeoning literature, Villarreal's novel *Pocho*, published in 1959, holds a secure position not only as the first Mexican-American novel, but also as a powerful statement on the enigmas of coming-of-age in the United States. My concern in this essay is a thematic analysis of the novel and its confrontation with the cluster of ideas provoca-tively, if diffusely, known as the American Dream.

Despite its historical importance and dramatic force, Villarreal's novel is not well known even among specialists in American literature, nor has it received more than cursory critical mention. This initial essay on the novel, therefore, will begin with a narrative overview of *Pocho* and the development of its young protagonist, Richard Rubio. For all its latent

From *Contemporary Chicano Fiction: A Critical Survey.* © 1986 by *Bilingual Press/Editorial Bilingüe.*

political significance, *Pocho* is a novel of initiation and, true to its genre, intensely personal. Understanding young Richard's character as it unfolds is fundamental to measuring the social ideology of *Pocho* and its contribution to an emergent Chicano literature.

The scene of the novel is the Santa Clara Valley of California during the late 1920s and 1930s. There Richard, the only son of Juan and Consuelo Rubio, searches for his identity while pulled between the old country ways of his parents and the mercurial new world south of San Francisco. The first chapter actually begins a generation earlier in Ciudad Juarez, Mexico, during the early 1920s, with a heroic depiction of Juan Manuel Rubio—a one-time cavalry officer in the army of Pancho Villa that liberated Juárez from the Díaz regime in 1911 and assaulted Columbus, New Mexico, in 1916—who dreams of returning with his deposed leader to again purge the *gachupín* (Spanish) stain from the land. A virile country warrior in huaraches and sombrero and the lover of many women, Juan Rubio symbolizes the Mexican past in the days of the Revolution. After casually killing the city-bred lover of a cantina dancer, Rubio is forced to cross the border into El Paso, where he stays until cut adrift by the assassination of Villa in 1923. "Thus Juan Rubio became a part of the great exodus that came of the Mexican Revolution. . . . It was the ancient quest for El Dorado, and so they moved onward, west to New Mexico and Arizona and California . . ." (pp. 15–16). In Los Angeles Rubio's tirelessly faithful wife finds him once more. The birth of a son, Richard, two months later on a melon farm in the Imperial Valley stirs a new family pride in him and a love for his wife that is intensified by their exile. He stops drinking and gambling, becomes discreet in love affairs and eventually surrenders the nomadic life of the migrant laborer for a home in the prune country of Santa Clara to the north. There, rubbing his sore knees, this man of the gun thinks: *Next year we will have enough money and we will return to our country*. But deep within he knew he was one of the lost ones" (p. 31).

With the second chapter, the novel shifts from the father to the son, from the Mexican past to the California present. The abruptness of the transition caused one reviewer to complain that "the story begins unnecessarily with Richard's father in Mexico." Thematically, however, the transition establishes important generational conflicts, the loss of the old world values and the suspension of Richard between the cultures. The first chapter of *Pocho*, like the documentary interchapters of *The Grapes of Wrath*, portrays for an unaware audience the backgrounds of immigration to the Southwest, both the causes of uprooting and the subsequent erosion of the elder generations. It is more properly an historical introduction than the first chapter of

Richard's life. Yet this is his legacy—a lost world refracted through prisms of memory and nostalgia.

Chapter 2 depicts Richard, nine years old, in an early stage of consciousness. Although labor strikes, violence and Communist rallies in the Depression year 1931 provide a context of social turmoil, the focus of this chapter is Richard's inner world. From the outset he shows the characteristic introspection and distance that make him more a spectator of the world than a participant. Reading the scenes of his spiritual awakening, one is immediately reminded of *A Portrait of the Artist as a Young Man*; in fact, Joyce's novel of initiation may be the most appropriate literary comparison for this similarly episodic work. Like Stephen Daedalus, young Richard agonizes over the immensity of God, suffers the guilt of childhood sexuality, mistakes the laughter of his teachers for ridicule, flees abusive adolescents, fears the dark, and strives to unriddle the natural universe through language and sign. Richard's troubled soliloquy on creation, time and sin, as he makes his way home from his first confession—the first of his age group to learn the catechism—has a distinctly Joycean cadence and imagery;

> *God made the world. Who is God?* But if He was good and kind, why did He make darkness? Night was the scariest time of the day, because a day is twenty-four hours and night is a day. But not daytime. He was scared at night because he could not see and he was frightened now because he could not know, and somehow God was in the middle of the whole thing. To do "bad" things had something to do with being alive, but really what were "bad" things? (p 37)

Richard's spirit wilts at the thought of hell and damnation but flowers again before the textures and pulse of the natural world. "His every sense responded to life around him": to the "mild, almost tangible wind [that] caressed his face and hair like a mother's hands, washing him clean as it fondled him and passed to who knows where"; to the sadness of "the wake of trampled grass he created"; to the bounding jack rabbit, and the green bugs, and the multicolored birds that lend "their opulence to the scene" (p. 32). He is certain that someday he will learn to ask the questions that unlock the mysteries of creation and empty sky.

At the center of Richard's life stand his protective, superstitious mother, part of the mystery of birth and priesthoods, and his authoritative father, whose smell "the boy . . . associated with his happiness" (p. 43). Often, Richard finds a refuge from the raucous world with Marla Jamison, the teenage daughter of a small farmer who opens to him her home and its world of books. Immured by family, social class, religion, and his own sexuality, Richard nevertheless readies himself even as a small child to fly from the labyrinth on the wings of art.

The theme of imprisonment and flight continues in Chapter 3, but as Richard matures, the sheltering arms of his family begin to fall back, exposing him to a harsher cultural orphanhood. Painfully the parents watch their child grow away from them. "We cannot teach you the things that you want us to teach you," Consuelo grieves, "—we cannot guide you, we cannot select your reading for you, we cannot even talk to you in your own language" (p. 61). Juan Rubio refuses to take his son out of school for work, sacrificing himself for the next generation. Undirected, Richard vacillates between the English and Spanish languages, between independence and family responsibility, between his father's proud hope that he will return to Mexico as a doctor or lawyer and his mother's plaintive warning that he, the only son, must go to work after secondary school and begin his own family. "Angry that traditions could take a body and a soul—for he had a soul; of that he was certain—and mold it to fit a pattern" (p. 63), Richard shuns both the fatalism of his mother and the materialism of his father. "Ah Mamá!" he cries. "Try to understand me. . . . I do not want to be something—I am." When she admonishes him for "that kind of feeling against the family and the custom"—"It is as if you were speaking against the church"—Richard flees deeper into a realm where his parents can neither lead nor follow him:

> "Mamá, do you know what happens to me when I read? All those hours that I sit, as you sometimes say, 'ruining my eyes'? If I do ruin them, it would be worth it, for I do not need eyes where I go then. I travel, Mamá. I travel all over the world, and sometimes out of this whole universe, and I go back in time and again forward. I do not know I am here, and I do not care. I am always thinking of you and my father except when I read. Nothing is important to me then, and I even forget that I am going to die sometime." (p. 64)

Someday he might even talk with God. Only with Mary, his slender Anglo-Protestant confidante, can he share the world of imagination; and to her he reveals his secret ambition to write books when he grows up.

Shackled by language and tradition, Richard's mother and father fall by the wayside along his pilgrimage toward self-realization. True to the second-generation immigrant experience, he begins to look for mentors and models outside the family. The first of these is the agnostic Portuguese cowherd, João Pedro (Joe Pete) Manõel Alves, whose story is told in Chapter 4. Because of homosexual incidents as a university student in Lisbon, Joe Pete was banished by his aristocratic father, a marquis, and after years of teaching philosophy in São Miquel, the Madeiras and Africa, took up a reclusive life in the Santa Clara Valley. Pan-like, he enthralls young Richard with his erudition and wondrous tales of Iberian royalty. The lad becomes a devotee to his poetic vision and Whitmanic compassion. "There was an innate communicableness in the small, honest face that made the man speak out and say things he had withheld even from himself" (p. 81). Finally, however, in loneliness and sexual distress, Joe Pete gets young Genevieve Frietas pregnant and then goes mad. He too fails Richard. Nevertheless, like George Willard in *Winesburg, Ohio*, the boy has shared an "adventure" of his people that he can later tell the world.

The destruction of Joe Pete drives Richard further inward, hardening his resolve to rise above the mysterious force "of tradition, of culture, of the social structure of an individual" (p. 95). He feels more and more alienated from his decaying family, and in Chapters 5 and 6 he turns instinctively toward the popular heroes, icons and formulas which the dominant culture offers. In the midst of domestic chaos, "He sat at the table with his chin in his hands and said aloud, in *English*, 'I am Buck Jones and Ken Maynard and Fred Thompson, all rolled into one—I'm not Tom Mix, too, because I don't like brown horses'" (p. 96, italics added). Like every twelve-year-old American boy, he idolizes the man on the *white* horse, not the *brown*. In his search for fathers, Richard turns to the mythos of the culture for the guidance his parents are unable to give.

Traditional guides to life fail the young Mexican-American. At an early age he learns, first, "that one should never discuss matters of sex with one's parents. Second, one should not, on penalty of going to Hell, discuss religion with the priests. And, last, one should not ask questions on history of the teachers" (pp. 85–86). It is expected that Richard's mother cannot select readings for him; more crushing, however, is the failure of the public educators to provide the standards of belief and behavior he hungers for. Teachers encourage his reading, but do not direct it. The only works prescribed are the novels of Horatio Alger, given him by a dear old librarian. "Funny about her, how the Horatio Alger books meant as much to her as the Bible meant to Protestants" (p. 108). Richard follows the adventures of Alger's trusting young heroes in his tangled desire to learn the rules of his world, yet he rejects the ethos of dutiful service to one's superiors. He does not aspire to become the gardener on a rich man's estate, as the well-meaning librarian recommends. Nor does he wish to study automechanics or welding because these are good trades for Mexicans, as his high school counselors advise. He spurns all efforts to reconcile him to the "Mexican" role in the social-economic pattern of America. In a scene echoing the "battle royal" in *Invisible Man*, Richard is coaxed to join the boxing game and fight his friend Thomas Nakano. "'How about it, kid?' asked the man. 'I'm giving ya the chance of your life—it's the only way people of your nationality can get ahead'" (p. 106). Richard walks away laughing at the absurdity. Even as a twelve-year-old, he is less trusting than Ralph Ellison's high school valedictorian and more emancipated from the stereotypes of ethnicity. One by one, he abandons the potential mentors who fail to perceive his *self*.

As Richard grows into adolescence, the foundations of family and church continue to erode beneath him. The last link with Mexico is cut when Juan Rubio buys a house. Outwardly the family prospers and assimilates to its new culture, but the "strange metamorphosis" that takes away tradition without imposing new controls is fatal to its integrity. Richard's mother changes completely. She learns from her neighbors that in the United States women are individuals and have rights. While this releases her sexually, it also transforms the once submissive and fastidious woman into an unhappy termagant who challenges her husband's discipline of the children, gossips, argues and keeps a dirty house as "a symbol of her emancipation." As authority and happiness slip through his hands, Juan Rubio turns to other women once more, his "raucous, infectious laugh" gone, his once solid body become flabby. All discipline disappears "and even the smallest child screamed at either parent, and came and went as she pleased." But "no one could be blamed," the author adds, "for the transition from the culture of the old world to that of the new should never have been attempted in one generation" (pp. 134–135). (The same breakup of the male dominated family and the rise of a trenchant matriarchy is seen in other uprooted ethnic groups, e.g., the "Jewish Mother" syndrome and the disproportionate number of Black female heads of households.)

In the latter chapters of *Pocho* the conflict between Richard's inner and outer realities intensifies. As he grows towards manhood, he confronts both the significance of his social acts and disturbing new currents in the community. In Chapter 8 he becomes intimate with the scrappy hoyden of his boyhood clique, Zelda, and agrees to take her for his "girl" on the condition she will stop "laying pipe" with the other fellows. With Zelda he loses some of his restlessness. The mating ritual they enact seems to establish the traditional authority of the male and the sexual fidelity of the female. Yet Richard maintains his customary distance, even as Zelda becomes wholly obedient.

This friendship, like that with Mary, is destined to be outgrown and left behind.

At the same time, the town of Santa Clara also is changing. While soldiers walk the streets following the Conscription Act of 1940, the main change in Richard's life, told in Chapter 9, is his confrontation with "the race." His home in town and childhood gang of Anglo, Japanese and Italian friends had sheltered him from much association with other Mexicans. When large numbers of migrants from Southern California now settle in the valley, he begins "to attend their dances and fiestas" and to seek out their company. Ever uncertain of his own identity, Richard is "obsessed with a hunger to learn" about the new breed of young men and women he meets:

> They had a burning contempt for people of different ancestry, whom they called Americans, and had a marked hauteur toward Mexico and toward their parents for their old-country ways. The former feeling came from a sense of inferiority that is a prominent characteristic in any Mexican reared in southern California; and the latter was an inexplicable compensation for that feeling. . . . The result was that they attempted to segregate themselves from both their cultures, and became truly a lost race. (p. 149)

Richard considered his identity a personal matter, to be nurtured both in family traditions and in the values of American culture—until someday it should burst from its dark chrysalis. His angry friends, to the contrary, seek a group identity through repudiating both their parents' customs and the new society.

The *pachucos*—or zoot-suiters, as they were called after their billowing pegged pants and fingertip black coats—were rebels without a cause, the raw seeds from which the Chicano would later emerge. After first finding them ludicrous and brutal, Richard comes to appreciate that "in spite of their behavior, which was sensational at times and violent at others, they were simply a portion of a confused humanity, employing their self-segregation as a means of expression." He learns their polyglot of "English and Spanish syllables, words, and sounds"—"unintelligible to anyone but themselves"–and disparages "whites" in their presence (pp. 149–150). For a time he hangs suspended between the friends of his youth and the angry pachucos, dressing and acting in such a way as to offend neither. As community tensions increase, Richard is mistaken for a pachuco hoodlum and beaten by the San Jose police. A militant strain enters his character as he is

ground by conflicting loyalties; nonetheless, he sustains his brittle affirmation: "Never–no never–will I allow myself to become a part of a group—to
become classified, to lose my individuality" (p. 152). A "protective shell of
cynicism" grows over his innate idealism (p. 164).

In Chapter 10 Juan Rubio leaves his family for good. Richard, torn by
personal affection for both his mother and father and for the values that had
once been theirs, rejoices at his father's renewed manhood. In their tearful
departure, Juan Rubio exhorts his son to be true to himself and let nothing
stand in the way of his determination to be a writer, "be it women, money,
or—what people talk about today—position" (p. 169).

In the last chapter of the novel, the legacy of the father threatens to
fall upon the son. From picking fruit, following his graduation from high
school, Richard moves on to lucrative wartime work in a steel mill.
Inexorably, it seems, he yields to his mother's will that he should take
responsibility for the family and, as the eldest son, provide for his sisters.
"Slowly the temporary aspect of the situation was giving way to perma-
nency" (p. 174). His dreams for writing, like his father's visions of return to
Mexico, begin to fade. Finally he does start spending time in the library
once more, and even enrolls in a night course in creative writing. But the
course teaches him little, and it pains him that his liberal classmates want
him to "dedicate his life to the Mexican cause" (p. 175). Unprotected by
family, church or school, he can no longer mistake the spectre of his own
existence: "He was now a part of the infinite nonentity—the worker, the
family man. He had slowly dropped into oblivion even in his mind, the one
place where once he had soared above the multitude" (p. 180). His only
flight is the war, and impulsively he enlists in the Navy. What lies on the
other side he does not know; he only knows, like Stephen Daedalus from
Dublin, George Willard from Winesburg and Ellison's Invisible Man, that
"for him there would never be a coming back" (p. 187).

This simple narrative critique should awaken in readers of American
literature a sense of déjà vu, for *Pocho* is a typical American story. We are
ready now to take a systematic look at the ideas surrounding the novel and
its place in the history of the American Dream.

Mexican-Americans are one of the last great folk migrations to the
United States. At the turn of the century the number of residents of
Mexican background in the Southwest did not far exceed 100,000;
however, the upheaval of the Mexican Revolution—combined with the
poverty of the Mexican states, the birth of the Southwest as an economic
empire and, after 1942, the government subsidized bracero program—
opened floodgates from the south through which poured nearly 10 percent

of Mexico's total population. Even while the immigration restriction acts of the 1920s stemmed the transoceanic flow, this new tide surged. Today more than five million Mexican-Americans form the nation's second largest minority, and the Mexican dream of the El Dorado to the north remains a major challenge to social planning in the border states.

Immigrant families like the Rubios, who joined the great wave of the 1920s, now have reached their third generation in the United States. Their experience, therefore, might be compared to patterns of acculturation in other immigrant groups, fomulated tersely in "Hansen's law" that "what the son wishes to forget, the grandson wishes to remember." This theorem refers to the phenomenon observed by historians and sociologists that the *first* generation (grandparents), uprooted from their ancestral culture, remain fundamentally estranged from the new society regardless of economic attainment; the second generation (parents), embarrassed by their forebearers' backwardness and eager to prove themselves "American," pursue the goals and behavior of the majority culture in an exaggerated way; the third generation (children), sensing their parents' rootlessness, look again to the grandparents for clues to their moral identity and seek a synthesis of old and new values. (The transition from second to third generation attitudes is evident today in the unfashionableness of the Melting Pot concept and the emergence of Pluralism and the Mosaic as rival national symbols.) In the Mexican-American community, the *pelado* of the first generation looks forward to the *Chicano* of the third. Between stands the American son of Mexican parents, the hyphenated Mexican-American called *pocho*.

The setting of Villarreal's novel in the 1930s and its actual writing in the 1950s bracket an extended second generation of assimilation when the Mexican-American community, with such exceptions as the pachucos, accepted the public attitudes of conformity and patriotism. The agonies Richard suffers are those both of a novice seeking his cultural birthright and of a generation suspended between two cultures. Richard dramatizes dialectics of:

Self-determination	and	Tradition, Filial Piety
The Individual		The Community
Personal Freedom		Social Responsibility
Teachers, Schools, Libraries		Parents, Home
Father		Mother
English Language		Spanish Language
Free Thought		Catholic Creeds, Confession
Dreaming, Reading, Writing		Working

Childhood Friends	Pachucos
United States	Mexico
Flight	Acceptance

Their synthesis awaits a third generation.

In important respects, however, the Mexican-American has proven an exception to the rule of intergenerational change. Sociologists have discovered that Mexican-Americans hold onto their language and cultural habits more tenaciously than other immigrant ethnic groups; in general they have been the slowest to assimilate. On the basis of the 1950 census data, Mexican-Americans "constituted the only major ethnic group with no substantial intergenerational rise in socio-economic status." Among the factors retarding acculturation are the proximity of the fatherland and the continual nature of Mexican immigration and repatriation, which have prevented the ultimate cutting of ties, physical and psychological, that propelled other immigrant groups into the Melting Pot. Absence of an educational tradition has been another important deterrent. The group's perception of opportunity has been further limited by the concentration of Mexican-Americans in rural areas and agricultural jobs, in contrast to the predominantly metropolitan and industrial thrust of European immigration. Richard Rubio, given his urban setting in the most liberal state of the Southwest, was exceptionally well exposed to ideas of mobility and change.

The root cause for the culture lag, finally, may be a fundamental difference in world view between dominant America and the Mexican-American people. While comparing the value orientations of the two cultures, Florence Kluckhohn identified the following differences of approach to five basic human problems:

Problem	Mexican-American Response	American Response
Man's relation to nature	Subjugation-to-Nature	Mastery-over-Nature
Essence of human nature	Mutable Good-and-Evil	Evil-but-Perfectible
Man's relation to man	Lineality (group, family)	Individualism
Preferable activities	Being	Doing
Time orientation	Present-Time	Future-Time

The progressive orientation and success ethos of American core culture contradict the traditional world view of the Mexican-Americans, with its emphasis on continuity, community and the obligation of one's assigned role.

By the late 1960s, however, there were signs that a "take-off stage" had been reached. In her study of the attitudes of Mexican-American high school seniors in Los Angeles, Celia Heller found expectations of high "relative" mobility. Subsequent work has demonstrated not only that the education gap narrowed between 1950 and 1960, but also that median income and home ownership "of Mexican-American individuals in the Southwest rose at a substantially higher rate than that of Anglos," and that moderate occupational upgrading also occurred. In *New Converts to the American Dream?* Professor Heller asked what effect the militant Chicano rhetoric of the late sixties might have on the incipient drive towards individual success.

> At a time when the climate of opinion is not conducive to the traditional rhetoric of the American dream, making it sound old-fashioned and dated, many Mexican-American youths are laying claim to that dream. . . . The process of responding to the American ideology of advancement, observed in all other immigrant groups is being similarly reenacted here, although it took longer to get underway. What typically took place in immigrant groups in the second generation is now occurring among third- and fourth-generation Mexican Americans. As a phenomenon of noticeable proportions, it is new among Mexican Americans. Also, these third- and fourth-generation Americans are facing the problems of marginality and assimilation which other ethnic groups met in the second generation.

She went on to speculate:

> By focusing attention on the incipient Mexican-American militancy and not bringing to light the beginning "success story," the mass media may play a part . . . in the extinguishment of the embryonic achievement orientation.

Pocho issued from a period when the ideology of personal advancement was still much alive. A tributary from the premilitant fifties, it fed into the mainstream of American literature just above the gulf of sixties and seventies revisionism. From its origins America has been a nation of immigrants, and, as if to satisfy Thomas Jefferson's call for a revolution each generation, continual social and political change has kept the crucible churning. At heart, our imaginative writing has been a "second-generation" literature, preoccupied with the struggles of rebirth, identity and acculturation. The typical protagonist is a stalwart, introspective young man like Richard Rubio, stripped of his past, who leaves home to seek his destiny in the new world lying open before him. When his parents are not entirely absent, they are ineffectual guides on new frontiers; at best they offer a memory of unrecoverable harmony. The young man, actually or metaphorically, is an orphan.

Chicano critics who discuss Villarreal's book approach Richard's ambivalence as part of "the alien[ation] in both worlds that many social scientists speak of when they portray the Mexican American." Such an attitude enables scholars to mark stages in the evolution of Chicano literary consciousness; however, it threatens to narrow the interest and achievement of the work by tying it too closely to a particular ethnic strain. The same motifs of ambivalence, alienation and brooding introspection on personal freedom run through Henry Roth's *Call It Sleep*, Budd Shulberg's *What Makes Sammy Run?*, Saul Bellow's *Dangling Man*, and other "second-generation" novels. They are the core of the novel of initiation, and in one form or another they constitute the classic tradition of American literature since the time of Hawthorne and Melville. The greatness of American ethnic and regional literature has been its ability to dramatize the universal dilemmas of self-awareness in a specific social context. Richard Rubio joins a long line of novices who have sought their spiritual birthright in America.

Bereft of the past, the young American must seek a new "father." When Richard finds he cannot discuss sex with his parents, religion with his priest or history with his teachers, he stands naked before the symbolic abstractions of the culture itself. The story of American literature has been just this initiation of expectant youths into the corporate myths of America and the psychological and metaphysical mysteries they conceal. A culture as idealistically conceived and committed to personal progress as the United States particularly needs a unifying myth to direct its energies. Since *Father Abraham's Speech* (1759), such a mythology has appeared. Its Old Testament is *The Autobiography of Benjamin Franklin*; its New Testament the synoptic writings of Horatio Alger; and its Book of Revelations the apocalyptic visions of Arthur Miller's *Death of a Salesman*, Norman Mailer's *An American Dream* and Edward Albee's *The American Dream*. Compulsively they tell the story of fatherless youths pursuing the chimerical patrimony of the culture and honoring its abundant opportunities–or not–through their discipline and success.

"The American Dream" is a particularly appropriate image for Richard

Rubio's experience, because *Pocho* is pervaded by the same air of unreality and half-sleep that surrounds every effort to lay hold on the substance of America. The structure of the novel is fragmentary; Richard's glimpses of reality are fleeting and unconsummated. By nature dream is not a negative state; it is a psychological bridge from sleep to reality and back, during which passion and will weigh the demands of the waking world. *Pocho* enacts this dreamlike ritual of segregation from the past, transition and awakening to a new reality—except that Richard never fully awakes.

Like Jay Gatsby, Richard builds his identity as best he can from the cultural debris around him. Young James Gatz of North Dakota, before he became "The Great Gatsby," forged his life models from the ragged ends of the Benjamin Franklin legend and Hopalong Cassidy books. Richard Rubio of Santa Clara, through his omnivorous reading and reverie, also imagines truths unseen by the human eye. His lodestones are artifacts of the culture: at first limp books cast off by teachers, *Toby Tyler*, or *Ten Weeks with the Circus*, or rescued from the city dump and smelling of garbage; later the popular culture of small town library shelves and radio programs, *Tom Swift* and *The Rover Boys*, stories of Buck Jones, Ken Maynard and Fred Thompson; all culminating in the adventures of Horatio Alger. Such stuff dreams are made of in America. Because Richard's parents cannot instruct his reading and imagination, teachers and librarians become his cultural mentors. But they fail in their appointed task to educate the boy because of their own ignorance of his spiritual needs and the duplicity of their culture. The heroes and images of success they offer do not lead him out of sleep into action. Celia Heller put this phenomenon in sociological terms when she reported:

> Thus we have found that the schools have managed to instill the goals and values of success. But they have failed drastically in developing behavior conducive to advancement The result is a rising appetite for socio-economic success without a corresponding development of the capacity to satisfy it.

Books are one means of bridging the gulf between individual dreams and collective realities. Unfortunately, the books given to Richard by his teachers and librarians are from the wrong phase of the American Dream to suit either the contemporary milieu or Richard's special temperament.

The author seems to have had the success dream of Franklin and Alger in mind when writing his book. The historical formula requires leaving one's father, journeying to a new city, learning the dictates of life from a series of mentors, seeking education, seizing opportunity, rising to middle-

class substance through luck and pluck, and perhaps sealing the achievement through marriage. Richard breaks the formula of course at crucial
points: he's hampered throughout by uncertain will, vague opportunities,
careless mentors, and his own sensual impulses; nor does he leave home until
the end. But sufficient vestiges of the pattern remain to identify the dream
that has defaulted. Villarreal's protagonist bears the name of both Richard
Saunders (Franklin's persona in *Poor Richard's Almanac*) and Richard Hunter
(the hero of Alger's most famous novels, *Ragged Dick* and *Mark the Match
Boy*). He is a shrewd and detached lad, "not showing his impatience, quietly
calculating until he saw what he wanted" (p. 51). Like Ragged Dick, he learns
manners and behavior from daughters of the Protestant gentry: first the
courageous Marla Jamison and then ethereal Mary who announces her
intention to marry him. Furthermore, Richard looks for a mentor outside the
family and finds him for a time in Joe Pete Manõel.

The most interesting images of the dream of material success appear in
the episode of Mat Madeiros' drayage barn in Chapter 2. Madeiros rose from
poverty to moderate wealth by cashing in on the booming hauling business
during the 1920s. Confident of the future of the machine, he bought a Reo
truck and soon "had visions of a fleet of trucks and an important position in
the community." When the Depression struck, he was forced to "put his rig
up on blocks" and go to work in a cannery. But he regarded this as only a
temporary setback, even while his savings disappeared. The Madeiros barn
was next used as a meeting place for the Unemployed Council of Santa Clara
County. When Communist organizers from the city took over, "the wall
behind the table was bedecked with bunting, of which a red flag with
hammer and sickle was the centerpiece," and "Mat's truck was once more on
the road. Working parties forayed the bakeries for stale bread, the dairies for
skim milk, and any place where they might find something to help feed the
people" (p. 48). Ostensibly, Mat's truck and drayage barn were transformed
from symbols of private enterprise into a badge of communal action. The
author's imagery, however, discloses the material dream that continued to
run through the people's thought. The "red flag with hammer and sickle . . .
always reminded the child [Richard] of the picture on the box that held his
father's indigestion medicine" (p. 48). Thus, the symbol of communal action
becomes Arm and Hammer Baking Soda, a mark of dyspeptic middle-class
America. Likewise, one of the most popular musical settings for lyrics of
protest was the bourgeois "Stanford Fight Song." At heart the people were
still buying the dream.

Whatever might be the validity of the entrepreneurial dream of Mat
Madeiros, it was the wrong dream for Richard. Richard's soul was attuned,

even as a child, not to the American Dream of material self-advancement that characterized the nation during the age of Alger, but rather to a more profound American Dream of spiritual self-realization that preceded and outlives its narrower economic expression. When Consuelo Rubio warns her son, "I know that we cannot live in a dream, because everything around us is real," he declares: "'I do not care about making a lot of money and about what people think and about the family in the way you speak. I have to learn as much as I can, so that I can live . . . learn for *me*, for *myself*—'" (p. 64). Richard is an Emersonian. His repeated assertions of the importance of the individual soul, like the following passage—

> I can be a part of everything, he thought because I am the only one capable of controlling my destiny. . . . I will not become a follower, nor will I allow myself to become a leader, because I must be myself and accept for myself only that which I value and not what is being valued by everyone else these days. . . . (pp. 152–153)

—echo Ralph Waldo Emerson's proclamations on self-reliance, individualism, friendship, and unity with the Over-Soul. Compare, for example, this passage from the essay on "Self-Reliance":

> Live no longer to the expectation of these deceived and deceiving people with whom we converse. Say to them, 'O father, O mother, O wife, O brother, O friend. I have lived with you after appearances hitherto. Henceforward I am the truth's. . . . I appeal from your customs. I must be myself. I cannot break myself any longer for you, or you.'

The importance of the *self* requires that Richard transcend the hereditary bonds of family, church, school and society until he can express his own intuitions. When the church forbids him from reading the scriptures, he steals away to study the Bible. From Catholic dogma to the inquiry of Protestantism to free thought is a natural spiritual evolution. Likewise, he successively outgrows his parents, his duty to dependent sisters, his childhood gang and adolescent girl friends in the course of personal emancipation. At the end of the novel the process of liberation is still underway. In his introduction to the 1970 paperback edition of *Pocho*, Ramón Ruiz spoke of "that sense of inferiority that settled down upon Richard in his lonely battle with reality" (p.xii). There is no indication in the novel itself, however, that the author wished Richard not to have asserted his spiritual independence.

His liberation from tradition is a painful but fundamental process.

In their essay "The Militant Challenge to the American Ethos," Armando Gutiérrez and Herbert Hirsch assailed American ideas for "destruction of the culture [of Mexican-Americans] coupled with the concomitant destruction of individual identity." The central questions are, first, whether the American Dream retains its power to unify diverse peoples around new cultural symbols and loyalties and, second, whether it enables individual self-discovery or is merely imperious, prescriptive and culturally appetitive. The family, ethnic community or social brotherhood is potentially just as tyrannous towards individual freedom as the dominant culture. This is the theme of works like *A Portrait of the Artist as a Young Man*, *Winesburg, Ohio*, and *Invisible Man*. The tragedy of the American Dream for Richard Rubio is not that it frees his mind from old ties and sends it exploring the possibilities of *self*; this is its excellence. The tragedy of the Dream is that it has not simultaneously given ethical norms by which this freedom might be embodied in action; thus, Richard's *anomie*.

It is no doubt because the normative standards for belief and behavior are less certain in complex modern America than they were in the expansive nineteenth century, that the countermythos of Aztlán has such appeal for Chicano polemicists. The myth of Aztlán calls forth the romantic vision of a great *indígena* culture in the Southwest before the coming of the Spanish and the Anglo-Americans. In the mind of Chicano poets and critics like Luis Valdez, originator of the Teatro Campesino, the mestizo who crosses the border today from Mexico into the occupied ancestral lands of the Southwest may suffer a "spiritual regression," but the European remains "the eternal foreigner, suffering from the immigrant complex. . . . His culture, like his name for this continent, is imported." Chicanos did not come to America, the poets claim: America came to them. The poetry of Aztlán calls to mind the bloodconsciousness of D. H. Lawrence and William Carlos Williams, who mythologized redskins and the spirit of the Southwest as a counterpoise to a mechanistic paleface culture. The cultural traits which Florence Kluckhohn identified as retarding Mexican-American assimilation in the United States—communalism, a circular view of time, emphasis on Being rather than Doing—have become the basis for a mystagogic religion aimed at recreating the "universal man." The Chicano, writes Guillermo Fuenfríos,

> is by nature a pluralistic man, a universal man, combining the racial strains and cultures of the entire world in his own person. José Vasconcelos coined the term "La Raza Cósmica" to describe him. The term is apt. . . . It is no wonder that he has successfully

resisted the best efforts of the North American to melt him down into a mere American.

At first this manifesto may sound like the cosmic decrees of Walt Whitman. But where Whitman chanted his song to the Self, the future and the new American, the poets of Aztlán extol an ancient race that preceded America. Luis Valdez asserts with fervor:

> Now the gringo is trying to impose the immigrant complex on the Chicano, pretending that we "Mexican-Americans" are the most recent arrivals. It will not work. His melting pot concept is a sham: it is a crucible that scientifically disintegrates the human spirit, melting down entire cultures into a thin white residue the average gabacho can harmlessly absorb. That is why the Anglo cannot conceive of the Chicano, the Mexican Mestizo, in all his ancient human fullness.

Can this mythos, this merging of "Indio mysticism . . . with modern technology to create *un nuevo hombre*," sustain itself? Or will the Cinco de Mayo celebrations, like St. Patrick's Day and Oktoberfest, be absorbed by dominant America as one more bright color in the fabric of national life? To affect the lifeways of its people, a myth must *emerge* with primitive strength. Efforts to create new myths have not been very successful as cultural amalgamation continues to take place. The demise of Yiddish Theatre in our time stands as a challenge to the prophets of Teatro Chicano.

In a provocative essay, "National Development and Ethnic Poetics: The Function of Literature in the Liberation of Peoples," Jay Martin has weighed the relation of national aesthetics to cultural development by comparing American literary nationalism between the 1770s and the mid-1840s to the contemporary Black Aesthetic and the Americanidad Aesthetic of Latin America. The impulse of literary nationalism, he has decided,

> originates when a formerly colonized people begin to achieve political equality with their former oppressors. Its function resembles magical thinking—it is to persuade the newly liberated group that the former oppressor is decadent and powerless and that the new nation has replaced the old on the historic stage— that a new race of men has appeared to redeem the world. It is, in short, an expression of the new nation's sense of its own value while it is still vulnerable.

Once economic independence and social equality are achieved, the aesthetic loses "its force as an instrument of liberation" and disappears. If, on the other hand, the progress towards social and economic equality with neighboring cultures is arrested, then the aesthetic eventually will turn upon itself through private mythologies, surreal images and racial memories that dismiss the importance of economic achievement. The function of Chicano poetics in the liberation of its people has been only partially revealed; however, recent works like Ron Arias' *The Road to Tamazunchale* show an inclination to escape from the novelistic world of man and society into the imaginary dramas and private language of myth.

When introducing the novel, Ramón Ruiz warned the reader to keep in mind, "lest he misunderstand and misinterpret its major premise," that the ambivalence in *Pocho* reflects "the ambiguities and ideological confusions inherent in Mexican-American thinking" during the assimilationist phase in which Villarreal was writing (p. viii). Today the Chicano's "commitment to unity of 'race' places loyalty to the community above all else"; a generation earlier, "in rebellion against his dual heritage, Richard [stood] defenseless, an insecure and beaten young man" (p. xii). The point of this essay has been to suggest that Richard Rubio is not so time-locked as Professor Ruiz and many others may believe. He is a universal man. As such he suffers an existential insecurity against which no community can protect him but which has been brilliantly dramatized during a century and a half of American literature. We do not know that Richard has been beaten; however, we also do not know at what point along the social and metaphysical frontier of America he will emerge from his rites of passage. That story still has not been told.

NASARIO GARCIA

The Concept of Time in Nambé–Year One

Time is a complex phenomenon, and scientific, philosophical and meta-physical theories are testimony to its complexity. Scholars from Plato, Plotinus, and St. Augustine to Bergson have yet to agree on a precise defini-tion. Time continues to be a mystery to man, but it need not be treated only on a theoretical plane. Many fiction writers in modern literature have devel-oped systems within which events unfold, and one of the built-in components has been time. To it the writer ascribes values or measurements according to his concept of time as it relates to the events depicted and the characters involved. My intent in this study is to show how Orlando Romero deals with time on three dimensions in the novel *Nambé–Year One* (the title itself is a clue to the complexity of time). I shall call the three categories Cyclical Time, Abstract Time, and Retrospective Time.

Cyclical Time

Cyclical Time is probably the least complicated. It can also be classified, measured, or horizontal time. Other critics and writers have labeled it clock time, true time, chronological time, conceptual time, and so forth. Notwithstanding the mulitiplicity of labels, Cyclical Time denotes objectivity, for it is absolute, conventional and fixed. It moves in a linear form uninter-rupted and unaffected by external objects or events. Transience, sequence and irreversibility characterize it further as moving on a continuum.

From *Contemporary Chicano Fiction: A Critical Survey.* © 1986 by *Bilingual Press/Editorial Bilingüe.*

Nambé–Year One, an autobiographical novel about Mateo Romero, in reality Orlando Romero, begins in early spring and ends in early spring (a letter dated July 1975 at the end of the novel serves as an epilogue) within a three year cycle. From the outset Mateo Romero alludes to Nature's "cyclic pattern." He traverses many obstacles in real life and whatever transpires in between in no way impedes the natural flow of time. Years, seasons, months, weeks, days, hours, minutes and seconds come and go routinely as life in the village of Nambé progresses, but, as he says, "Here in Nambé everything evolves in and around cycles" (p. 13). If Mateo did set back the clock, time would continue to elapse.

However, mechanical gadgets to measure the regularity of natural or invented events are not typical in Mateo's household, and for that reason time appears to go unchecked. He says: ". . . in this house there are no clocks or other man-made devices that try to measure time" (p. 13). Yet, there must be calendars because generally Mateo is very conscious of the chronology of time. He utilizes events such as Easter, Ash Wednesday, and local fiestas as signposts for the synchronization of time in Nambé.

If we parallel the continuity of time with man's existence on Earth, then the scope of time that Orlando Romero uses falls within a traditional mold of beginning and end, or ". . . the cyclic patterns of life and death" (p. 100). Time does not stand still in the world of reality. It is inevitable and the ultimate result for Man is death. Mateo recognizes this, so he is not afraid to die, for death does not symbolize the discontinuation of life. It represents the start of a new life, reincarnation. As he says: "Death is not dying, but coming back again to nourish living things" (p. 15). Death also represents the idea that past, present and future converge simultaneously to assure the perpetuity of his being. He reflects: "When I have completed my turn, I shall be buried under the apricot tree. My rot shall enrich its roots. But, tomorrow, I must water all the trees, the garden, and also the thirst of ancestral memories that go down one thousand feet below Nambé" (pp. 13-14). Death becomes indistinguishable from the beginning of life and cyclical in nature because "the end will be like the beginning" (p. 25).

In assessing the contributions of the old people of Nambé who are dying—the completion of their life-cycle on Earth—Mateo does not shrug them off lightly. Their death is recognized as a tremendous loss, and he bemoans the far-reaching implications for *hispano* culture. The present, past and future converge again: "If the old people are dying too, and with them the wisdom of the ancients, who will show the children the real sun that gives life to Nambé?" (p. 17). Mateo furthermore laments the fugacity of time, and he views his life as inane, in addition to feeling guilty because of not having left a legacy: "How quickly my life has passed, and I've not composed a great symphony, or painted a mural masterpiece reflecting the life of my people . . ." (p. 172).

Life is circumscribed by a beginning and an ending, and years, seasons, and the like are but entities that constitute the whole. That is Cyclical Time, a kind of whirlpool of life whose movement and energy ultimately create a depression in the center as motion ceases. Thus, in *Nambé—Year One* one has Giant Cycles (Life-Death) made up of many Medium Cycles (Year-Year), with Miniature Cycles falling within a year's time span.

Abstract Time

Unlike Cyclical Time, Abstract Time is not measurable and is much more complicated; its abstractness emanates from personal and subjective value judgments. Critics and writers have categorized it as psychological time, private time, inner time, or perceptive time. No matter what classification one adopts or invents, Abstract Time is man's personal clock that measures time according to his perceptions rather than by conventional means. Values attributed to circumstances surrounding events of the past become important. In order to bring to the present a fictional past, a writer must rely on past memories.

Since memories tend to be somewhat vague in the writer's mind, regardless of the time that has elapsed between the writing and the actual occurrence of the event, he avails himself of his greatest literary weapon–imagination. Imagination affects memories and the values linked to them. Imaginary embellishment of memories in the abstract world of time is unavoidable. Three values germane to the complete understanding of Abstract Time in *Nambé—Year One* are the emotional, mental and physiological, and physical conditions as they relate to some of Orlando Romero's characters.

Time does not discriminate; it is ruthless in its physical encounter with Nature and Man. Time is all-powerful; it vanquishes and overcomes and destroys. Mateo, in talking about New Mexico, the ancestral land of serpents and ghosts, expresses that, despite Nature's fortitude, time is as destructive to It as it is to Man: "The rugged Bandelier Canyon vibrates. . . . The giant walls of the canyon, sharp and ravaged by time and the elements, destroy the twentieth century" (p. 30).

In the mystical land of New Mexico, Man and his legendary past are inextricably bound to the soil (*la tierra*); and the inhabitants of the village of Nambé are testimony to this unique relationship and dependency. Man can endure punishment inflicted by time but, unlike Nature, he eventually succumbs to it. The people of Nambé are no exception and the physical consequences of their suffering are evident. This is particularly true of those persons who become legends in their own right. Time does not spare them either.

La Bartola (*La Llorona*) is one such individual who, because of the mystique associated with the *llorona* in New Mexico, is shunned by her neighbors in Nambé and normally lives in isolation. *La Llorona* is very much a part of New Mexico's culture, and physically La Bartola in her old age becomes indistinguishable from the soil. As Orlando Romero says: "She looked like her adobe house. It was so weathered by time that most of the mud plaster was cracking and the wood of the windows had turned a soft, wild nappy gray" (p. 59).

But *La Llorona* is not the only person who forms part of the *hispano* culture in New Mexico. No village is ever without a *viuda*. A widow is very much an integral part of *hispano* culture and in most cases she is venerated, not scorned. Orlando Romero talks about *La Viuda* as an anonymous, nameless creature; the reason, no doubt, is to underscore her importance collectively instead of fragmenting the concept of *viudez*. By and large the widow leads a very introspective and personal life, in which time is relative. The punishment—or martyrdom—is partially self-inflicted, although culture is also responsible because mourning is inherent in it; hence the consequences for the *viuda* which are "total remorse, total isolation, total penitence . . ." (p. 163). All of these things contribute to physical deterioration, but time is the most devastating. *La Viuda* has been "bent by time" in ".. . the vast loneliness of her house" (p. 163).

One of the by-products of solitude is mental and physiological agony incurred by circumstances surrounding isolation, in which case time seems even more abstract. As Mateo states: "In my restlessness [physiological] I imagine [mental] the hour, for in this house there are no clocks or other man-made devices that try to measure time" (p. 13). Five minutes under duress may seem like an eternity and therefore not indicative of true time because the conscious activity is altogether different.

Proper conditions can also engender an inordinate expansion of time in the mind of an individual. Mateo, in recalling an unpleasant episode with his father, draws upon the expansion of time: "Centuries later, at age twelve or so, I hit him with a piece of firewood as he was about to beat my mother" (p. 26). The expansion of time is seen moreover in the context of Man's wisdom. In Nambé the person who stands out in that category is Don Agustín. His knowledge has transcended so many decades that his name strikes a legend remembered only in time and space. According to Mateo's grandfather, Don

Agustín is ageless: "My Grandfather says he [Don Agustín] is about one-hundred-fifty years old. Everyone in the village knows he is a man of wisdom" (p. 93). Don Agustín himself talks to Mateo not in literal but abstract time: "'Mateo, today for the first time in over a hundred years, I feel a little old but yet full of joy to see you a grown man and as exciting a child as when I used to hold you in my arms!'" (p. 97).

Feelings and emotions are values inherent in Abstract Time too. They are symptoms that emanate from within, or as the *hispano* would say, from the "heart and soul." Mateo's "adobe soul and spirit" rest in his adobe house ". . . where time means nothing and everything . . ." (p. 9). However, it is the place where memories and nostalgia abound with emotion: "Its walls are alive with the tears of years forgotten to the meaningless word we know as time. It was fact. . . . It caught time itself, made it stop, and its haunting memories were left as reminders" (loc. cit.). Mateo's soul at times reflects antiquity, but his spirit is rejuvenated. He states the following: "My years have been measured at twenty-seven though my soul is older than the world . . ." (p. 17). He talks about his "weary yet joyous soul" (p. 21) and how time is meaningless in a world of illusion in spite of the many spirits he evokes from his adobe milieu. Time is priceless, an abstraction, to say the least, but "that's the way it is in this land of paradoxes, enigmas and solitude. In this land, time means nothing and everything. Every second is burdened with joy and sorrow" (p. 94).

Love causes joy and sorrow and makes time insignificant; love is witnessed in relatives, friends, or children. There is no question but that time that is lived and enjoyed intensely tends to elapse much more quickly, while in memory it lasts a lot longer because "only the memory lingers, always memory. It stays behind and sometimes jumps ahead of time, which we consider more valuable than wealth" (p. 57). Mateo constantly reminds us of this fact ". . . as if the time we shared with our loved ones will far outlast the time created by men . . ." (p. 80). Mateo recalls his first love affair with an Indian-Irish girl as a means of measuring time: "She was my first. This is the way time is measured here. In seasons, love, joy, and pain" (p. 15).

Mateo asserts over and over the validity of time in its abstract form, saying that time is "precious and enigmatic" (p. 138). Conversely, if time is imbued with boredom, time passes slowly. In the final analysis, Abstract Time is very personal because, "Each one of us lives in his own time. Each one of us lives in his own world. It is the health of our own past and the health of our own world that will determine our future" (pp. 141-142).

Retrospective Time

Retrospective Time may be defined as the block of time that the author selects to describe past and present events in a novel. Time, in this case, does not command a true beginning or a definite ending because something precedes and something follows. Because of the author's choice, time is irreducible and constant, yet he may wish to restrict or to expand time itself within that time frame either to underscore or de-emphasize certain episodes and thereby achieve the proper fullness and continuity in the work. In that context, time can vary in degree, with the basic difference being that here, unlike in Abstract Time, it is the reader who is affected (provided there are no external distractions) and not the hero or characters.

Retrospective Time, then, once the author establishes its boundaries, is not altered. In *Nambé–Year One* it covers twenty years. This period can be placed between 1955 and 1975, a time span that begins when Mateo Romero is seven years old and ends about the time he is twenty-seven. To be sure, the reader experiences two decades in a few hours of reading. It is worth noting, moreover, that Mateo's age span is both arbitrary and coincidental, which is in keeping with the concept of Retrospective Time, because his physical presence on earth does not start or end at age seven and twenty-seven, or in 1955 and 1975, respectively. His intellectual and spiritual *raison d'être* does; it begins on the day he finds his identity and roots: "I am the incarnation of his wild-blood [his grandfather's] . . . There is Indian in us . . . I felt it the night I was seven years old" (p. 12).

Where short periods of expanded or reduced time within Retrospective Time affect the reader, the author strives to bring into focus particular events that add texture and tempo to the novel. To do this he resorts to devices concerning time. These may include time-shift, flash-back or historical reference. These devices are all important in *Nambé—Year One*.

Orlando Romero employs what I have chosen to call historical reference. This does not mean historical citations *per se*; instead, they are references made to history in a broad and purposely vague way. (This vagueness is in concert with the concept of time in general.) For example, in *Nambé-Year One* Romero does not refer directly to episodes in history, but the general and implicit hints that he does use manifest an impact on and an importance in the artistic development of the novel.

He begins his novel by purposely introducing the reader into a world of historical significance that sets, to a degree, the tone and prepares the reader for the kind of atmosphere that is prevalent throughout *Nambé—Year One*. He narrates: "In the time of the Gypsies and Payasos that wandered through the mountains of Northern New Mexico, there was one particular enchantress who came from Spain" (p. 7). An amplification of the importance of the history of New Mexico in the novel is further witnessed in the longstanding archeological and anthropological vestiges of the Native American. As Mateo says:

> This is the land of Serpents and Ghosts. Ghost of Indians in their caves, children playing and crying. Old, ancient people dying, being reborn in the blackness and stillness of cave society, as the great, primal essence is absorbed. The paintings in the caves remain as proof of man's mystery, love, and involvement in the sometimes bewildering events in nature. Here, man has taken a bit of himself and painted his fancy, fantasy, and his reality." (p. 30)

However, as Mateo proclaims, Man has a way of neglecting or distorting history: "There is an invader in this stream. He devours the young of the Rainbow and Cutthroat trout. He was brought here in the 1880's, but is considered by many as a native" (p. 31).

Time-shift is the other technique that Orlando Romero uses, and he does so successfully in giving balance to the structure of the novel. This device is a deliberate fragmentation of the sequence of events or the natural flow of time in a novel. It is time in the past laden with feelings that remain in the past. Two good examples are Romero's references to a couple of letters by Juan López Romero (Mateo's great-grandfather) that Mateo examines surreptitiously in the attic of his house. The first letter, dated October 18, 1863, is to a woman in Santa Fe who is ill and for whom help will come from a *curandero* enroute from Mexico (pp. 45–47). The second is a love letter written on August 21, 1862, addressed affectionately to Flor (pp. 47–48). The date indicates a time-shift within a time-shift. That is, the more recent letter comes first in the novel's narrative. This is a conscious interruption of the continuity of time and events that Romero uses by accentuating that interruption with two letters from yesteryear, out of sequence, and not within the 1955-75 time period chosen as Retrospective Time for the novel.

The last device that Romero employs in dealing with Retrospective Time is flash-back; it is the depiction of past events inserted into a present situation. Unlike time-shift, where the emotional impact of the situation remains in the past, flash-back deals with events of the past, but the feelings are brought to the present. For example, Bartola, the *Llorona* in the novel, encounters Mateo one early spring or summer day and tells him about the calamity that befell Tres Ritos in years past. "'In the middle of January,'" says Bartola, a "'up in Tres Ritos, that's where we lived, a terrible plague terrified all the villages. Little children died every day. . . . We weathered that cruel winter of death, sorrow, and haunting, restless spirits'" (pp. 63-64). It is also a winter that brings back memories for Mateo in reflecting on his love for his Gypsy, his idealized love and Muse:

> It was at her doorstep, in the middle of Winter, that a small snow-filled man melted. He disappeared into the flagstones by her door. His little pebble eyes remained along with the same warm smile that caused him to melt. There in the middle of a cruel physical Winter, the bronze, golden sun of Nambé penetrated the solitude of enigmas that constitute living in the land of ancient ghosts and paradoxes. . . . Only the memory lingers, always a memory. It stays behind and sometimes jumps ahead of time, which we consider more valuable than wealth. (p. 57)

After studying the dimensions of time in *Nambé–Year One* several observations and conclusions come to mind: first, Nambé, a Tewa word (*nambay-ongwee*) meaning "people of the roundish earth," prompts us to reflect briefly on the title of the novel as it relates to our study on time. Nambé implies antiquity, things of the past. Similarly, "year one" conjures up a kind of mystery and uncertainty about the significance of time. It suggests moreover an epoch in the past, but is it 1 A.D. or 1 B.C.? Or is it perhaps a year in the future? A concrete determination of the date may be irrelevant. On the other hand, it could be the fateful year 2001. By that time Nambé, after having been ravaged and destroyed by time and melted into the earth from which it once rose, may be nothing more than a symbol of history, as has become customary with other villages in rural New Mexico. To be sure, Orlando Romero used year one deliberately to dramatize the spirit of time and how it defies a concrete definition and is therefore open to a multitude of analyses and interpretations by anyone who is interested. Year one quite simply heightens what Mendilow calls the vagaries and varieties of time.

Finally, we have learned that one should not take time lightly in a piece of literature, particularly the novel. Time demands more than casual attention. Cyclical, Abstract, and Retrospective Time and their respective nuances and preferences according to the values ascribed to them attest further to the complexity of time in the structure of a given work of art. Yet, in the total scheme of things, it cannot be controlled. Any manipulation of time is superficial at best, and this, coupled with all the other facets discussed in the course of this study on *Nambé–Year One*, accounts for the mystery that time generates and the bafflement it creates in human behavior, whether it concerns the writer, the critic, or the reader.

EDUARDO SEDA BONILLA

On the Vicissitudes of Being "Puerto Rican": An Exploration of Pedro Juan Soto's Hot Land, Cold Season

When they are true to their calling, Latin American writers and intellectuals must live the passion which Leopold Zea in *Latin American Mind* considers the fate of *visionarios*. In English, the word visionary has the negative connotation of an impartial idealist. The closest approximation to the Latin American meaning of *visionario* in English is anti-visionary: he who reads the signs of his times, and takes advantage of it—in other words, the opportunist. In Latin America, when intellectuals are not *visionarios*, they become politicians and like a high proportion of politicians everywhere are materialistic, practical, cheap, and limited in vision. In responding with authenticity to their calling, *visionario* writers in Latin America become what Victor Hugo was said to be: "the conscience of his country" in his lifetime.

The genre of our writers is social criticism, as evidenced by Ciro Alegría, Jorge Icaza, Gabriel García Márquez, Mario Vargas Llosa, José Eustasio Rivera, Alejo Carpentier, José María Arguedas, Carlos Fuentes, Augusto Roa Bastos, Miguel Angel Asturias, Julio Cortázar, Rómulo Gallegos, Carlos Luis Fallas, and Juan Rulfo, just to mention a few. Puerto Rican writers follow the pattern set by fellow Latin American writers. The historical awareness of writers like Pedro Juan Soto, Enrique Laguerre, René Marqués, Abelardo Díaz Alfaro, César Andreu Iglesias, Emilio Díaz Valcárcel, Luis Rafael Sánchez, Edwin Figueroa, José Luis González and

From *MELUS: The Journal of the Society for the Study of the Multi-Ethnic Literature of the United States*, Vol. 6, No 3. ©1979 by the University of Southern California.

many others gives them the function of consciousness raisers, ahead and beyond the conservative thought of sociologists, political scientists, and other so-called behavioral scientists.

In Pedro Juan Soto's novel *Hot Land, Cold Season* the drama arises from the subject matter of racism, American brand, internalized by Puerto Ricans. It portrays the response to the nonwhite racistic identity imposed upon Puerto Ricans by North American categories of culture. The identity of individuals is derived from genetic inheritance in ignorance of all scientific evidence showing identity as the result of enculturation. Children of immigrant parents have always been told that their identity was derived from their genetic inheritance rather than from the enculturation given them in the behavioral environments of community, school, play and work situations. The deeper the internalization of the categorical postulates of the American culture, the stronger their pseudo-ethnicity.

Pseudo-ethnicity is indeed a very peculiar component of the naive realism imbedded in the cultural optic and praxis of the United States. Upon internalizing this peculiar cultural postulate of their identity, persons born in the United States of America think and feel that they are Italian if their parents were Italian, even if the only thing they know to say in Italian is spaghetti and "Mama mia." When these pseudo-Italians return to Italy without knowing the language or the culture, they find that Italy is as foreign to them as it is to any other of their fellow pseudo-ethnics in the Land of Pseudo-Ethnia.

In the categorical postulates of American racistic thought, the descendants of the enslaved African population are believed to be African even if, when they go to Africa, they are perceived by Africans as nothing but Americans, which in truth is what they are. Commenting on this issue, Donald C. Leidel says that

> . . . it is a white-racist notion to think that Black Americans have anymore instinctive bonds with, say, Nigeria than white Americans have with Finland. Black Americans in Africa are in fact often seen by Africans as "white" because culturally they belong to the expatriate community.

North American racistic optic makes identity a derivation of genetic descent, denying the effect of culture on personality, and often going to the extremes of denying the existence of an American culture, as if the American people were a society of bees, ants or wasps. Just like the children of any other immigrant group, children of Puerto Rican parents are made to believe they are Puerto Rican by the reason of genetic inheritance, in total disregard of their enculturation in neighborhoods they share with Blacks and other pseudo-ethnics. Paradoxically, the more North American, the more Puerto Rican they think they are, looking at themselves from a perspective that views identity as derivative of genetic inheritance.

Here in Puerto Rico, we accept as Puerto Rican all those who integrate themselves into our cultural milieu, no matter where they or their ancestors came from. This is the reason why in Puerto Rico there are no "Italians," even with all the Italian surnames we have. We have no Irish, even with all the Murphys, O'Neills and MacAllisters, no "French," no "Russians," no "Spaniards," no "Africans," despite the popularity of the Afro, which is more North American than apple pie. Africa has many cultures and many languages. There is no one culture that could be identified as African.

The United States is a land of pseudo-ethnics, i.e., culturally assimilated but socially segregated identities. Cultural assimilation in the melting pot implies social segregation and racistic hierarchy. This racistic hierarchy is often called a "pecking order." Socially segregated yet culturally assimilated pseudo-ethnics are placed in a status hierarchy, the top position of which is occupied by the Anglo Saxon protestants. At the bottom of the "pecking order" are placed the dark Mediterranean and Eastern European populations. Mexicans, American Indians, Blacks and Puerto Ricans are set apart in a different league, characterized as non-white with their own "pecking order," with "Japanese" on top and Blacks on the bottom. Many so-called white ethnics on the lower rungs of the hierarchy have engaged in a struggle to be included in this caste line so they might profit from federal funds assigned for programs for the disadvantaged. Women have also moved along the same line.

There are many Puerto Ricans in Puerto Rico who are not aware of the phenomena of pseudo-ethnicity that prevail in the United States. They are not aware that the Puerto Rican identity of many of those who come back home is a simple derivative of the American racistic cultural optic and praxis, and that their self-presentation as Puerto Rican is a dramatization of the categories of culture of the United States. In other words, *their Puertoricanness is a fiction* created by the racistic categories they have acquired in the process of enculturation for the second generation and even for the first generation.

The United States of America lacks a national name identity because both "United States" and "America" are generic terms. United States citizens have remained nameless in the history of a world upon which they themselves have strongly imprinted a pragmatic view. A name of an object is not the object, but unlabeled objects resist placement in categories and become vague as the solipsistic "I am who I am." We are of course assuming that "American" is not a proper name for the inhabitants of the United States, since it is a generic name for the inhabitant of the whole continent: North, Central and South America. There are, of course, the derisive nicknames such as Yankees, *gringos*, rednecks, and lately "whites," used by the so-called non-whites. But these are not place names.

Facing the ambiguity of object categorization for the place of their destiny, migrants from Puerto Rico and their relatives at home invented their own terms. Migrants leaving Puerto Rico were said to go to *El Norte* and, later on, *Los Neuyores*. The latter term was first used for New York, but since New York was conceived as the whole country, migrants returning from no matter what part of the United States of America were said to return from *Los Neuyores*. Eventually *Los Neuyores* was the generalized term for the place that Puerto Ricans went to when they left for mainland U.S.A. *Neuyorican* was the expected coinage. *Neuyorican* is often incorrectly used as if it were interchangeable with *Neorican*, which is the term coined by Enrique Laguerre in reference to those Puerto Ricans who have undergone soul transmigration and become one hundred percent "American" without ever having left the island (see Enrique Laguerre, *El fuego y su aire*). I first heard the term *Neuyorican* used by Manuel Maldonado Denis.

Hot Land, Cold Season portrays the traumatic experience of children of Puerto Rican parents who encounter Puerto Rico with an American cultural script: i.e., a repertoire of linguistic and interpersonal praxis which they assume to be Puerto Rican on the basis of the fiction of racism imbedded in the American culture and in which they have formed their outlook and praxis. With the influx of thousands of returned migrants and their children to Puerto Rico in the last decade, this confusion of cultural stages and the consequent disappointment and despair takes on the proportion of a Tower of Babel.

The narrative of *Hot Land, Cold Season* begins in Kennedy Airport, where Eduardo, a young man born in Puerto Rico but reared in New York from the age of eight, waits for a flight back to Puerto Rico to visit his brother, Jacinto. The brother and his wife Adela have moved back to and settled in Puerto Rico for good. Jacinto has made up his mind never to return to the United States, even for a visit. It is not clear if Jacinto did not want anything to do with New York or if his actual resentment is only against his father. Jacinto had had a fist fight with his father two weeks before his return to Puerto Rico. However, Adela, who did not want to return to Puerto Rico at the time, continues to hope that they will go back for a visit to New York.

One of Eduardo's reasons for going to Puerto Rico has to do with the rift between Jacinto and his father. Eduardo hopes to soften his older brother's attitude toward their alcoholic father. He plans to visit in Puerto Rico for four weeks, and to return to New York to begin his freshman year in college.

In the plane, after take-off, Eduardo strikes up a conversation with a tourist. The tourist inquires what Eduardo's nationality is. Amazed that the man could not guess the fiction he takes as self-evident and true as *mancha de plátano* (the indelible stain from green bananas), he muses, "Can't he tell just by looking at me?" Eduardo assumes, like any other North American, that behavior is a derivative of race and not of culture. Neither does he realize the extent to which his culture has become American. Part of that Americanization is the assumption that Puertoricanness is derived from a "race," invisible to all but those tutored in hypodescent. This knot of contradictory assumptions will remain as the central thread of the drama. When the freckled-faced tourist closes his eyes and sleeps, Eduardo's mind wanders back to the first trip, when his family moved to New York ten years before. His mother then spoke of her hope for a better college education for the children. She also spoke of parks and beaches, nice schools, nice jobs— but deep down her main reason for coming to the United States was to get her husband away from the bottle.

Passing reference to New York is made in Eduardo's reminiscences about his sister Lavinia, who married an "Italian" psuedo-ethnic, and whose son, Ralphie, in an early identification with the aggressor, called her family "Spicky Spicks." There is also reference to Willy, a veteran of World War I, who drank two bottles of rot gut every evening and tipped his hat to every lady going by on the street. Willy ended up falling from an elevator shaft and breaking four ribs. Eduardo recalls Lefty Fernández who jumped off a roof before his 17th birthday. Lefty's sister had become pregnant by Carl Livingstone, a neighborhood bully. When his sister told Lefty of her pregnancy, he grabbed a butcher knife, met Carl at the corner of Madison and 112th street and, after a brief struggle, stabbed him to death. Lefty then ran to a roof top and jumped to his death. Further horrors are recalled as Eduardo muses about the time that Jacinto and Adela moved to an apartment where armies of cockroaches and rats scurried about the attic at night.

The scene then changes to Puerto Rico, where the familiar uproar starts the moment when returning Puerto Rican migrants glimpse the island emerging as an outline in the blue Caribbean waters. The airport scene is realistically portrayed with the confusion and commotion of passengers and people waiting for passengers, the free drinks for tourists, and the emotionality of returned migrants upon seeing their beloved country again. While stepping off the stairs of the landing ramp, Eduardo nearly trips over an old man who had gone down on his knees to kiss the earth. Other Puerto Ricans are elbowing their way through the crowd of tourists to meet relatives and friends, embrace them, shed a flood of happy tears, or rush frantically back and forth in search of people they had promised to meet in the airport.

Here Eduardo's crypto-racistic, fictitious self-concept becomes invisible again when the Puerto Rican porter, upon returning his baggage, asks another porter to hand it to the "American kid." Then, in the airport parking lot, ready to go, Eduardo uses the word *garpante* to describe Jacinto's old car. The latter does not remember the meaning of the word and coldly refuses to understand Eduardo while rebuffing him with "that is not Spanish." Like many other return migrants, Jacinto lives with his wife and children in Levittown.

The story unfolds as an anatomical dissection of Jacinto's choice to become a Puerto Rican and live up to the commitment of that choice. Jacinto is the prototype of a biographical and historical option taken by many who, like him, become Puerto Rican, shedding the optic of the North American culture, in which they were "Puerto Rican" in name only, and adopting a Puerto Rican identity in language, in culture and in life projects. Our prodigal son had a hard time learning first things first, i.e., that Puertoricanness is not a matter of race; it is the outcome of a culture. He must learn the Spanish language and the optic and praxis of a culture that he assumed he knew on the basis of crypto-racistic, pseudo-ethnicity.

Like any other human identity, the Puerto Rican identity is option lived in commitment and not a biological heritage. Race is a social fiction, not a biological determinant of behavior. Human behavior is a function of history in its cultural transcendence. Man is a creature of his own creation in history, not a product of biological inheritance. Racism is a cultural fiction intended to make all futures a repetition of the past, as with animals. Human beings can become whatever they make up their minds to be, as long as they have the courage to pursue that as an option in the exercise of freedom. A biological definition of identity is a denial of that freedom.

I will not mention the names of those I have known personally who were raised in the United States, and later made the choice to live in Puerto Rico as Puerto Ricans. Most of them do not want to be reminded that once upon a time they called themselves Puerto Rican and in doing so were reinforcing a North American definition of identity which was crypto-racistic.

The American milieu, like that of any other country, acculturates immigrants in the first generation and enculturates their children in the postulates that hold together the intersubjective world of that society.

Social segregation in a racistic "pecking order" is often confused with resistance to cultural assimilation. Ethnic identity is then reified in stereo-typed tokens such as knishes, *bacalaítos*, or Saint Patrick's Day. Yet, there is effective resistance to acculturation among those groups who partially recon-struct their system of life in ethnic communities. Brentwood is an example of such a community. Such is the case with orthodox Jewish communities, the French Canadians, native Americans, Mexicans, and other ethnic enclaves, where a system of life parallel to the main culture remains. Even there, they must find ways of adjusting to the dominant culture of the United States. Without the support of the community, there is little likelihood of not becoming culturally assimilated.

Their courage to be true ethnics might have given strength to the possibility of authentic cultural pluralism in the United States in contrast to the prevailing practice of crypto-racism that generates pseudo-ethnicity in the melting pot of anglo conformity. Their courage to be and their determi-nation to engage in the commitments and responsibilities of their choice might have been a lesson to those melted into the culture of the U.S.A., who assume themselves to be ethnics in North American terms. Support for the pseudo-ethnic misconstruction of reality for children of Puerto Rican parents finds patronizing support among those who would lead us along the path of assimilation to the language and culture of the United States, because the racistic optic blurs their understanding of culture, because of the profit accruing to the con man playing "Be my guest," or because of purposeful Americanization of Puerto Rico.

The image of Puerto Rico seen through the eyes of Eduardo is first that of Levittown with all the houses made from the same mold, on the same size plots, with the same fences, and similar cars. Returning to the *barrio* where he was born and raised until the age of eight, he is met, as though he were an American tourist, by a group of shoeshine boys. Here, in his own home town, the shoeshine boy remarks *sotto voce* that Eduardo sounds almost like a "gringo." The remark costs the shoeshine boy the tip Eduardo had planned to give him. His home community is not what he had dreamed it would be. The discordant reality is pieced together with naked, barefoot children and the polluted river. The aristocratic house of Doctor Boneta had been converted into a gas station. The ever-present signs of poverty, indo-lence, and the deterioration of human dignity are a far cry from the idealized image Eduardo had formed of the community from far away. Eduardo wonders if an old lady, Doña Caridad, "would be capable of ordering Monsita [her daughter] to sleep with a man so they'd have something to eat?" When he tells Doña Caridad that his parents are planning to return to

Puerto Rico, the old lady begs him to warn his parents not to return to Puerto Rico but to stay in the United States. "They'd be better off if they stayed up north." Her image of "up north" is the old myth of El Dorado, where the streets are paved with gold. What a contrast to the mud of El Babote, literally the big drool. Eduardo was there as evidence to prove the myth, with his opulent attire, his wrist watch, his wad of dollars, his discreet, anonymous present of a bag of groceries for Monsita's family.

Eduardo's Puertoricanness, derived from American cultural assumptions, becomes invisible again when Quico Artaud wonders rhetorically, "You are more American than Puerto Rican, are you not?" Yet, Eduardo's determination to sink his roots in Puerto Rico is strengthened by the hope of studying engineering, to help the people whom he always considered to be his people, and who are so badly in need of help. That night, he writes a letter to his parents asking them to move back to Puerto Rico. He does not suspect how difficult is the way back to Puertoricanness because he mistakenly assumes that he is already what he must become.

When Eduardo goes to Mayagüez to seek admission to the University of Puerto Rico's College of Engineering, he tries in Spanish to ask a girl where the Registrar's Office is. "Excuse me" (he can not think of the words in Spanish, so he continues in English), "Where is the Registrar's Office, please?" The girl gives him a blank look and he stands stammering and gesturing for some time, feeling like a fool for not being able to make himself understood, almost like a deaf mute. "Oh, you mean la Oficina del Registrador?", she finally says in Spanish, and tells him where to go.

The central issue of the book is the confusion which the American crypto-racistically-conceived-self-concept of Puertoricanness generates when actualized, as if indeed race had anything to do with human behavior. This drama is now lived by thousands of children of Puerto Rican parents raised in New York who assume on the basis of the North American criteria that the way they behave is a product of genetic inheritance and not the outcome of enculturation. The central issue is eventually crystallized in Eduardo's mind when he asks his brother, "If I am an American, a gringo, a Yankee down here, and up north I am a Puerto Rican, a spik; what in hell am I really? Who am I? Where do I belong?" (breaking into English).

His older brother's answer is that for him, being Puerto Rican involves a choice in the exercise of freedom. "You have to make up your mind that you are going to belong here, do you understand? It has to come from inside you. Otherwise. . . ."

The "otherwise" choice is a halfway station, a place where a world constructed with categories of North American culture is suspended over the world of Puerto Rican reality, an alien intruder with an outlook and values which do not ever quite reach the standards of Puerto Rican culture, except as a model for those Puerto Ricans in pursuit of Americanization.

Since the categories of reality and the optic and praxis of this sector of children brought up in New York are North American, despite their having been conned into believing otherwise either by opportunistic Puerto Ricans or by racistic North Americans, they drift toward becoming the bored tourists looking for excitement in a world for which they have no commitment nor attachment. Here, the author brings into view a portrait of an alien world of returned migrants, marginal to Puerto Rican society, peopled by those who remain unaware that for them to become Puerto Rican involves a cultural choice and a commitment They continue taking their Puertoricanness as biologically given.

The halfway choice presented in *Hot Land, Cold Season* is a no-man's land of uprootedness and marginality. The marginal groups meet in secluded places with dimmed lights, strip-tease, naked dancing, and retreatism of every possible kind. They are, to themselves, Puerto Ricans, yet Puerto Ricans on the island do not and can not see them or relate to them as such. Some become bitter, others defiant. When Eduardo asked Fran if she had been called American, she answered "Well, if they don't like it, they can lump it. . . ."

The author's understanding of the phenomenology of pseudo-ethnicity is portrayed in a scene where a girl, in imitation of Juliette Greco, sings in French. The girl defines her predicament: "We are not Americans, because in New York we are called Puerto Ricans. We are not Puerto Ricans, because in Puerto Rico we are called Americans." Faced with the need to choose from a position of "neither Puerto Rican nor American," they fell into the vacuum of "men without a country." In that vacuum, it is hard to see that men are, as Sartre has argued, their options, not products of their genes. Soto's characters must choose with conscious awareness of culture. The choices are not unlimited. There is Jacinto's choice which I believe has been the choice of many eminent university professors and outstanding Puerto Rican writers, poets, artists, journalists, and leaders. By contrast, there is the choice of Ziggy Benítez and company to remain marginal, scooping the crust of the pie of the "best" of two worlds without belonging to either. Then there is the choice of Eduardo, overwhelmed by the confusion, incapable of taking the option of his brother Jacinto, and disgusted with the sick option of Ziggy Benítez. The climax of the novel portrays Eduardo in total disillusionment and in a desperate retreat, trying to return to his home, New York, at any cost and inconvenience. His wallet and his watch are stolen when, in disgust, he leaves the company of Ziggy and walks in a state of drunkenness into the night of San Juan. At last he reaches the airport. His belongings disappear, but he is oblivious. He has only one purpose, a fixed obsession to return home on the first available seat on a standby flight, at no matter what price.

The outcome of Eduardo's choice to go back to a home that will never be acknowledged to be his by those who share it with him as fellow-traveling pseudo-ethnics, such as Italians, Jews, Anglo-Americans and Afro-Americans, is not explored in this novel. Neither has this choice been followed up and analyzed in sociological research. What happens to the Eduardos when they finally succeed in re-entering the land of pseudo-aliens? Will they continue thinking with North American categories of pseudo-ethnicity that they are Puerto Rican? Will they find comfort in the fact that people around them cannot see anything wrong with that crypto-racistic conception and would consider any identification other than Puerto Rican as "passing," a hideous crime in that culture?

The portrayal of Eduardo's predicament represents that of 45,000 children born on the mainland of Puerto Rican parents, who have returned to Puerto Rico and who live the identity crisis presented by Pedro Juan Soto in *Hot Land, Cold Season*. Many of them refuse to speak Spanish and are given special instruction in English in the company of *Neoriqueños*, who are elated to have a chance to learn English with those who speak it like United States natives, called here "Continentals." They live the standby drama of Eduardo, waiting for the first chance to go "home.") Some do return to New York, and later on come back to Puerto Rico to re-enroll in the school left, in some cases, months before, to the utter confusion of themselves and the school personnel.

The radical Puerto Rican student group considers them cultural aggressors and despises them, not out of snobbery, but from resentment for their strengthening the hand of those Puerto Ricans who have undergone soul transmigration to become 100% Americans: the *Neoriqueño* group who sees in them the model that "Puerto Rican Americans" should imitate. Manuel Maldonado Denis mistakenly argues that the *Neoriqueños* (Americanized middle-class Puerto Ricans) is the sector that rejects children of returned migrants.

> La presencia de estos puertorriqueños que han arribado a Puerto Rico y que no saben español ha generado toda una dialéctica de chauvinismo y prejuicio social y racial entre considerables sectores de la población puertorriqueña, sobretodo entre las capas medias. Resulta chocante que quienes más estridentemente pregonan su filoyanquismo sean

a su vez los que rechazan una persona porque habla inglés.

Maldonado Denis has obviously not visited public school Papa Juan XXIII in Bayamón where the children of returned migrants have the support of the "phyloyanqui" *neoriqueños* in violent confrontations with the radical *independentista* groups who accuse them of "stomping their feet on the flag of our country Puerto Rico."

In a study in progress, we have found so far that return migrants live the initial period of return to Puerto Rico in exuberant happiness. Some describe this as a tourist euphoria, basking in our sunshine, enjoying our scenery of palm trees, blue waters, and white sandy beaches, blue skies, and a countryside full of lush vegetation. Then comes the realization that the vacation is over.

After the initial stage of blissful happiness, many of these children of returned migrants realize that Spanish is not their best language and that they feel insecure in a world constructed with categories of reality that are alien to them. They view the behavioral norms, and the physical condition of schools lacking in gymnastic facilities, and the non-permissive educational environment, as oppressive and restraining compared with the school "back home." This is not the mere contrived snobbery which Manuel Maldonado Denis portrays in his latest writings. At this point, they start their frantic struggle to return to the United States, a struggle which includes despising everything that is Puerto Rican and over-identifying themselves with "America."

It is said in the schools where children of return migrants are concentrated that they respond to the felt rejection by accentuating the traits which differentiate them from Puerto Ricans and stressing dissimilarities, since the enemy is perceived to be the Puerto Rican from the island (*los de acá*). In a total definition, everything about the enemy is bad. Scholastic achievement in the migrant group suffers from the impact of this situation and it is to be expected, although there have been no reliable studies showing that the drop-out rates, as well as the prevalence of alienated behavior, is especially significant among the children of return migrants.

Many things these children do or do not do are misinterpreted or rejected in a behavioral environment constructed with categories of culture that they do not understand. Children of return migrants often misinterpret the incompatibilities that result from stage misplacement as equivalent to what happened to them in the United States, when "whites" rejected them by calling them dirty Spiks and other derisive names. They experience not being seen as Puerto Rican as a re-run of the earliest drama of their lives, when Anglos and other pseudo-ethnics refused to acknowledge them as fellow Americans no matter to what degree of Anglo conformity they might pattern their lives. Since they were once refused identity credentials in a racistic context, they assume the rejection here is as hypocritical and fallacious as it was then, when it was a cover-up for racistic prejudices. They would not live the nightmare of not-American, not-Puerto Rican, who-am-I, if efforts were made to make them aware of the power of choice in the exercise of freedom.

Since they mistakenly assume they are Puerto Rican and find support and propitiation for this mistaken American postulate from those who see in them the model of Americanization for Puerto Ricans, their prospect of acquiring Puerto Rican culture and becoming full-fledged Puerto Ricans becomes a political game of many hands. Those who play in that game destroy the opportunity of these prospective Puerto Ricans to become Puerto Rican in the light of conscious choice. In some schools in the San Juan Metropolitan area, they gravitate together in opposition to those who call them *gringos* and press them to abandon their American life style and language. Fist fights and rock and bottle throwing sometimes break out in the schools between students from the two groups.

Many Puerto Ricans born and raised in Puerto Rico are not aware of the enormous psychological price paid by return migrants raised as "spiks" in the streets of New York. Most Puerto Ricans on the Island tend to interpret the New York experience through the character of Maria in *The West Side Story*, ignoring all the other characters of the play, as well as the implied statement on race in the song "To be White in America," which Puerto Ricans are not. News media tell us only of "success" stories. Most Puerto Ricans in Puerto Rico are not aware of the fact that Puerto Rico for the return migrants is the dream of the home they never had in the land of Pseudo-Ethnia.

Awareness of the root of the matter lies in the understanding of culture. This is likely to misfire in the face of racistic definitions of culture and high pitched emotionality. A significant portion of the children of returned migrants live only for the moment when they can return to the mainland, in a state of mind like that so masterfully portrayed by Pedro Juan Soto in the character of Eduardo, who is willing to leave behind his luggage and belongings, just so long as he can get the first empty seat on the first flight out. The struggle to return usually ends in the second year, when they generally become culturally integrated as Puerto Ricans. For those who insist on returning, like Eduardo, the eventual outcome is one of homeless uprootedness, a pattern not just for children of return migrants, but for many migrants of the first generation. Filomeno Santos

Chico in the village of Tipan voices this pattern in these words:

> "Damn it, guys, I can't get used to being here and can't get used
> to being there! I can't stand it in either place, men!"

For the children of migrants, the homeless uprootedness is a bit
different from that of their parents, since once they lose communality with
Puerto Ricans in language and culture, they have to avail themselves of the
American language and culture, where their postulated Puertoricanness is a
function of paradoxical pseudo-ethnicity. In their "America," they will never
be considered American except as hyphenated pseudo-ethnic aliens. This is a
hard truth to face, but only truth will liberate men. In giving men the capacity
to choose with conscious awareness and responsibility, we attempt to increase
our awareness of the dangers of possible cultural extinction, should our people
continue on the path of Americanization. Eduardo and those like him are
opening for Puerto Ricans a path to a hell of cultural assimilation paved with
the good intentions of brotherhood-in-name not in substance.

The options are not infinite. They are limited by the dialectics of
history. There is the option of those like Eduardo, who assume they are
Puerto Rican from an American cultural perspective. There are those like
Jacinto who Celia Cintrón and Pedro Vales have portrayed as "burning
their bridges behind them." People like Eduardo can remain Americans by
an understanding of the concept of pseudo-ethnicity or they can become
true Puerto Ricans by adopting the culture of Puerto Rico. Led by those
who play "Be my guest" to Eduardo's type, we will all eventually be Puerto
Rican in name only, joining the Americans in the myth that there is a
Puerto Rican racial inheritance that determines the behavior of Puerto
Ricans. This can be for Puerto Ricans the first step towards full and foolish
Americanization. Since a person in the American culture is assumed to
inherit the ethnic identity of his parents, and genetic inheritance cannot be
altered, we will be led to accept the false assurance of cultural continuity
which is ethnocidal in its consequences.

VERNON E. LATTIN

Time and History in Candelaria's
Memories of the Alhambra

A commonplace of literary criticism is the importance of time in the modern novel. With Bergson and Proust standing in the background, one thinks of Joyce, Woolf, Mann, and Faulkner to confirm this point. In the shadow of such giants, the recent development of the Chicano novel with its branch, the New Mexican Chicano narrative, goes unnoticed. However, a work like Nash Candelaria's *Memories of the Alhambra* must be read because it is one of a growing number of Chicano novels exploring time and history from a new perspective.

The New Mexican Chicano holds a unique position in American history and American letters. The Chicano looks at history and himself from multiple and often simultaneous angles of vision. From the first angle of vision he looks back to Spain and his emotional ties to Europe, to the Spanish language and customs, and to the early Spaniards in America such as Cortez, Coronado, Oñate, and Vargas. The date 1492 is etched into his soul. Perhaps he can trace his ancestors to the early settlers of New Spain. This emotional tie is reinforced by a prevalent Anglo racism which considers Spanish superior and Mexican inferior.

A second angle of vision turns toward Mexico, and his *mestizo* reality. Historically, the New Mexican territory was for a short period of time part of Mexico, and the New Mexican was a Mexican citizen. The New Mexican, from this angle, identifies with Mexico and sees Spain as the conquering country and the history of New Spain as the history of lies. As the Mexican

From *Contemporary Chicano Fiction: A Critical Survey*. © 1986 by *Bilingual Press/Editorial Bilingüe*.

writer Carlos Fuentes has said, "We are very conscious of the silence behind us. Our history is not written and these are a pack of lies concomitant with our abundant defeats. We have to rewrite it all over again." The Chicano therefore joins the Mexican in seeing the Spanish language as the language of the conqueror and in taking pride in his Indianness.

Still another angle of vision results from the fact that in 1846 Mexico was defeated by the United States and that what is now New Mexico became part of the United States. As Candelaria has written: "Although Mexico lost this war, not all Mexicans lost their homeland as the New Mexican and Californian did. That is, the new migrants do not carry this defeat in their psyche as the New Mexican does." From this angle, English is the language of the conqueror and Spanish is held in esteem.

When Carlos Fuentes says that Americans have never had to quarrel with their history because, except for the Southerner, they have never been defeated, he fails to account for the Chicanos and Native Americans who are defeated "American" people. Candelaria himself, who is married to a south-erner who traces her history back to the defeated South, is very sensitive to this "quarrel." However, the New Mexican Chicano's quarrel is different. The double conquest (1492, 1846) creates ambiguities and uncertainties beyond that of the Southerner (one defeat, same race, same language), the American Indian (one defeat, one linguistic rape, one clear enemy), or even the Black (transferred to a land away from his native language and most cultural ties).

Finally, the modern Chicano must turn to see himself as an American living within a dominant Anglo culture. Today many New Mexican Chicanos, whose grandparents may have spoken no English, themselves speak little or no Spanish. Educated in English-speaking schools, they read history from the conqueror's perspective, and they remember the Alamo rather than the Alhambra.

Candelaria's novel deals with time and history from this multiple perspective. Having been influenced personally by the accumulated past of Spain, Mexico, and the United States, he speaks of Cervantes, Fuentes, and Faulkner as literary influences. His sense of the historical past, however, is balanced by an awareness of time as continuity and repetition.

Memories of the Alhambra has a circular structure, moving from the death and burial of José Rafa's father, "The patriarch was dead," to José's own death and burial at the end of the novel. This circular pattern includes a series of repeating episodes, images, verbal echoes, and thematic motifs reflecting a theory of the recurrent cycles of time as well as a sense of unity and wholeness that contrasts with the hero's fragmented self, his entrapment with clock time. The novel's thirty chapters are presented from three points of view (José, Theresa, Joe) which are echoed in other trilogies of the novel (Father, Son, Holy Ghost; United States, Mexico, Spain; past, present, future; Spanish, Indian, Anglo), all reinforcing the separateness and division of José, but also reminding us that the three can mystically be one, that time and eternity can be reconciled.

The first three chapters of the novel, told from the successive points of view of José, Theresa, and Joe, establish the quest motif and refer the reader to the different concepts of time operating within the novel. Candelaria's basic understanding of time is that it is subjective and emotionally based: "All three characters flit back and forth in time guided by their feelings that revolved about the meaning to them of 'Mexicanness' and coming to terms with it and the Anglo world." Yet within this general understanding of time, each character has his or her own concept of history and time; one can most clearly trace these attitudes toward time by following each individual's quest.

The novel begins with José in the present, being driven by his son from Los Angeles to his family home in Los Rafas (Albuquerque), New Mexico, for the funeral of his father. Suddenly transported in memory back to his childhood sixty years ago and then to the time forty years ago when he first moved from Los Rafas and broke with family and tradition, he realizes that now everything is different, changed: the city, his siblings, himself. Only the dust blowing on the way to the cemetery seems permanent and the same. After the funeral his old friend Herminio Padilla comes up to him, but he cannot "pierce the layer of years that covered the familiar voice with this alien flesh" (9). These reminders of lost time and mutability increase as he returns to the family home and views his greedy sisters and brothers, who do not even seem to be "members of the same race." The chapter ends with José standing by his mother in his childhood home, although not now at home at all, looking out the window, past the orchard, "toward the river," the symbol of both continuity and change, the ambivalent image of time as both dura-tion (Bergson) and flux (Heraclitus). Stirred by all that has happened this day, he thinks: "And he had never traced back to the root of things, to the begin-ning—back to the conquistadors—back to the hidalgos, hijo de algo, son of someone" (12).

José's quest is doomed to failure because he is trapped by his view of lineal, chronological, clock time. His concept of self in time is actually spatial: he wants to find the exact place and date of this origin. To find himself he needs to know the when and where of his racial history. He is, in Sartre's term, "haunted" by a dead past and thus has as future only loneliness, fear, and death. Seeking an order that is spatial, he wants to arrange his life into neat successions of dates and categories. Specifically, as a Chicano, he wants to separate the Spanish from the Indian, to find his true origin in Spain at a specific date, linked to a specific father-figure. Bergson's concept of *durée* or Sartre's sense of an existential future are beyond his conscious powers.

José's attempt to place himself in space and time begins with "Alfonso de Sintierra," a *historical* consultant whose name means "without land," and who uses the "de" to signify "of someone, of someplace." For his $300 José gets a "top-heavy genealogical tree whose limbs, branches, twigs, and buds showed a complex tangle—a regular bird's nest of kinship" (22). This chart is not home (nest) for José since it is a spatial tangle (web, trap) whose few dates only keep José searching for himself. In chapter two, as Joe is questioning Sintierra in his search for his missing father, Sintierra points out that José Rafa, "a great-great-great something or other" has inscribed on a rock in Arizona: "Pasó por aquí." Later, when Joe asks Sintierra if José had indicated what he planned on doing with the genealogical information, Sintierra answers, "Pues no. No más pasó por aquí." This Joycean pun reveals the essential nature of José and raises the whole question of man's mutability: José is a man who is only passing by in this world, caught in time with no sense of future or timeless existence. He is all flux, "no más pasó por aquí."

José's journey takes him first to Mexico and then to Spain. Throughout his search he is continually made aware of important dates, dates which in Faulkner would suggest a timeless moment in history. For example, in Mexico, Gómez, the supposed genealogist who turns out to be a limousine driver, reminds him of 1531 and the miracle of the Virgin of Guadalupe. The Basilica of Guadalupe is built on the site of the ancient Aztec temple of Tepeyac. Here Juan Diego met the Virgin Mary and began the conversion of Indians to Catholicism. To the fiercely Mexican Gómez, this event is a second betrayal: "We were betrayed by the Aztec woman, Malinche. Now the second. Betrayed to the Church by another woman. Hijos de la chingada. First they take the balls from your body, then they take the balls from your soul" (42). This event is real for Gómez because it lives in the present as a timeless moment, part of his racial history. But for José, who cannot integrate the event into his concept of self, it is merely a fixed date that proves that Mexico is not the home he seeks: "All wrong, we Spanish beat them. We were conquerors" (44).

José flees Mexico and his terrifying dreams of "an endless search—seeking, asking but never finding" (49). Trying to find in Spain his link to the conquistadores, he travels to Madrid, Granada, Sevilla, and finally Extremadura. The most significant event in Spain is José's meeting Señor Benetar. While they listen to the song ""Recuerdos de la Alhambra,"

Benetar, who is of Moorish descent, tells his tale. When the Moorish kingdom of Granada fell in 1492, his people were given the choice of leaving Spain or becoming Christians. They stayed, but always with the belief that the Moors would reconquer Spain. Finally, Benetar's father "accepted himself as a Christian Spaniard," abandoning the dream of reconquest. The son, who returned to Africa and the Muslim religion, rejected both the solution and the father. Now, however, Benetar comes back to Spain and accepts it as his home.

Pondering Benetar's story, José realizes for a moment the "magic" of 1492. "The Moors defeated and Christianized. . . . When Catholic-Islamic-Jewish Spain had become one nation—politically and spiritually. While in the New World they had initiated another trilogy of culture—Spanish, Indian, and later Anglo. As if the one God, the true god, sought balance" (159). This moment of awareness created by the unity of the song, which is of time and yet beyond time, by the magic of the timeless date which marks not a separation but a new unification, does not last, however; almost simultaneously he hears in his memory another tune of forty years ago, sung by an Anglo at Joe's first job in California:

Mexico Joe.
Mexico Joe.
Crossed the river near the Alamo.
Go back Joe.
Not so slow.
Across the river back to Mexico. (160)

With this song, panic and hatred assault José, destroying his moment of timelessness; ironically his thoughts flee back to his first success at his job of cleaning fish: "But he had shown them. They had let him help the *time-keeper*. . . . He had done the work so well, known his numbers so well, that soon he was helping the bookkeeper" (160, my italics). José is forced back into his prison of time, again unaware of time as more than sequential counting, life as more than timekeeping.

The above incident shows that José's cage of time and history is built with the pain and conflict of racial memories. Throughout his life he has been tormented by his race and the conflict of the New Mexican as Spanish, Mexican, Indian or White. This nationality "game" is repeated as a motif throughout the book, preventing José's accepting himself and finally killing him. As a second grader he feared the Anglo teacher's game of asking "about what it meant to be a citizen of a country. About nationality" (25). In high school, he worked in an Anglo drug store and wished he were light-skinned like Herminio. His Anglo boss knew he was "Mexican" yet was confused because José acted "Anglo" during a race riot. When he arrives in Mexico, the cab driver compliments him on his good Spanish and immediately identifies José as "Cuban." In Spain, significantly sitting across from a statue of another endless quester, Don Quixote, José is approached by a dwarf with whom he is soon playing the nationality game. The dwarf proudly identifies José as from Mexico!

These repeating episodes of nationality are the cumulative experiences that keep José forever on a treadmill of time and pain. His thoughts of going "on like this forever—unfulfilled" are images of the self trapped within itself, the past as overwhelming. Only in his dying thoughts does he come close for a moment to the possibility of home and peace: he goes back to his childhood when he and Herminio stole watermelons and then went swimming in the Río Grande. This is the same river he saw from his mother's window at the beginning of the novel, and he now recognizes it as a giver of life, "Feeder of cornfields, Sweetener of melons. Cooler of boys at the end of the hot summer days" (176). In a Proustian memory, he again feels the water, tastes the sweet melon, hears the laughter of childhood "along the banks of the quiet river. Flowed with barely a ripple, following the waters toward the south. Toward the river's home, its final resting place—the Gulf of Mexico" (126). Here the river images the movement of time to a point where time ends, where the river is at rest in the sea (ironically the Gulf of Mexico). Even in this final image of home and rest, however, José still expresses limited concept of chronological time, time that can only stop, but which does not suggest a future or a repetition of time in a finer tone. José's life ends thus with a tragic question, "Where is home?" unanswered as he hears the bus driver announce "Sevilla in thirty minutes" (176).

The second point of view in the novel, the second concept of history and time, is that of Theresa. Theresa's quest is simpler and yet in many ways more profound. On one level her "quest" is often a running away from homes and a rejection of her past, both resulting from the scar she carries with her from childhood which prevents her from ever fully entering into the timeless reality she desires. This can be seen in the novel in the form of a series of earthly homes. Although her family has lived in New Mexico for over two hundred fifty years, she does not feel that "it was her home" (13), and her individual memories are often of moving. She remembers her childhood home, where her father was "mean and drank," as a place from which she wanted to escape (she climbed out the window to meet with José). She remembers the "home" of the Anglo for whom she cleaned and who fired her because she stole the can of tuna she was supposed to feed the cats. She remembers José's family home when he first took her there to meet his parents: "Theresa stared hard at the house, hoping to see what secrets it must hold that would foretell her future" (58). She remembers being told in this home that she was not good enough for José and that she should forget about marrying him. After their marriage, it was Theresa who convinced José to reject the adobe home the Rafas wanted to build for them on family land, and when they arrived in East Los Angeles, it was she who refused to live in the run-down home José wanted to rent. Theresa keeps the family moving to better homes and better neighborhoods until the present time of the novel, when she is temporarily home in an Anglo neighborhood in Whittier. From this home José runs away to find himself.

Basically, one part of Theresa is a woman trying to escape her past history, seeking security and a sense of "being" in different homes. Significantly, one of the songs attached to her memory is about traveling on Route 66: "Gallup, New Mexico, Flagstaff, Arizona. Winona. Kingman. Barstow. San Bernardino." She avoids the chronological past, always seeming in a state of "becoming." Running counter to this escapism, however, is a deeper awareness of timelessness, a sense of racial roots which cannot be measured in clock time, and a religious faith which assures her of an eternity outside of time. She achieves this understanding once during a visit to her grandparents in the Sangre de Cristo Mountains. Theresa has gone to her grandparents' house because she has miscarried and feels a deep sense of sin and guilt over her seduction of José and subsequent pregnancy. As she arrives in the mountains, she sees her grandparents' home, "Man-made, yet made from the earth so that it took its rightful place among the beans, chili, and corn in the small field." Repeating the image of the nest which was used iron-ically for José's genealogical chart, this house has a "nesting quality of comfort and refuge" (68). Life here is rooted in the past only in terms of the natural cycle of events and has a regularity that gives time itself a sense of eternity. Her grandmother, who measures time by generations of people and the changes of the seasons, seeks eternity in God.

Finally, a bird, a symbol that links the earth and sky, people and nature, time and eternity, serves as a catalyst to Theresa's understanding of her grandmother's sense of time. While talking to her grandmother, Theresa sees a one-legged bird, a friend of the grandmother, hop up to be fed. The bird intuitively accepts his place in space and time; he is at one with nature and all life. As Nana says, "He goes on living the best way he can." A few days later, while returning home from church with her grandparents, Theresa again encounters One Foot. Suddenly, in an epiphany, she moves beyond time into the eternal. "It was as if they were all one—the adobe church, the path, the two old people, the singing bird, the valley itself. As if they all throbbed with that same vibrant energy, that same vibrant life" (75). With this sense of oneness of eternity, Theresa finds a sense of peace and tries to live the rest of her life, like One Foot, as best she can, trying to help José break his barriers of time and Mexicanness, to make him see that all people are one and that time can be absorbed by eternity.

However, although Theresa does the best she can, her sense of eternity is never complete because she cannot escape her fears. Perhaps the image that best summarizes Theresa's struggle with time and eternity is her stealing holy water from the church to baptize her agnostic son's children. The drops of water symbolize eternity, but in this world they must be stolen. As a crying baby brings back these memories of baptism, she in turn recalls her grandmother and her own limited success in imitating her timeless existence: "What a beautiful old lady she had been. If I could only have been like that, she thought. Well, I tried. I tried. A sadness softly enveloped her, and tears ran down her cheeks" (109–110).

The novel's final point of view is that of José's son Joe, who throughout the novel is like Telemachus, seeking his missing father. He must come to grips with his individual personal history and with his father in that history. Joe's story is also about the generations of fathers and sons in an eternal pattern of love and hate. The book opens with Joe driving José to José's father's funeral and ends with Joe's son driving Joe to José's funeral. The pattern repeats itself.

Joe's story begins in chapter three as he sits in "his suburban ranch house" and hears by phone of his father's disappearance. By the end of the novel he has moved a long way toward understanding his place in time, as far as from his suburban home to the adobe home "that time had passed by," the home which belongs to his uncle Carlos:

> Even from inside he knew that it belonged to the earth. He felt from it a solid, heavy inertia that said: This is where I belong. No stone castles as in Spain on this new frontier, but the earth itself. Leaving no monuments after man has gone. For then the elements will erode what was man-made, giving it back to the earth from which it came It is proper that it should be so. (189–190)

This image obviously contrasts with his father's inability to find a place, a home, but also with Theresa's image of her grandparents' home. While

Theresa's grandparents' home suggests a lasting security, an eternal rest, this image suggests an infinite series of cycles of time that subsume the individual into the whole. Each return renews and begins a new pattern of time, neither ending chronological time nor replacing it with eternity.

To understand Joe's journey toward this concept of time we need to understand his attempts to deal with his personal history that places him within the conflicts of Spanish, Mexican and Anglo identity. As a child he constantly overheard his father and brothers arguing whether they were Spanish, Mexican, Indian, or American. He experienced this conflict physically in Albuquerque when his cousins fought him because he could not speak Spanish. In Los Angeles he had to fight the Anglos who called him dirty Mexican. Later, his own father drove away his girlfriend Isabella because she was Mexican.

Although while growing up Joe has learned to hate his father and has seen him as a traitor, he finally comes to realize he must accept and understand his father's pain if he is ever to understand himself as his father's son. He says, "I start out thinking about my father and his Mexicanness . . . and end up thinking about myself" (86). He finally learns that his quarrel with his father is also a quarrel with history, a battle that cannot be won without a pragmatic acceptance of the past and a positive existential movement toward the future. He first comes to understand this in college, where he realizes that even with his liberal white friends he is a Mexican, their token. Although he cannot fully identify at this point with the Chicano Movement, when "El Chicano" asks him "¿eres Mejicano?" he can answer "Sí." (He wanted at first to say, "Hell no. I'm an American.") His freedom to answer yes moves him from the past into the future: "As if the bogeyman that had hung over his father for his entire life, and over Joe for so many years, had disappeared with that simple word: yes" (92).

This is Joe's pragmatic solution to his personal and racial history. In contrast to his father, who is on an endless search for the missing thread of his life, Joe escapes the labyrinth of time by simply stopping to look for himself. He finds it easier to say "Mexican" to the nationality game, and then forget it—to look toward a future where all Latinos are one: "Hispanos. The new race. The way of the future" (184). After his father's death he can formulate more clearly the intuitive understanding of his college days, realizing now that a new history can be written, the history of losers, Indians, Mestizos, Blacks, Southern Whites, who could form a new "pantheon, the rainbow of humanity as losers. . . . The brotherhood that would not be forged in peace had been forged in loss. If they could only recognize it" (181).

Complimenting this new view of history is Joe's growing awareness of time as cyclical. His accord with historical and personal time is pragmatic and oriented toward the future, yet he finally knows that no accord within time is permanent, no more permanent than an adobe home or man. Rejecting the Catholic Church, he cannot accept his mother's faith in an eternity beyond time, so he seeks a ballast to counter time's swift movement and the image of the river in constant flux.

Ultimately all time is caught in the pattern of death and birth. As his father before him had done so many times, Joe, at the end of the novel, looks out toward the Río Grande and thinks: "Like the river, life flowed on. Its headwaters replenished by the winter snows. Its winding course fed by the freshets of early spring. Surging with gathering strength toward the ocean where storm and sun sent it upward to the sky and moist clouds drifted back toward the source to begin the cycle again" (191). This last image of the novel looks back on all the images of rivers and water, revealing more fully Candelaria's final view of time.

Each of the three characters in Candelaria's novel must face an individual sense of time, his or her racial history, and the question of timelessness. Trapped and doomed by his chronological sense of time, José cannot escape his racial history and loses his quarrel with time. Theresa, who flees from home to home, still manages through her faith to grasp as much of eternity as her history allows. Finally, more fully representing Candelaria's view, Joe comes to practical terms with his individual and racial history, accepting his personal memories without being consumed by them. Moreover, rather than transcending time, he accepts time as a recurrent cycle. *Memories of the Alhambra* is both a uniquely New Mexican Chicano novel structured by the conflicts inherent in New Mexican history and a universal novel reflecting Everyman's struggle with mutability and death.

MARTA E. SANCHEZ

Inter-Sexual and Intertextual Codes in the Poetry of Bernice Zamora

In *Restless Serpents*, her first collection of poems, Bernice Zamora presents us with a poetry of conflict. Most of these poems attempt to redefine relationships between men and women, and the conflict which propels them, as sexual. Sexual dilemmas motivate Bernice Zamora to articulate an *unsaid* of male-female discourse: her poems convey what women have not said to men, or what men have not permitted women to say or, what men themselves traditionally have not said.

The *unsaid* in Zamora's poetry is linked to problems both of sexuality and textuality. The poetic discourses of her fictional feminine speakers are responses to prior utterances or actions performed by males. The man's utterance or action constitutes a sexual or "male" text. The intelligibility of Zamora's poetry depends not only upon the presence of this sexual or "male" text but also upon the presence of a literary text. Zamora recurrently employs the strategy of taking up another poet's work to generate her own poetic text. Her poems thus become dialogues, at times even quarrels, with specific precursor poems. As such, Zamora's poetry raises questions of intertextuality, or the notion of how particular texts reject, modify, or transform features of anterior texts that inspire them.

The three poems chosen as the core poems for this discussion attempt to define inter-sexual relationships between men and women as well as intertextual relationships between a text and its literary source. "Sonnet, Freely Adapted," "California," and "Gata Poem" present three

From *MELUS: The Journal of the Society for the Study of the Multi-Ethnic Literature of the United States*, Vol. 7, No 3. ©1980 by the University of Southern California.

women speakers with different responses to male discourse.

These poems also represent the two distinct literary and cultural traditions shaping and influencing Zamora's poetry: English-American and Mexican-Chicano. "Sonnet, Freely Adapted" and "California," written in English, are attempts to rework previous texts. The writing of "Sonnet" is prompted by the poems of Shakespeare, and that of "California" by Robinson Jeffers's long narrative poem "Roan Stallion" (1926). "Sonnet" and "California" are implicit responses to their literary antecedents, and as such they represent Zamora's own attempt to articulate an *unsaid* in male literary discourse. In "Gata Poem," Zamora makes the strategic decision to write in Spanish (with the exception of one line). Though no specific literary text seems to motivate "Gata Poem," its poetic register is Chicano tradition, language, and culture. My specific contention about these poems is that, while they question and challenge male discourse at inter-sexual and inter-textual levels, they are also characterized by an identity and connection with male-dominant forms of expression.

> *Sonnet, Freely Adapted*
> > for J. R. S.
> Do not ask, sir, why this weary woman
> Wears well the compass of gay boys and men.
> Masculinity is not manhood's realm
> Which falters when ground passions overwhelm.
> O. no! It is a gentle, dovelet's wing
> That rides the storm and is never broken.
> It is whispered, secret words that bring
> To breath more hallowed sounds left unspoken.
> Men, sir, are not bell hammers between rounds
> Within the rings of bloody gloves and games.
> Men, sir, aught not rend the mind round square's round,
> Spent, rebuked, and trembling in fitted frames.
> > So, I return, sir, worn, rebuked, and spent
> > To gentle femininity content.

The inter-sexual code in "Sonnet" is male heterosexuality versus male homosexuality. The contextual indicators of the first two lines point to a heterosexual male who inquires of the woman speaker why she persists in keeping company with gay men. We may even presume that this male has made a "pass" at her and been rebuffed. Irked, he then inquires why she prefers gays to real *machos*, like himself.

The woman's discourse is a direct reply to the man's inquiry. The woman-speaker is "weary"—either tired of defending herself against the advances of heterosexual men or tired of being asked by heterosexual men to justify her preference for gay men. In turn, she replies that she is more comfortable in the presence of gays ("wears well the compass"). She argues for a notion of an unconventional masculinity which encompasses the opposing qualities of gentleness and strength (the dovelet's wing riding the storm). This masculinity, she continues, "brings to breath" or gives voice to sounds "more hallowed" than those actually spoken by traditional men. The homosexual male is closer to her ideal than the heterosexual male, who aims to fit himself into typically masculine roles ("bell hammers between rounds"). The woman is implying that men like her addressee think they are masculine only if they are violent, fighting *machos*. But since the "sir" does not share her view of things, she withdraws to "gentle femininity content." Her resolution of the inter-sexual conflict with the heterosexual male is to retreat into relationships with male homosexuals or women because they are, supposedly, "content" with their gentleness.

A central ambiguity of the inter-sexual relationship elaborated in this poem concerns Zamora's use of irony. Does her use of the archaic sonnet genre result in a flat, two-dimensional irony, or does she employ the form to gain critical ironic effects in the communicative circuit between the woman-speaker and her male addressee? Throughout the first eight lines, Zamora knowingly fails to fulfill the maxim of manner, which governs how a modern woman in a similar situation and with similar motives to those of Zamora's speaker responds to a male making such an inquiry or wishing to flirt. Zamora intentionally flouts the maxim of manner by attributing archaic language and syntax to her speaker.

One implication of this flouting is that Zamora achieves distancing effects in her speaker's discourse. The polite, formal, and emotionally subdued tone of the archaic mode allows her speaker to say what she wants to say without saying it too directly. Too blunt an answer will only anger the male and prevent him from listening to her argument. Though the speaker's archaic diction and syntax ("Do not ask, sir", "manhood's realm"; "gentle dovelet's wing") probably sounds "prissy" and effeminate to her male addressee, a modern audience will catch the humor and sarcasm behind it. The repeated use of "sir" is ironic for it does not mean to the woman-speaker what we assume it means to the male addressee—rank, respect, and manhood. The speaker pretends the pose of a woman who suffers a rebuke whereas she really intends her words to serve as a rebuke to him.

Changes in tone appear in the woman's discourse which subvert her ridicule of the man. In lines 9–10, "Men, sir, are not bell hammers between rounds / Within the rings of bloody gloves and games," the woman shifts from a highly archaic, lexical and formal language into a modern colloquial and oral word usage. At a first level meaning, these lines say that men are not instruments of physical conquest. The second level meaning is subliminal because in colloquial speech, "hammer" is the male organ and "rounds" designates female genitals. These lines also say that men are not instruments of sexual conquest making the "rounds" among women. The woman shifts into an oral language that her modern macho addressee understands and uses. These oral, popular references jar the hitherto continuous flow of the archaic mode, causing gaps and discontinuities in the woman's ironic pose. In effect, in shifting over to the colloquial mode, the speaker's ironic mask drops, creating a rift in the communicative circuit. Ironically, the woman-speaker establishes her own identification with male discourse.

At an intertextual level, this poem is also Zamora's quarrel with the conventions of the traditional English sonnet. The fact that she makes her interlocutor feminine and her addressee masculine in a form traditionally and primarily employed to express a man's love for a woman is in itself a deviation from the expectations of this archaic genre. This reversal produces irony, for a woman is addressing a man—not to idealize him but to chide him. Tension and contradiction also result when Zamora casts unconventional content within a conventional frame. She argues against the rigidity of conventional roles for men and women; yet she casts her ideas within the tight and closed form of the sonnet ("the fitted frame"). These deviations suggest a quarreling with the conventions of the Elizabethan sonnet and courtly love. The "sir," implicitly, is Shakespeare, and Zamora is saying: "Women, sir, not only men, can use this mode, and not for the purposes of praising men but to rebuke them."

The abrupt intrusion of the oral and popular into the sonnet undermines the fictional woman-speaker's criticism of the man, and it also modifies Zamora's intertextual dispute with Shakespeare. The shift in mode creates gaps and discontinuities in her discourse, rupturing the dialectical tension sustained throughout the first eight lines. One possible reason for this breakdown may be the sexual ambiguity surrounding the figure of Shakespeare, who is well known for taking the position of the opposite sex to create ironic tension in his address. A second reason may be that Shakespeare, the "universal" and "sensual" poet, is ultimately a *regional* poet to Zamora.

The precursor text in the next poem is Robinson Jeffers's "Roan Stallion." Like "Sonnet, Freely Adapted," "California" attempts a dialogue with its parent poem. It succeeds in articulating the dilemma of a woman who becomes the center of physical, sexual warfare between two male powers.

California
"The night-wind veering, the smell of the spilt wine
  drifted down hill from the house."
Two gods lay at my feet; I have
  shot one, and that one killed the other.
Each in his turn, each in his fashion of late
  laid over me splitting hairs, splitting atoms.
The dog, dead too, leaped to his death.

Beasts they were, both of them beasts—one
  of the wind and rein, one of the night and wine
  and all of us pools in the moonnight.

My child stands witness to one aimed shot, three
  flamed and freeing ones, and one that plunged
  my wailing will to the center of this bloody corral.

California, the heroine of "Roan Stallion," is the daughter of a Scottish father and Spanish-Indian mother. California is married to Johnny, an Anglo gambler and drunkard who uses her to satisfy his lust. Johnny brings home a roan stallion, who represents pure sexual potency. California has a mystical sexual encounter with the stallion. One night California becomes the center of physical, sexual warfare between Johnny and the horse. Johnny, lusting to do with California what he has seen the stallion do with his buckskin mare, wants to sexually abuse California; but since California presumably has had a liberating experience with the stallion, she repulses him and escapes to the corral. Johnny and his dog Bruno pursue her. The dog leaps at the horse and Johnny dashes for California but falls under the stallion's forehooves. California, armed with a rifle provided by her daughter, aims and kills Bruno. The stallion tramples Johnny. The poem terminates with California firing three bullets at the horse.

The woman's victory over the male in the battle between the sexes is one reason why Jeffers's poem interests and concerns Zamora. The first two lines of quotation of Zamora's poem are the two final lines of "Roan Stallion." The technical fact of making Jeffers's final lines her first two lines suggests that Zamora is critical of Jeffers for ending the poem where he does.

"California" is Zamora's attempt to "complete" Jeffers's narrative. She retains the plot, characters, and even the terms of "Roan Stallion" but means them in a different sense than the precursor poem, as though Jeffers had failed to go far enough. Zamora writes her own sequel to Jeffers in order to give the woman the final word.

As an autonomous unit, this poem does not seek a language of precision; instead it seeks a language of suggestion. It evokes indefinite impressions of moment, place and action. Physical energy, violence, and conflict are also evoked. The images cluster around the liberation of physical, sexual energy: "splitting hairs," "splitting atoms," the spilling of wine and blood; the release of sexual impulses ("laid over me"); violence and death. The first lines summon up a concrete image of a landscape (sound, smell, color, movement), probably in California.

While their specific identities would remain unknown without prior knowledge of "Roan Stallion," we could infer that the "I" is a woman and the "gods" are masculine. The woman's discourse mocks and satirizes the male powers, for "gods" are not supposed to die. Some relationship between the terms "gods" and "beasts," is intended: the subject of the first stanza is "two gods" and that of the second "two beasts." The nature of this relationship is not explicit, but we can infer that the woman further satirizes the "gods" by reducing them to "beasts," in the line "Beasts they were, both of them beasts." The rhetorical emphasis on "beasts" and "both" leaves no doubt that the woman thinks these male powers are "beasts" and not "gods" in any sense. They have in common the nature of "beasts" but are nevertheless distinct from each other: "One / of the wind and rein, one of the night and wine." The pun on "rein"—"rain" is a clue that one of the "gods"—"beasts" is of the outdoors.

Even without Jeffers, then, "California" has some autonomy: it is a discourse spoken by a woman with a child who explains why she has shot two males. The primary point to mark here, however, is that even without Jeffers, the reader can determine that the nature of this woman's dilemma, like that of the woman in "Sonnet, Freely Adapted," is sexual. Her resolution of the inter-sexual conflict is to literally kill her male sources of oppression.

When seen against the backdrop of Jeffers's poem, Zamora's "California" is primarily a discourse that transforms "Roan Stallion." Zamora introduces four transformations. The first concerns the attribution of a "consciousness" to the original California which is absent in Jeffers. Jeffers's California is a *told* consciousness. Jeffers never allows his protagonist to articulate a critical stance toward Johnny and, much less, the stallion. Zamora's character, in contrast, expresses a critical and condemning tone toward her oppressors. She speaks what Jeffers's heroine might have said had she been permitted a voice in the matter. Zamora thus voices a silence in Jeffers, presenting a California who enlarges and extends the original.

The second transformation is the equating of both man and animal at the level of *beasts*. In Jeffers, Johnny is presented, in metaphorical terms, as a "beast"; so Zamora's calling him a beast is nothing new. However, her reference to him as "god" is a new dimension. This reference is satiric, mocking him for thinking himself a god and behaving as though he were one, whereas in actuality he is crude and vulgar. When Zamora's California insists in line 8 that both gods are "beasts," she deflates the aura of "godliness" surrounding the stallion in Jeffers. By demystifying her counterpart's perception of the stallion as god, she thereby reduces the stallion to Johnny's level. If the concepts of "god" and "beast" are in conflict in Jeffers with respect to the stallion, Zamora's transformation is to equate man and animal at the level of beast, thus providing a critical dimension absent in the original poem.

The next transformation hinges on the interpretation of the last "one" in the line "one that plunged / my wailing will." The identities of the referents of the previous *one's* in lines 11 and 12 are accounted for in Jeffers.

The "one aimed shot" is the bullet California used to shoot Bruno; the "three flamed and freeing ones" are the bullets that killed the horse, which in turn kills Johnny. The last "one" has no clear corresponding referent in Jeffers. Rather than referring to an actual bullet within Zamora's perspective, it reflects the existence of a consciousness who knows that something—some unidentified presence or power—beyond the desire to escape her husband's lechery has driven her ("plunged my will") to the center of the "bloody corral."

Finally, Zamora removes all traces of ambiguity in the original California's motive for killing the stallion. In "Roan Stallion" Jeffers leads us to believe that California's motive for shooting the stallion is "some obscure human fidelity" to Civilization. Caught between Culture (Johnny) and Nature (the Stallion), California must opt for Culture. Jeffers's reader, however, is left to wonder whether an instinct that the stallion, too, was her sexual oppressor did not also prompt California's action. No such ambiguity exists in "California." We are certain that Zamora's protagonist shoots both man and beast because each has oppressed her sexually.

These transformations in Zamora's discourse suggest a dialectical response to Jeffers. Her discourse criticizes his, but her criticism also implies that his discourse has had significant impact on her. The conflictual relationship between Zamora and her intertextual choice is, at deeper levels, a conflict between written literary discourse and oral discourse. If we are

unaware that Jeffers is the literary source for this poem when first
confronting it, we are uncertain as to whether the quotation marks refer to
written or spoken discourse. It is only upon learning that they are the final
lines of "Roan Stallion" that we know for certain that they are written
discourse. The lines which follow are Zamora's rendition of California's own
spoken words, left "unspoken" by Jeffers. California's speech in Zamora's
poem corrects and undermines the dominant written text.

The transformative relationships suggest that Zamora's involvement
with Jeffers is more intense and conflictual than her relationship to
Shakespeare. Zamora goes as far as she does with Jeffers because Jeffers, a
modern U.S. poet who writes about northern California, offers Zamora a
congenial poetic mode. The northern California landscape, the dramatic
persona of the native woman, and the theme of male sexual domination of
women constitute material that interests and provokes Zamora. Whereas
Shakespeare, the "universal" and "sensual" poet may be remote to Zamora,
Jeffers, the "local" and "minor" poet is major to her.

Even though Shakespeare and Jeffers represent two divergent literary
strands, the English and the American, the frame of these first two poems is
the dominant English-speaking cultural heritage. Yet Zamora is a Chicana,
bilingual and capable of biculturalism, as she displays in *Restless Serpents*.
The frame of the third poem is the frame that has not been utilized in the
first two poems:

Gata Poem

> Desde la cima me llamó
> Un hombre perfecto, un chicano
> Con cuerpo desnudo y tan moreno que
> *He glistened in the sun like a bronze god.*

> —Ven, mujer.
> Ven conmigo.

> Se me empezó a morir como una gata
>   en la noche
> Y yo misma era gata vestida de negro.

> —¿Que quieres, señor?
>   ¿Que quieres conmigo?

—Quiero cantar eternamente contigo
   lejos de la tristeza.
Quiero enseñarte un sol tan brillante
    que debemos verlo con alma escudada.
Quiero vivir contigo por los nuevos mundos.

—Ven, gatita.
Ven conmigo.

     Y me fui

My translation follows:

Cat Poem

From the summit he called me
A perfect man, a chicano
Naked, and so brown that
He glistened in the sun like a bronze god.

—Come, woman.
 Come with me.

He began to die on me like a cat
   in the night.
And I also was a cat dressed in black.

—What do you want, sir?
 What do you want with me?

—I want to sing with you eternally
   somewhere far away from sadness.
I want to show you a sun so brilliant
   that we must see it with a guarded soul.
I want to live with you in nine worlds.

—Come, kitten.
 Come with me.

    And I left. *or* And I went.

"Gata Poem" portrays sexual rivalry in terms of verbal play between a chicana and a chicano, the goal of which is to determine who decides the rules of the sexual contract. The epitome of chicano machismo is the chicano on the summit. The pun on *cima / sima* enriches the poem. *Cima* means pinnacle; *sima* means abyss. Thus, if our experience with the poem is purely an auditory one, the chicano's location is ambiguous; is he above or is he below? The oral dimensions of *cima* reverberate even when we read the poem. Only by reading do we know for certain that the chicano is above.

The ambiguity about the chicano's location may be a sign of a consciousness or an impulse that desires to question the dominant social codes defining boundaries between men and women in a chicano context. Such an impulse is certainly congruent with a dominant theme in Zamora's poetry. The impression that the chicano is below is only a possibility on the poem's oral plane. The issue is settled in the poem's written plane. What is interesting is that from the poem's onset, tension is established between two antagonistic statements and codes pulling in opposing directions: "Chicano is below"—the oral code, and "Chicano is above"—the written code.

The first three lines of the narrator's discourse is presented in reflective, meditative language. Their purpose is to present the myth of the chicano as a "bronze god." The speaker's abrupt shift into English (line 4) breaks the flow of her preceding phrases which construct the romantic, sexual image of the chicano—up until the word *que*. The effect of the English interruption at this strategic point in the rhetorical structure is to disrupt the effect of the preceding romantic lines in Spanish. The code-switch introduces a slogan which sounds more clichéd in English and provides the only clue in the opening stanza that the chicana is critical of the romantic rhetoric within which the chicano can imagine himself as a "bronze god."

Stanza two is the first instance of dialogue. The man utters an abrupt, straightforward directive to the woman, indicating his position of power over her. Stanza 3 interrupts the dialogue and returns to the woman's meditative, romantic discourse which initiated the poem. These lines correspond to her sexual fantasy, since they separate the man's command from her question to him in stanza 4. They involve a different level of signification, suggesting a "surreal" scene in the juxtaposition of disparate images: death, a cat, blackness, night, a woman and a man. Through an elaborate metaphor, the chicano is transformed into a feminine animal. The man "dies" as a female cat would "die" in the night. In a Chicano and Mexican context, associations link *gata* to a stray female cat wandering the streets and indiscriminately copulating with any male cat. In line 7, the word *morir* means what "to die" means in 16th and 17th century literature—sex. The image transmitted is of the Chicano "expiring" on her as a female cat "expires" in the night. In the following line, male and female are linked in a common symbol. She speaks of herself also as a *gata*, thus identifying with the chicano.

Stanza 4 returns to direct, declarative language. The woman answers the man with a question. Her manner of answering suggests that she too has some measure of power. She is not responding to his command without questioning it.

The communicative circuit seems to break down in the next two stanzas for it is difficult to distinguish the two voices, male from female. The last line, "Y me fui," is also not attributable; not with respect to voice, for only she could think it, but with respect to content: does she decide to submit to the chicano's sexual call (in which case, "Y me fui" means "I went"), or does she assert her own separateness from him (in which case, "Y me fui" means "I left")?

Interpreting the poem loosely, we could argue that the chicano enunciates stanzas 5 and 6. Possibly threatened by the woman's stern tone of answer in stanza 4, he changes his formerly terse style to a more softened endearing tone. He then reiterates the command in stanza 6, only this time he uses the diminutive *gatita*. If he does actually speak these lines, her answer "Y me fui" must logically relate back to his command, suggesting her acceptance of the *macho*.

A closer look at the different levels of language in the poem and sex changes in stanza 3 raises the possibility that the chicana may be the speaker. Stanza 5 is presented in romantic, flowery language. No precedent exists for the chicano using it. She, in turn, has used romantic language in stanza 1 (3 lines) and in stanza 3. The contradiction of stanza 1 can now be stated. Even though the chicana is critical of the romantic myth of the chicano as "bronze god," the myth is also her fantasy because it is presented in romantic, flowery language which corresponds to her imagined voice. Stanza 5 might very well also correspond to her dream of what she would like him to promise her— "eternal songs" and "brilliant suns." So, this stanza could constitute the chicano speaking but only through her voice. The stanza's content which is an answer to her question and the double hyphen preceding Quiero (— "Quiero . . . ") are elements pointing to a male voice.

The sex changes also create ambiguities. In stanza 3, she performs within her own consciousness the metaphoric reversal of *gata* on him, not he on her. If stanza 6 represents actual spoken communication, only she can call him gatita. He, on the other hand, can only call her *gatita* if stanza 6, as was suggested of stanza 5, also represents her thoughts. The juxtaposition of stanzas 5 and 6—5 uttered as a commissive in elaborate language and 6 as a directive in statemental language (except for the metaphoric elaboration of *gatita*)—might cause her to conclude the following: "Though the chicano may promise me poetic floweriness, his vows still amount to commands." If she sees these words as a contradiction, "Y me fui" most likely means she rejects the chicano and goes off without him. The poem's typography reinforces this idea. However, the argument against this interpretation is that the diminutive gatita softens the commanding tone and turns it into an invitation. The inviting tone adds power to her fantasy of what she would like him to say. "Y me fui" would then more likely mean she goes with him.

It is impossible to decode the poem completely at the inter-sexual level because no matter which way we argue, indications are always present to suggest the opposite view. What we can argue is that even if the chicana follows the chicano, her discourse suggests enough consciousness to make us suspect she does not follow uncritically.

A consciousness and awareness of the English dominant tradition framing the first two poems is present in "Gata Poem" in the bilingualism of the title and the code-switch from Spanish to English in stanza 3. Since the majority of lines in "Gata Poem" are in Spanish, it would seem that Chicano textuality is being privileged over Anglo textuality. Yet, even within the internal frame of the lines in Spanish, there is a conflict between an oral and popular poetic language and the dominant "literary" tradition. The interpretation of stanza 3 depends upon the decoding of two words: *morir* and *gata*. The decoding in both instances relies on specific presuppositions. In the case of *morir*, the modern reader must shift from a current usage of *morir* ("death" / "expirar," " fallecer") to an archaic, literate usage ("sex"). Since Zamora knows English literature, she could assume that the reader will make an interior code-switch, meaning that he or she will shift first from Spanish into English and then link "die" with "sex."

The second presupposition is that the reader will know the meaning of *gata*, which comes not from dominant, literate English-speaking tradition but from an oral, popular Spanish-speaking Chicano tradition. *Gata* colloquially designates either "prostitute" (*puta*) or "servant," both of which connote a subservient position for woman. Thus to decode stanza 3, the reader must be privy to these interpretations for *morir* and *gata*.

A secondary conflict within the lines in Spanish is a tension between a romantic-metaphoric and a direct-statemental Chicano discourse. Up until stanza 4, these two types of discourse alternate: romantic (except for the English line), statemental, romantic, statemental. The romantic discourse is presented as meditative, or unspoken narrative, reflecting the chicana's state of mind, whereas the statemental discourse is presented as spoken dialogue (either chicano's or chicana's). Like the two voices, they are difficult to separate in stanzas 5 and 6. The language of stanza 5 is romantic hyperbole, but its form of presentation insinuates spoken discourse. Stanza 6 appears to be spoken but the insertion of *gatita* links it to romantic discourse, which up until now has been presented as unspoken. The last line "Y me fui" is direct, statemental discourse, but retains the non-spoken and meditative feature of the romantic narrative. Although the line's typography may suggest a desire to break and reject the conflict of its own prior language, the conflict between the two types of language is present to the end.

"Gata Poem" is the most inter-sexually ambiguous of the three poems, though "Sonnet, Freely Adapted" also contains unresolved inter-sexual tensions. All three poems give evidence that the primary determinant of Zamora's poetry is *sex*. This is true whether she writes in English or in Spanish, whether she grounds her poetry in an English-American "learned" context or in a socially defined phenomenon such as *machismo*. The hesitations and contradictions marking "Sonnet" and especially "Gata Poem" suggest a feminine consciousness which is reflecting critically on the issue of sexual relationships between men and women. They suggest, moreover, a consciousness unable as yet to resolve dilemmas with respect to male-female conflicts. Zamora's dilemma is only part of a larger social dilemma confronting modern women, especially Chicanas in a struggle to define and redefine traditional sexual roles assigned to men and women by a male-dominated society.

These poems also reveal a young Chicano poet in transition, absorbing and resisting influences, attempting to define her own feminine voice in relation to her intertextual choices. choices that come from two distinct traditions. The rhetorical and linguistic resources Zamora relies upon to develop and expand her poetic universe come either from the dominant English-speaking cultural heritage or from the language of a social group that derives its poetic vitality from oral and popular culture.

Regardless of the language Zamora employs, two distinct forms of expression intersect in her poetry: a written and "literate" mode (sometimes archaic) and an oral, popular, modern mode. "Gata Poem" is also the most intertextually ambiguous, for it involves conflicts on two distinct levels: a conflict within Chicano culture itself. The latter conflict is suggested by the unresolved tensions created by the two types of Chicano discourse.

While the inter-sexual ambiguities may relate to an, as yet, unresolved attitude toward the male in general and the Chicano male in particular, the intertextual ambiguities, especially those characterizing "Gata Poem," may suggest the dilemma of an intellectual Chicano poet caught between two traditions, unable yet to define clearly her relationship to these traditions and the audiences each one implies.

EDWARD ELIAS

Tortuga: *A Novel of Archetypal Structure*

Tortuga, Rudolfo Anaya's latest novel, once again treats the experiences of a young man growing up. The crippled boy/protagonist, aged sixteen, makes a pilgrimage through the desert to a hospital in southern New Mexico for crippled and orphaned children, where he seeks a cure for his paralysis. Tortuga, as the boy is nicknamed because of the body cast he wears throughout much of his stay in the hospital, functions as protagonist and first person narrator; the reader watches him pass through one maturing archetypal experience after another as well as interact with that tragicomic group of fellow patients—long-term and terminally crippled children—that populate the fictional world of the novel. Through his eyes, the reader meets these poor, forgotten members of society that, even in their youth, embody all the problems, fears and hopes of their adult counterparts in the outside world. The novel recounts the struggle of young Tortuga to heal himself spiritually and physically in order to walk upright in "the path of the sun" as a charismatic hero/leader whose destiny is to sing prophetically to mankind of human suffering, regeneration, and the possibility of "resurrection"—all of which he will experience in his own flesh.

Anaya is as successful in this novel as he was in *Bless Me, Ultima* because of the skillful way in which he recounts the experiences and perceptions of his young protagonists, his constant intermingling of reality and illusion (the world of dreams), his frequent use of poetic images, and the grounding of the narrative in the ethnic and geographical milieu of

From *The Bilingual Review/La Revista Bilingüe*. Vol. IX, No. 1. © 1982 by The Bilingual Review/La Revista Bilingüe.

New Mexico. The novel definitely reflects a Chicano worldview but transcends it by being structured in its entirety around stock, archetypal myths. This study will examine how the protagonist, Tortuga, is an archetypal hero (yet a character unique to Anaya's style because of his epiphanic fusion with the landscape) functioning in a fictional environment or world that is equally mythical in its composition.

The novel begins with the crippled hero's difficult pilgrimage through the New Mexico desert (from north to south) to reach the children's hospital where for over a half a year he will remain isolated from all his past life in order to discover his destiny and learn to accept it. The boy goes to the hospital in an ambulance driven by Filemón, a counterpart of the mythical boatman that traversed the river Styx. Upon arrival, Tortuga is christened with a new name and a new identity inasmuch as he is "buried" in a cast that covers his entire head and reaches to below the waist. The simile of the boy with the turtle is easily comprehensible since this shell encloses and shelters him for the needed escapes into frequent reveries and for the long period of purging. The boy's challenge and purpose will be to strengthen himself sufficiently to crack the protective yet punishing shell and be ready to leave that secure hospital environment in order to immerse himself in the world again, this time as a self-assured adult. While the boy arrived helpless, immobile, and not in control even of his own body, he will leave erect and grown-up after his mythical search and quest are completed. For this purpose he left behind family and hometown (retaining only the sayings and teachings of his elders) and became closely identified and bonded to an imposing mountain, also named Tortuga, source of healing thermal waters, and to a terminally ill patient named Salomón.

The reader is quickly introduced to the soliloquies of a key figure in the novel, Salomón, who will be crucial in Tortuga's discovery of himself, his destiny, and of the world. Salomón speaks as an oracular voice disembodied from a credible character. His counsel is akin to that of the wise Solomon of biblical texts; the Salomón of Anaya's novel, however, is only a crippled boy in an iron lung who, while awaiting the end of his terminal illness, reads voraciously. It is Salomón's first soliloquy that initiates Tortuga into the world of suffering and waiting in the hospital, and into the search for a destiny. The two characters' lives and thoughts become intertwined and one is given the impression that Tortuga must carry on the work of Salomón and live for him once he has been properly schooled and strengthened. Understandably, all of Tortuga's wisdom will come via Salomón's teachings; the latter will function as the classical holy sage who primes the younger man for adulthood. Salomón's speeches are initially represented in the text by cursive type in order to signal their dream-like nature; in later passages this device is discontinued. The sage's words then appear constantly in the narrative as if they were reflections of Tortuga's conscience, his reveries or intuitions; in fact, the sage's teachings are disconnected from actual meetings or dialogues between the two characters.

Not only is Salomón the benevolent sage and guide but he also represents that feared and devouring monster who protects a sacred space. His territory in the hospital is that of the wards of the most sadly incurable children, an area never visited by other patients of the institution—indeed, a territory that is set apart as if it were sacred. It is a place that inspires fear and depression. Tortuga's first meeting with Salomón is in this area of dark wards lined with life-sustaining machines, and it renders the hero physically ill and depressed for days.

There is also present in the novel the classic figure of the silent, strong, redeeming woman whose love and nurturing sustain and save the protagonist. Ismelda, the nurse's aide, is all-knowing about the mysterious inner workings of the hospital and its inmates' lives. She is "the path of the sun" mentioned frequently in the text, the sustaining love force vital to Tortuga, yet she is ethereal and untouchable, the ideal love that stands at a distance. When Tortuga lives out his first sexual encounter it will not be with her but rather with another patient who is faceless in the narrative.

Ismelda represents the forces of good that lead the protagonist to a positive self-realization, to that coveted path of the sun. There is mention once of *la llorona*, who appears in a nightmare sequence; she is the antithesis of Ismelda. *La llorona* represents death, destruction, non-Christian forces, the negative powers of the nether world. Her domain is in the vicinity of the trash heap where she encounters Tortuga and attempts to claim him for her own; he is able to escape her grasping and clawing by confessing his Christian faith and by physically fighting her off while teetering symbolically atop a narrow path at the edge of a cliff:

> . . . You, my son! she cried as we met on the narrow path. She reached out to grab me, mistaking me for her murdered son, scratching at my face and eyes with long, black fingernails, crying like a wild witch . . . and I fighting back, driven by terror . . . No, no, I am not your son, I am not your son, I am my mother's son, I live, I believe in the holy Trinity which I now call to dissolve you, to make you disappear! (p. 66).

There are other events in the novel that mark key stages in the development of the boy/hero, some relived in dreams, others accomplished in reality. Thus, present events such as the painful physical therapy sessions trigger the memories of his painful birth, when he was almost strangled by his mother's umbilical cord, and his sucking at the breast of a wet nurse.

> I only knew her milk was as bitter as the milk of her goats, and her smell was as strong as theirs. . . . Later, no one spoke of her [the midwife and wet nurse], she took no credit for the delivery, the birth which was so close to death because the umbilical cord came wrapped around my neck, suffocating me, drowning me . . . I came like a hanged man into the world, my mother said later, and it was only the swift fingers of the two old women which saved me . . . I remember the old woman's sour breath when she breathed into my mouth to pump up my lungs, I remembered her eyes staring at me, coaxing me to breath . . . and then there was the scream that came from the pit of my stomach as I was startled into life . . . (p. 86).

It is in a movie theater that the young man lives out his first sexual encounter, described in a sequence of passionate images that take place in Tortuga's mind, on the film screen, or in actuality. By this point in the novel (pp. 149 ss.), dream sequences are so commonplace that the narrative moves from the real to the imagined without need of signaling the transition.

The day of first communion is relived again in a dream sequence that becomes poetic and allegorical. This scene as well as that of the first sexual encounter are significant in that they are both rites of passage that mark adult stages in life, choices directed to a higher moral life style in the one case, to adulthood in the other; in both instances there occurs a subsequent loss of innocence.

Toward the end of the novel, Tortuga, again in a sequence that is half nightmare and half real, finds himself living out the required traditional descent into hell and subsequent "resurrection." Pushed by Danny, a deranged fellow patient, into the hospital therapeutic swimming pool that is filled with the healing waters of the "magic" Tortuga mountain, the boy begins to drown because of the weight and immobility of his body cast. He is saved, however, just before asphyxiation; by then the waters have accomplished their task of crumbling the tortoise-like plaster shell surrounding the boy to give birth to the new man. From this moment on, Tortuga begins to walk and prepare for his eventual release from the hospital in the spring—as was predicted at the beginning of the novel. This passage gains fuller meaning in light of Salomón's teachings about the origins of man:

> Yes, Tortuga, long before his word was flesh the sea covered
> the earth, and men and turtles were brothers in the sea. Together
> they ruled the world of the fish . . . But the world was dark and
> so our grandfather called them forth from the sea. He opened a
> hole in the waters and for the first time man and turtle saw the
> bright sun and the clear sky. Man stood upon the back of the
> turtle and climbed into this world of light. Immediately he was
> blinded by the sun, he lost his golden scales and his skin turned
> dark and hard. But he was determined to walk upon the earth and
> to explore this new land of the sun. He called his new life
> 'walking the path of the sun' and he sang its praises (p. 68).

We go on to read that man wanted to share this new life with the turtle
but most of the shelled creatures were afraid and remained in the waters
protected by their thick shells. It becomes clear why Tortuga assumed that
temporary identity in his development and needed to lose his shell in order
to grow fully into manhood.

The environment that forms the backdrop for the narrative helps
complete the mythical archetypal structure that gives the novel its framework. The internment in the hospital, the cast, and the near drowning in the
pool are all symbolic settings needed for the withdrawal of the hero, his initiation, and later trials. This future leader and hero, in particular, needs the
withdrawal and seclusion from the world to prepare himself for a later public
life. The value of the many dream sequences Tortuga engages in is that each
one is a reaching back into the inner self (at times to contact the voice of
Salomón, who also functions as a directing conscience) in order to emerge
with a greater self-awareness and a knowledge of that ultimate purpose in life
that Tortuga calls his destiny.

The boy's destiny and progress are connected in many ways to the reactions of the magical mountain, which is present in the story as much as is any
one of the characters. Both boy and mountain are connected to the natural
weather cycles, so that animal and mineral nature reflect and duplicate the
climactic conditions. Is it not during springtime, when all life is born again,
that Tortuga emerges from the hospital healed?

The presence of the ideal woman is essential to the existence of the
classical hero; she is his moral guide to steer him from the path of danger
and evil. Ismelda is introduced from the beginning of the narration and the

relationship between her and Tortuga blossoms immediately. He senses the important role that she is to fill in his destiny but only comes to be fully aware of it as the narration unfolds. The woman is constantly aware of her divine mission to minister to her hero and master. She is delicate and pure, both the *curandera* and the seer, the mother figure and the lover. She is not tarnished by lustful sexual encounters but is present in image form in her hero's mind while he lives out his first experience. Some of the encounters between Tortuga and Ismelda are described in extremely poetic terms wherein she, in particular, assumes a new identity that is more than human, analogous to that of literary characters of centuries past. The following excerpt is taken from a scene that develops in Tortuga's mind; in the sequence all the characters in his normal hospital existence take on new identities and roles. The ambulance driver, Filomón, has transported Christ across the desert to a sanatorium occupied by patients crippled by the pharaohs; Christ himself is one of the crippled, bent bodies found in the scene, as is Ismelda, who appears dressed in veils and numerous jangling bracelets, in a Middle-Eastern fashion:

> What did it mean? Ismelda smiled. The date palm was heavy with fruit . . . bees buzzed in the sun. It was a journey, and I had come to one station, and this young woman of the desert who bathed me with the water from the springs and dried my broken body with her long, dark hair was mine. I would take her with me. Come with me, I said and reached for her hand . . . she was a desert bride, clothed in a flowing white gown. My white stallion waited nervously, pawing the wet earth of the oasis pool, anxious to feel my weight and the weight of my bride, ready for flight across the desert (p. 96).

The world of the hospital is itself a self-contained unit that is a microcosm of the larger world outside. Thus, each character created by Anaya serves a purpose, and all of them, by the narrator's own admission, are intertwined.

> They didn't understand what Salomón was working. Perhaps it wasn't affecting them, but I felt it was drawing me into a complex web. Somehow Ismelda and Salomón and Filomón and all the others I had met were bound together, and the force created was sucking me into it. When Ismelda sat by me I felt another presence hovering over us. When I looked into her eyes I often saw the outline of the mountain (p 101).

Characters' names are symbolic of their condition or role, such as Tuerto, Mudo, Ronco, Sadsack, Dr. Steele (the backbone of the hospital and chief physician who heals Tortuga). They all serve to demonstrate and prove to Tortuga the human condition. Each character recounts bits of his life with events that led to his present condition of paralysis. Even this common malady seems to be symbolic; it is representative of another underlying impediment in the personality of the characters that holds them back from living their lives fully away from the shadow of the hospital. The entire working staff of the hospital has a residual condition caused by paralysis that continues to bind them to the same community they serve. One of the characters, Mike—the rational voice—points this out; the cushioned world of the hospital is nearly impossible to leave, and few former patients seem to do so. That is why it is vital that Tortuga shed his shell and join the living in the outside world. He must now choose the path of either remaining a turtle or a lizard that crawls, or instead progress to the point where he finds and walks that "path of the sun" of which Salomón speaks.

Symbolically, just before Tortuga is well enough to be discharged from the hospital, the moral issue of the existence of good and evil in the world—once heatedly debated by the boys in Tortuga's ward—reaches a peak; the terminally ill patients in iron lungs all die because of a power failure in their wards. This event causes a crumbling in the morale and structure of the hospital that parallels the melting away of the boy's plaster cast. As the investigation begins, Tortuga receives his clearance to leave the institution, cross the desert, and return home.

The large group of universal literary *topoi* in Anaya's novel establishes it as an accomplished work that transcends the specifically Chicano. Nevertheless, its uniqueness lies in the fact that the entire work springs from the Chicano ambience that colors it.

Although the work is written entirely in English, the title is a Spanish word; many of the names of characters are characteristically Spanish, as are their nicknames. The foods for which the patients yearn are New Mexican (chile, beans, chile verde, menudo). It is this diet that the characters say they need in order to feel whole. So it becomes evident that within the structure of the state institution there is yet another subgroup of the Hispanic population.

Hispanic folklore and tradition emerge strongly in many ways. Tortuga comes to the hospital with the legacy given him by his parents; his father had always spoken of the need for a man to learn and fulfill his destiny. His mother spoke of carrying out God's will, very much in adherence to the

Catholic tradition of New Mexico. One perceives as well the respect and value placed on family relationships, on the teachings of elders. At the end of the novel it is an old man who sends Tortuga his legacy—that artifact which will help him fulfill his destiny. The blue guitar (which also appears in Anaya's second novel, *Heart of Aztlán*) will be essential for the boy to sing the songs of life learned during his pilgrimage and his tutelage by Salomón. The hero's constant reveries—the dream sequences—that are an integral part of the narration are very much in keeping with the Hispanic custom of telling and retelling tales, embellishing them, and learning a lesson from these allegories.

Tortuga's concern with the presence of evil and injustice in the world leads to a heated discussion among the boys in his circle that centers on God, free will, and the fate of the terminally ill patients. This concern with religious matters, along with Danny's obsessive misinterpretation of religious belief and practice, also reveals characteristic elements of the Hispanic tradition.

Lastly, to more definitely root the novel in the New Mexico that Anaya loves and knows so well, the whole geographical setting of the story is situated in the state. The presence of Jerry, the Indian boy who dies in freezing weather while attempting to return home, further ties the characters to the Southwest.

The prophetic Salomón, who appears to be more the voice of Anaya than a developed, credible character, continues the character line of Ultima in Anaya's first novel. He is the *padrino*, the elder sage and holy one, the teacher who makes boys into men.

The lessons gleaned from Anaya's novel are positive and beautiful. Out of the suffering, pain, and loss experienced in the hospital are born new hope, new life. The hero survives admirably; he chooses the path of the sun, walks in the truth and the light. In *Tortuga*, Anaya offers his readers a character and a novel that is replete with pictorial images, beautiful metaphors, peace, and a final joy.

TOMAS RIVERA

Richard Rodriguez´ Hunger of Memory
as Humanistic Antithesis

Although I was born in Texas, had lived in many states in the Midwest and had not lived in any Spanish-speaking country, until then, my public voice as well as my private voice was Spanish through my first eleven years. It was in the fifth grade, that *eureka*! to my surprise, I started speaking English without translating. I suppose that at that time I had two public voices as well as two private ones.

Hunger of Memory is an exceptionally well written book. It is a profound book, a personal expression which one learns to respect for its sensibility. To respect this type of sensibility is something I learned in the Spanish-taught "escuelita," which I attended before entering public school at age 7. What Richard Rodriguez has written has great value. However, I have difficulties with concepts in the book which I consider anti-humanistic. For several reasons I consider *Hunger of Memory* as a humanistic antithesis. This book has been controversial for the Hispanic in general and in particular to the Mexican-American or Chicano. This has been the case much more so, I think, because it seems to be so well accepted by the North American public as a key to understanding the Mexican-American and debates related to bilingual education and affirmative action. Thus, it is important to define and perceive the book from different vantage points. Hispanics, Chicanos, and Latinos are not a homogenous group. They are as heterogenous a kindred group as any that exists in our present society. They are at different

From *MELUS: The Journal of the Society for the Study of the Multi-Ethnic Literature of the United States*, Vol. 11, No 4. ©1984 by the University of Cincinnati.

levels of development, perception, understanding and as complex and therefore as complete as other human beings. Richard Rodriguez´ book is a
personal expression, an autobiography, and it must be understood as that in
its singularity. It should not be used as a single way or method of understanding the bilingual, bicultural phenomenon of the Hispanic group.

I do not know Richard Rodriguez. I have seen him on television. I have
read *Hunger of Memory* three times. I intend to read it again for it has much
to offer. The work becomes more with each reading.

Richard Rodriguez´ essays have a style and tone which complement
and establish his concepts. *Hunger of Memory* establishes its tone through
patterns based on the ideas of silence and the centrality of language—silence
versus non-silence, silence and active language, silence and culture, silence
and intelligence. The aggregation of silence seems to indicate that if a person
does not speak, he/she lacks intelligence. This is a view generally held by
many teachers in the classroom: how can one judge silence? If a child's hand
does not go up, if a question is not asked, the teacher's perception is usually
that there is a lack of intelligence. Richard Rodriguez insists on the presence
of his signal-silence and the public voice. If a person does not speak he/she
does not have a public voice. How can one have a personal voice only in
silence as the only true aggregate? The author indicates that Spanish was and
is his personal voice. But it is an inactive passive voice that became neutered,
sterile, and finally silent—dead.

I find underlined throughout the text a negation of what is fundamentally the central element of the human being—the cultural root, the native
tongue. As one reads each essay, one progressively recognizes that what is most
surprising for Richard Rodriguez is that silence and his basic culture are negative elements, regressive ones. This pattern of negation is softened somewhat
when he thinks of his parents and his love for his parents, but he ultimately
comes to the thesis that this silence and the consequent inactive community is
something regressive or negative. This dealing with silence reminds me of my
efforts in struggling with this phenomenon of silence when I studied in Mexico
and lived with Mexican families; especially in the rural communities, where I
tried to write about what I considered the impenetrable face/masks and their
silence. But I never thought for a moment that their masks did not conceal an
imagination or thought processes, not that they were not developing and
inventing constantly their own world view and perceptions. And that, although
they were not speaking to me and hardly to each other, they were not actively
thinking. Richard Rodriguez delves into silence, and writes from silence as
he himself tells us, "I am here alone, writing, and what most moves me is the
silence." Truly this is an active task for him. Yet, with regard to his own

family, he sees this silence as a non-force. He finally concludes simplistically, unfortunately, that his personal voice is Spanish and that his active voice is English. Surely, this is a humanistic antithesis.

It is necessary at this point to call attention to his development as a writer. He grew up and was taught in the humanities. The humanities have a clear base—at a minimum the explaining or aiding in the elaboration of a philosophy of life. Surely by the time one is twelve years old or so one has a philosophy of life. By then one has formulated and asked all the great philosophical questions and has even provided some answers. Whether one asks and answers in English or Spanish or in any other tongue is not important. The humanities, and certainly the study of literature, recognize this. As an educated scholar in literature, certainly, and much more so as a Renaissance scholar, Richard Rodriguez should know this. But his thoughts do not recognize this fundamental philosophical base. Clearly as a youngster of twelve or thirteen years of age he could not have, but certainly as an academic he could have reflected on the realities of his life, on the sensibility, and on the importance of what he did not know then and what he must now know. The humanities are also, to put it simply, a search for life, a search for form, but most significantly a search for wisdom. In this regard Richard Rodriguez starts out well. His search for life and form in the literary form of autobiography has as a premise the basic core of family life. But then Richard Rodriguez struggles with the sense of disassociation from that basic culture. Clearly, he opts to disassociate, and, as a scholar, attempts to rationalize that only through disassociation from a native culture was he to gain and thus has gained the "other," that is, the "public" world. Without wisdom he almost forgets the original passions of human life. Is he well educated in literature? For literature above all gives and inculcates in the student and scholar the fundamental original elements of humanistic endeavor without regard to race or language, much less with regards to a public voice. The most important ideas that the study of the humanities relate are the fundamental elements and values of human beings, regardless of race and nationality. Ultimately, the study of the humanities teaches the idea that life is a relationship with the totality of people within its circumstance.

Then we come to the question of place and being. In Spanish there are two verbs meaning "to be," *Ser* and *Estar*. This is quite important to *Hunger of Memory*. Being born into a family is equal to being, *Ser*. Education and instruction teaches us to be, *Estar*. Both are fundamental verbs. *Ser* is an interior stage, and *Estar* is an exterior one. To leave the *Ser* only for the *Estar* is a grievous error. Richard Rodriguez implies, at times explicitly, that the authentic being is and can only be in the *Estar* (public voice) and only there is he/she complete. And further, he states that authenticity can only come by being an exterior being in English in the English speaking world. In the Hispanic world, the interior world of *Ser* is ultimately more important than the world of *Estar*. *Honra*, honesty, emanates from and is important to the *Ser*. Richard Rodriguez opts for the *Estar* world as the more important and does not give due importance to the world of *Ser*. He has problems, in short, with the world from which he came. Surely this is an antithesis to a humanistic development.

As with memory, the centrality of language is a constant pattern in the book. For the Hispanic reader the struggle quickly becomes English versus Spanish. His parents do not know the grand development of the Spanish language and its importance beyond their immediate family. However, Richard Rodriguez should, as an educated person, recognize this grand development. Surely, he could have given credit to the development of a language that has existed over six hundred years, which has elaborated a world literature, which has mixed with the many languages of the American continents, which is perhaps the most analytical of the romance languages, and which will be of such importance in the twenty first century. Instead Richard Rodriguez flees, as a young man, from this previous human achieve- ment. This fleeing is understandable as a symbol of the pressures of the Americanization process. Yet, as a formally educated scholar, reflecting upon that flight, he does not dare to signal the importance that the language has. Instead he sees it as an activity that has no redeeming value. He gives no value to the Hispanic language, its culture, its arts. It is difficult to believe that as an educated humanist he doesn't recognize the most important element of Hispanic culture—the context of the development of the distinct religions in the Spanish peninsula—the Judaic, the Christian, and the Moorish. These distinct cultures reached their apogees and clearly influ- enced Spanish. As a humanist, surely he must know this. The Hispanic world has elaborated and developed much in the history of ideas. Richard Rodriguez seems to indicate that the personal Spanish voice lacks the intel- ligence and ability to communicate beyond the sensibilities of the personal interactions of personal family life. This is intolerable. Hispanic culture has a historical tradition of great intellectual development. He does not recog- nize the so-called "original sin" of the American continents. What is this *pecado original* that Hector Murena wrote about so eloquently? It is simply the act of transplanting the European cultures to the American continents. The conquest by the Europeans of what is today Hispanic America is one of the most fundamental struggles for justice. The Laws of Burgos (1511-1521), established in Spain before the conquest of Mexico, held above all that the

Indian was a man of the world. This was a fundamental axiom. The evolved mestizo nations struggled through a racist colonial empire, but there was a mixture of races. This was less evident in the English-speaking world. I mention this because it appears to me that one of the greatest preoccupations of Richard Rodriguez is that he "looks" Indian. He speaks of his father as looking and being white. He speaks of his mother as looking Portuguese. It surprises me that as an educated humanist in 1982 he would still have that type of complex, colonized mind. He feels out of place in Bel Aire in L.A. because he looks Indian. He worries about what or how he will be perceived by the "Anglo." These are honest and sincere perceptions. I respect his feelings. He does, however, remind me of students I had in the 50s and 60s who were struggling with their brownness.

The Hispanic colonial period evolved a racism based mainly on color and, of course, class. The colonial mind was preoccupied with color. When a child born to a couple was darker than the parents, he/she was called a "*salto atrás*," a jump backwards, but if the child was lighter, he/she was considered a "*salto adelante*," a jump forward; and if the child was the same color as the parents, a "*tente en el aire*," suspended. At times Richard Rodriguez clearly illustrates a colonized mind. His reactions as a young child are understandable. As a writer, however, while interpreting these sensibilities well, he fails to analyze those pressures that force conformity and simply attributes negative values to the language and culture of his parents, who have, as he states "no-public-voice."

It is well to recall briefly the formation of the Mexican nation and its history as it went from a political to an intellectual emancipation from 1811 to 1917. It took the Mexican nation over 100 years and 50 civil wars to evolve an independent, clear, and creative character. It is a unique nation. By 1930 the Mexican character was distinct—its art, music, literature, and culture were unique. It had developed a unique identity and character; it had accepted the mestizo. Surely, Richard Rodriguez must recognize, now that he is educated, that his parents came from a culture that was distinctly Mexican, and non-imitative, that his parents represent a culture with a singular identity. He offers, however, no recognition of the cultural uniqueness of his parents. Mexican culture had gone through its colonial and imitative period, its struggle for intellectual emancipation, and had arrived as an authentic, unique nation. His parents, therefore, recognize much better than Richard Rodriquez who the "gringos" are. This is a constant motif in the book. His parents know who they are themselves. They are no puzzle unto themselves. Richard Rodriguez says that change is a constant and should be constant and he argues that in order to change or to have the dynamics of change it is necessary to leave behind his Mexicanness, represented by the silence of the personal voice, the non-public voice, and his distinct cultural attributes. By gaining the other public voice, he asserts, he will become more authentic. Truly, this is antithetical to a humanistic education.

Richard Rodriguez' views remind me of two excellent books. The first one was published in 1930 by Samuel Ramos, *El perfil del hombre en la historia de Mexico* (The Profile of Man in the History of Mexico), and the other was published in 1950 by Octavio Paz, *El laberinto de soledad* (The Labyrinth of Solitude). *El perfil* discusses the inferiority complex of the Mexican. *El laberinto* reflects on the silence and the bursting out from that silence of the Mexican psyche. They are books eloquent in their perceptions of silence and the negativistic attitudes about the Mexican psyche. Samuel Ramos writes about *el pelado;* Octavio Paz has a marvelous chapter on *el pachuco* and now with Richard Rodriguez there is a total book on *el pocho* or what he considers to be *el pocho. El pelado, el pachuco* and *el pocho* can be considered alienated persons at the margins of culture. They do not represent the totality of the Hispanic culture in general, nor, in particular, the Mexican or Mexican-American culture. These are books about extreme people. What the pelado, the pachuco, and what Richard Rodriguez symbolize is a type of graffitti. By saying this, I do not seek to demean Richard Rodriguez' endeavor at all, but simply to point out that the most important element of graffitti is that it is an expression. Done in silence. Powerful. Exact. It calls out attention to itself as if saying "I want to understand myself," "I want you, the passerby, to understand me. I am at the (extreme) margin. I want to be; I hunger to be part of your memory." Graffitti beckons us. It calls to tell us that they *are* us—in an extreme way, that they exist between cultures, but outside a culture.

In spite of its humanistic antithesis, *Hunger of Memory* has an authentic dimension. Perhaps the most important element here is that Richard Rodriguez is a reflection of a North American education. Is he a reflection of the English professor or the place of preparation which doesn't really give him perceptions other than those of the English-speaking world? There is, ultimately, I believe, a lack of understanding of world culture; especially lacking is an understanding of the Hispanic world. It is a reflection of a North American education. He calls himself Caliban in "Mr. Secrets." Who is Caliban? He is a slave, a monster, a character in Shakespeare's last play. Caliban represents the puppet, the person who is controlled. Caliban in *The Tempest* was driven by material instincts only. "Mr. Secrets," the last chapter, is especially clear on this concept. Is Caliban a reflection of a North American education? Is it an indication of an education which refuses to acknowledge as important only that which is tied to the northern European cultures? Is it an attitude of non-inquiry in the teaching of humanities? Aren't racist impositions, Adamic and nativistic concepts and attitudes quite prevalent?

The great surprise of many of our students who study abroad is that of finding out that not everything is originated (truly) in the United States, and that in reality our cultural history is quite short and in many instances limited. Richard Rodriguez is saying that he now has a public voice, an authentic one. Before he did not. He now believes that he is more real, and this is absurd. The dimension that Richard Rodriguez gives the North American public in his book fits well within North American intellectual circles because he has ironically justified his context by "being" not one of "them," but rather by having become one of "us." The North American public accepts Richard Rodriguez quite well and much in the same manner that it accepted Oscar Lewis' studies of the poor in Puerto Rico and Mexico. In this manner, knowledge of the unknown is accepted, simplified, and categorized. One has to ask if Richard Rodriguez has a community now? Did he have a community in the past? Does he think that now because he has published and has been accepted as a good writer that he now has community? Richard Rodriguez exists between two cultures, but he believes it more important to participate in one world than the other. But it is possible to participate in many worlds profoundly and, without losing, but rather gaining perception and appreciation from all.

I want to place in opposition to Richard Rodriguez' work a body of Chicano literature which has precepts as profound and as well written. This body of expression has not had the same acceptance. Some of it is written in Spanish, some in English, and some in a mixture of both languages. It is not recognized well, basically because the works have not been published nor merchandized by major American publishing companies. In these Chicano works there is little hunger of memory, and much hunger for community. If Richard Rodriguez has hunger of memory, Chicano literature hungers for community. Those who labored, in the 1960s and 1970s and into the 1980s to establish a literature, accepted the task to develop a literature in the United States and that it was to be in languages understandable primarily to the Mexican-American community. The endeavor was a basic challenge to North American literary dominance. In 1965, there were few works written by writers of Mexican extraction in the United States. There were no courses being taught in Chicano literature. Today there are courses taught in Chicano literature in a total of 135 universities at the undergraduate and graduate level. It is recognized as a body of literature either as part of Mexican literature, as part of American literature, or as an offshoot of

Hispanic-American literature. It has several intellectual bases, but this literature does not interest Richard Rodriguez even as a curiosity—even though, paradoxically, he is now inextricably part of that contribution.

The Chicano writers I have in mind were hungry for community. The manner of establishing that community was through remembrance and rediscovery of commonalities of the culture plus the need to accept the community in all its heterogeneity—that is, with all its virtues, with all its flaws, with all its energy, with all its apathy. It was important to recognize and to develop the basic elements of our community. Martin Buber's idea that "Community is the aspiration of all human history" was clearly before us. The Mexican-American as part of human history had to develop that community, to be part of it, or leave it. Rebecca West says that "Community is conversation," and the Mexican-American community has not been silent since then. What the Chicano writer did was establish a community where there was a definite place, where dialogues could develop, and where the values of the community could be elaborated. There was little concern regarding acceptance by the larger/majority population. There is a more visible Chicano/Mexican-American community today because Chicano writers aided in underlining the realities that made up the community. Clearly Richard Rodriguez regards that community as living in silence. Actually that is why he is very alone. What one senses in *Hunger of Memory* is that his parents no longer speak. Ironically his parents speak louder than he. The sensibility of his writing effort, I dare say, does not come only from his training in the English language, but from those early day experiences when he was taught, I am sure, the way to invent himself in the world by his parents.

I said earlier that Richard Rodriguez reminds me of students I had in college in the 1960s who were embarrassed to organize themselves, who did not want to bring their parents to college to participate in college activities because their parents wouldn't know how to dress, and students who hardly respected the few Chicano professors who were then around. Truly, these students had the same type of colonized mind dramatized by Richard Rodriguez—honest, authentic, and naïve, particularly at this later date.

What *Hunger of Memory* therefore reveals is one more step in the intellectual emancipation of the Mexican-American. It represents a significant intellectual step because such views are so clearly articulated. His parents know who they are, who they were, and who the gringos were. They didn't stop talking to him because they didn't understand him, but because he no longer saw the significance of their life. Richard Rodriguez lost the memory of all the philosophical questions they had helped him face and answer long before he walked into the English-speaking world. A writer is lonely only if he has lost the sense of his community's aspirations and the integrative values. His parents are the thesis of his statement. Sometimes, he feels frustrated because they have not read García-Márquez, Rubén Darío, but then he never read these writers to them. He hungers for a memory that could be so close, yet he doesn't seem to realize that satisfying this appetite is within reach.

Hunger of Memory is thus a humanistic antithesis for several reasons. First, because its breadth and dimension is so narrow, unaware as it is of the traditions that should inform it. Second, it is ultimately an aggregation of cultural negations. Richard Rodriguez prizes as authentic only that which he learns in the classrooms. Third, he underlines the silence of culture as negative. Finally, Richard Rodriguez believes that it is only through English that he thinks he can elaborate what is correct and not correct for the community as a whole.

In his last chapter, "Mr. Secrets," as the family is leaving, and everyone is standing outside, his mother asks him to take a sweater to his father because it is getting cold. The last words of the book are "I take it [the sweater] and place it on him. In that instant I feel the thinness of his arms. He turns. He asks if I am going home now, too. It is, I realize, the only thing he has said to me all evening."

Here Richard Rodriguez tells us that his father has been silent all evening. What he doesn't tell us is that he (Richard Rodriguez) has also been silent. He does not tell us about *his* own type of silence. If he has a hunger of memory it is mainly because he does not choose to communicate his more intimate memories. Can anything be that painful? Where is the real *honra*, the real *Ser*? The only positive cultural attributes which he signals throughout his book are those relative to the English-speaking world. Richard Rodriguez understands the needs for memory, but does not dare recover it totally. Why? The title is the thesis, but the content is the antithesis of the very title. This is a classic work, 1930 Mexican vintage, clearly seeking approbation of an inferiority complex. As Samuel Ramos stated in *El perfil del hombre*, it is not that the Mexican is inferior: it's that he thinks he is inferior. This was the legacy of Spanish colonization. Richard Rodriguez apparently decolonizes himself by seeking to free himself from a personal voice, but in so trying he will likely enter another colony of despair.

GENARO M. PADILLA

A Reassessment of Fray Angelico Chavez's Fiction

Fray Angelico Chavez has had a long and remarkably distinguished career as a man of letters. A retired Franciscan now in his seventies, Chavez has proven himself a capable historian and scholar with *Origins of New Mexico Families in the Spanish Colonial Period* (1954), *Archives of the Santa Fe Archdiocese* (1957), *Coronado's Friars* (1968), *My Penitente Land (1974)*, and most recently, *But Time and Chance: The Story of Padre Martínez of Taos* (1981). Over a period of over forty years, Chavez has published five volumes of poetry, and one volume, *The Virgin of Port Lligat*, was recognized as a "very commendable achievement" by T. S. Eliot. During these prolific decades, he has also written a good deal of short fiction. Many of Chavez's stories appear in two collections—*New Mexico Triptych* (1940) and *From an Altar Screen: Tales from New Mexico* (1957). Other stories remain hidden away in various journals, as well as church magazines such as the *St. Anthony Messenger* and *Sodalist* where Chavez published regularly in the thirties and forties. In addition to these publications, there is a wealth of miscellaneous material—historical articles, biographical profiles, contributions to other books, scores of book reviews—for which Chavez deserves credit.

Yet, despite this outpouring of material about the Hispano experience in New Mexico, Chavez has been largely overlooked as one of the pioneers of Chicano writing in this century. Moreover, often charged with writing about the romantic, the wistful, the engagingly Spanish past in New Mexico, the social concerns that pervade Fray Angelico's work have been neglected by much recent criticism. Since he is a Franciscan, he is often thought to be too

From *MELUS: The Journal of the Society for the Study of the Multi-Ethnic Literature of the United States*, Vol. 11, No 4. ©1984 by the University of Cincinnati.

mystical, as in his poetry, or exclusively concerned with church-related history instead of with what Juan Rodriguez, for instance, calls "the specifics of the Mexican American experience." Other critics like Rodolfo Acuña, author of *Occupied America: A History of Chicanos,* actually dismiss Chavez's historical scholarship, saying that he "ignores history" by expounding the Spanish "fantasy heritage" and the "myth that New Mexicans peacefully joined the Anglo nation and 'became a willing enclave of the United States.'"

Chavez's poetry may indeed shun the world, for it does follow the meditative tradition of religious poetry and, as he says, the "pure English lyric" form in its offering of love and service to Christ and the Blessed Mother. Such otherworldliness, however, should not be charged to his historical studies. Unlike much of the poetry, Chavez's history is grounded in the world, even when that world is seen from a religious perspective. Fray Angelico's clerical training understandably informs his interest in church-related history, but that history has been conducted with painstaking archival research in such studies as *Archives of the Archdiocese of Santa Fe, Coronado's Friars,* and *But Time and Chance: The Story of Padre Martínez of Taos,* not to mention his voluminous historical articles for various publications. The story he records from such archival material is invariably transformed from dry documents—church records, exploration chronicles, letters, wills—into a colorful narrative pastiche of New Mexico's past four centuries. One such pastiche, *Coronado's Friars,* a study of the identities of the Franciscans who accompanied the Coronado expedition of 1540, is considered the definitive work on a "seemingly unsolvable problem," unraveled, not through scholarly luck, but through careful collation and reexamination of sixteenth-century documents that Chavez suspected were based upon an altogether distinct and previous source. That he chose to write primarily on early New Mexico history need not indict him for ignoring what we now recognize as intercultural tensions in the state; on the contrary, his study of the early stages of settlement often informs his understanding of events in the last century.

My Penitente Land, for instance, is written in the same spirit that early American historiographers reconstructed their people's errand into the American wilderness. Like them, he discovers parallels between life, landscape, and religious devotion in the Biblical Holy Land and in Hispanic New Mexico. Offering no notes at all, Chavez writes a sweeping profile of the Hispanic soul of New Mexico. A people's history, he insists, cannot be understood by merely "stringing out facts and dates." A meaningful history is one that seeks to record the internal dynamics of a people's "beliefs and yearnings," their spiritual history.

Given this intention, Chavez's *My Penitente Land* is a provocative, even controversial, quasi-literary history of a unique cultural and religious climate represented not only by penitent rituals but by an entire way of life. Unless we understand the manifold forces that shaped Hispanic consciousness in New Mexico, we simply fail to touch a people's historic essence, as have so many "American newcomers." He writes from an internal or spiritual perspective, Chavez argues, precisely because so many American historians, well-meaning or not, have so consistently mangled New Mexican history.

In upholding the dignity of his people, nevertheless, he does overemphasize the Spanish heritage of New Mexico. His preoccupation, for instance, with what he refers to as the "*castizo*" ancestory of many New Mexico families and village clans becomes offensive when he rather casually distinguishes between the refined manners of these "*pure*" *castizos* and the coarser, sometimes uncivil, basically "Indian" manners of the *gentízaros* who resided along the fringes of many settlements. Moreover, he notes but does not elaborate upon the abuses heaped upon these people of mixed Spanish-Indian blood by the *ricos*. While he admits that these "poorer and lowlier folks were made to feel that they were an inferior class among God's children," he only mentions their exploitation by the "*castizos*" for whom they were forced to labor in the fields, as servants in homes, or as livestock herders. But if he has little to say about class tensions in his history, his fiction, we discover, often revolves around such tensions.

As to the charge that Chavez is among those who expound the myth of the bloodless conquest of New Mexico in 1846, one can only say that he reports the fact that General Kearney's march into Santa Fe was not met by resistance, Governor Armijo and his soldiers beating a fast retreat to El Paso. He does go on to say that even though there was no bloodletting in this initial encounter, there later was, physically and certainly spiritually. While Chavez contends that in the main, New Mexicans accepted the new flag, or at least tolerated it, he points out that there was a good deal of self-serving betrayal on the part of the *ricos*:

> The New Mexican leaders were of little or no help to their humbler and poorer countrymen. In what we now call "vanity biographies" appended to regional histories of the times, they falsely claimed that their immediate grandparents had come directly from Spain. It was a handy way of disassociating themselves from their less fortunate cousins bearing the same surnames. . . . This, of course, helped them in competing successfully with the newcomers.

Finally, Chavez, drawing upon Biblical allusion again, rather sardonically refers to the American invaders as cultural "Philistines," crass and greedy. Among these Philistines were also the new non-Hispanic clergy, starting with Jean Baptiste Lamy, a French priest appointed first Bishop of Santa Fe in 1850, who disrupted long established religious practices.

In *But Time and Chance: The Story of Padre Martínez of Taos*, Chavez returns to documentary history to assess the rift between Bishop Lamy's Church and the native Catholic clergy and populace. A thorough biographical study of Padre Antonio José Martínez, the influential Taos priest who was excommunicated by Bishop Lamy for alleged ecclesiastical infractions, *But Time and Chance* lauds Padre Martínez´ clerical and political achievements, without romanticizing his life. On the old controversy over whether Martínez broke his vows of celibacy to sire a number of children, a contention that forms the basis of Willa Cather's vilification of Martínez in *Death Comes for the Archbishop*, Chavez deduces, on the basis of some dubious circumstances surrounding their baptismal records, that Martínez may well have been the father of one Teodora Romero's four children. In addition, he writes that Martínez had a streak of intellectual pride, tended to boast his accomplishments, and was manipulative in both civil and ecclesiastic affairs. Still, he gave freely of his inherited bounty, seldom pressed for tithing, frequently attended the sick, and traveled a wide circuit to bestow the sacraments.

Regarding the ecclesiastical charges leveled against Martínez by Archbishop Lamy and Lamy's henchman, Vicar Joseph Machebeuf, he was innocent. Chavez shows that Lamy and Machebeuf arrived in New Mexico already quite decided that the native Hispanics were primitive, grossly immoral, treacherous, and stupid; the clergy, moreover, were suspected of even greater moral terpitude, drunkenness and concubinage, for instance, as well as clerical incompetence. Their concerted efforts to scandalize the native clergy, and to denigrate the populace in sermons and pastoral letters, are scrupulously exposed as little more than self-serving and hypocritical sham, not to mention un-Christian behavior.

By way of illustrating the unscrupulous methods American historians used in vilifying Martínez, Chavez himself shows how easily fragmentary information can be summarily distorted. Since seminary days, Lamy and Machebeuf had had an *amitie particuliere*—a "particular friendship" that might be considered a bit too particular, too intimate. Just as they had defamed the native clergy's morals, so also might the almost inseparable pair's morals be questioned. To wit, in the text of one Christmas Pastoral Letter warning against various forms of vice, Chavez discovers an interesting discrepancy:

He [Lamy] warned them in all charity to avoid such scandalous occasions of sin as divorces, dances, and gambling, and ended with a quotation from I Corinthians 6; 9–10: *Be not deceived, neither fornicators, nor adulterers, nor theives, nor drunkards, nor railers, nor extortioners, shall possess the kingdom of God.* If the later detractors of the native clergy in general took this biblical citation as directed at them personally, which it most certainly was not, one could ask them with the same unfair reasoning why Bishop Lamy happened to leave out "nor the effeminates, nor sodomites" between the words "Adulterers" and "thieves." This would be entirely reprehensible, to say the least. But to the francophile biographers, it seems, everything was fair in love when it came to their French heroes—and in war when it came to the so-called Mexican opposition.

As a historian, then, Fray Angelico is hardly the humble, little brown-robed Franciscan, stooped in quiet prayer while oblivious to injustice and racial bigotry, even within his own Church. If he is too *castizo* and too defensive about the labeling of his people as Mexicans, it is largely because he hears well the reverberations of that word's other meanings, its intentional meanings. Among themselves people have long called themselves mexicanos, but when called "Mexicans" by the American invaders it was the innuendos that grated, the meanings that bruised—greaser! lazy! stupid! immoral! All epithets meant to dehumanize, and to rationalize land grabbing, cultural pillaging, thievery, and Aryan disdain. Such psychological defenses, quixotic as they might be, have played a significant role in this people's cultural endurance and distinct identity. As Chavez admits, this is not to say that people haven't come from Mexico, or that Mexico has not significantly influenced the way of life in the region. Nevertheless, three hundred years of life on that particular landscape has indelibly forged a unique regional consiousness. That is essentially what Chavez lays claim to in his history, and also in the fiction to which we now turn. For it is in the fiction that the dramatization of the Hispano's long tenure upon that landscape is best evidenced in its concrete socio-cultural realities and its spiritual nuances.

≈≈≈≈≈≈≈≈

On the narrative surface, Chavez's tales in *New Mexico Triptych* and *From an Altar Screen* are genial, easy to read, as though framed for adolescents. They often sound like traditional Hispanic *cuentos*, employing as they do provincialisms, archetypal characters and situations, and Christian morals. They are, in short, tales that read like Biblical parables and allegories. Their complexity lies not in language or character but in the implicit meanings of the parabolic structure itself. To follow Chavez, just as the "more or less exact date of each tale appears hidden somewhere in the background of each panel," so also do certain exact social and cultural issues remain hidden somewhere in the background of each tale's morality structure. However implicit, such issues are brought into sharper relief when Chavez's readers are willing to probe the background of a restrained, seemingly facile language.

Read chronologically as the settings progress from the eighteenth century to World War II, the stories and the village surroundings in which those actions take shape produce a *retablo* of interconnected panels that dramatize a people's cultural evolution. Most of the stories are, to be sure, about some human relationship gone awry, some moral lapse that is set aright through a visionary experience, usually the dreamlike appearance of a village patron saint, which restores grace and the moral sight of the characters. Even so, there is more complexity to this allegorical aspect of Chavez's stories than has been recognized by critics who have glossed over his serious social themes while commenting upon their "great charm . . . and droll wisdom." For it is in his fiction that Chavez's writing reveals a complex interplay between the artist's fictive imagination, his moral and religious perspectives, and his historian's knowledge of the troubling realities of New Mexico's intercultural conflicts. The stories subtly examine the tensions which have long existed within the Hispanic culture itself, as well as the tensions between the Chicano and what Chavez in *My Penitente Land* calls the "Philistine" American culture.

In the fiction that focuses upon life before the American occupation, stories such as "The Bell That Sang Again," "The Ardent Commandant," "The Black Ewe," the tensions within the culture itself, especially between classes, are played out in isolated Hispanic settings. Each of these stories pits an arrogant stranger, usually a Spanish officer sent to supervise the long established colonists, or a rich *patron*, against simple villagers or shepherds. In "The Bell That Sang Again," Joaquin Amaya, a dark-featured *genízaro*, fights to the death with a Captain Pelayo, a red-headed soldier born in Spain, who has openly flirted with Amaya's wife. Even before their duel, the stranger has incited resentment and anger in the village men by charming their wives with tales of Spain, while briskly ordering them about and letting fall "occasional slurs about their own unlettered speech or about their humble blood" (p. 6). A skillful adaptation of the well known *cuento* about a woman who keeps a secret assignation with a handsome stranger only to discover moments before she is seduced that he is the cloven-footed devil himself, "The Ardent Commandant" plays upon the colonists' long distrust of the Spanish officials arbitrarily imposed upon them by the Mexican Viceroys, many of whom were regarded as equal to the devil himself in their deceit, political greed, and carelessness of the colonists´ needs. Outsiders, however, are not the only ones capable of deceit. The *patron* who owns thousands of sheep as well as their shepherds in "The Black Ewe" sends a certain villager out to a distant range in order to seduce his young *genízara* wife. In this story the peonage system is exposed for its inhumanity, for even when the guilty lovers are discovered, it is the *genízara*, her dark hair mysteriously clipped to the skull, who must bear the public burden while the Spanish *patron* returns to his hacienda untainted. Still, his sin does not go unpunished altogether, at least symbolically, since his rich grazing land turns to desert following years of severe drought. The land itself thus recoils against his deceit.

The conflict between classes, characterized by the exploitation of the "lowly villagers" by Spanish snobs and self-serving *patrons*, is certainly at the core of Chavez's fiction here. Instead of ignoring history, he dramatizes the intracultural hostilities that have long brewed in New Mexico, hostilities that have, in part, shaped the consciousness of its people. Emblematic of the racial and cultural effects of such struggle, the two ill-fated adversaries in "The Bell That Sang Again" lie together in death, "Joaquin with a military dagger completely buried in his throat, while next to him lay the Captain with a hunter's knife pushed deep under his ribs" (p. 12).

As village life moves closer to the present, after the American invasion, the trials Chavez's characters undergo become less centered in an enclosed area of cultural experience and more entangled in the web of corrupting American influences. Stories like "Wake for Don Corsino," "The Lean Years," and "The Angel's New Wings" simultaneously examine internal cultural erosion and the disruptive external influences for which the railroad, Bishop Lamy's snobbish clergy, and Christmas tinsel are the chief metaphors. Finally, "The Colonel and the Santo," a story set after World War II, dramatizes some of the cultural misunderstandings that continue to strain Chicano and Anglo relations.

Although "Wake for Don Corsino" is a comic tale about a drunk who startles neighbors when he abruptly sits up during his own *velorio*/wake, this *cuento* also provides a sharp satire upon the negative effects of American technology and the capitalistic impulse upon Hispano mores. Like a "faint trailing moan of a locomotive" (p. 65), the American presence begins to resound throughout the territory, not through any direct interaction between Chicanos and gringos, but through subtle references to the railroad that quickly followed their arrival. The railroad, an early symptom of Yankee ingenuity in the West that has become a metaphor for social struggle in other Chicano fiction, is pictured as having "lately spun its threads of steel across San Miguel County" (p. 65). The spider image here is illustrative of Chavez's chagrin with an American commercial enterprise that brought with it a poisonous economic reality for the Hispano.

Don Corsino, who has become the village drunk after the death of his wife, is described as having lost all of his cattle and horses "since he became a daily customer at the saloon, another institution that came with the railroad to Las Vegas and spawned little offshoots in scattered villages like El Piojo" (p. 66). The railroad has been double-edged in its dealings with Don Corsino, for while he has been drinking himself into a stupor in the saloon brought by the railroad, his neighbors, one of whom hypocritically chants *alabados*/religious ballads at his wake, have been stealing his livestock piecemeal and peddling them at the "railroad stockyards in Las Vegas" (p. 68). While no claim is made for pastoral innocence in these villagers, the railroad, and the material greed that fuels it, tears across their common grazing land, breaking a cooperative economy for a handful of silver coins.

In another story set soon after the American occupation, Chavez's social perspective becomes sharper, even openly sarcastic. "The Lean Years" takes aim at the corrupting effects of railroad expansion, the wholesale land-grabbing that dispossessed village people of their homes, and the American clergy's attempts to rid the Catholic Church in New Mexico of its "superstitious ways," as well as of its native clergy. The story about a man's renewed love for his crippled wife, Chavez's tale may also be read as a social allegory in which an old, largely uninterrupted village culture is crippled under the weight of time and the invasion of a foreign culture intent upon establishing a new social and economic order.

Set in the period after Jean Baptiste Lamy was named Bishop of Santa Fe in 1850, the story describes the trip a newly arrived French priest makes to a secluded village to say Mass. Not so much intolerant as condescendingly impatient with a people he regards as culturally primitive and theologically unsophisticated, the priest, a figure of Lamy himself, views a hand-carved *santo*, a statue of San Jose, that adorns the village chapel as an "ugly monster . . . with its stiff poise, its cheap tin coronet . . . and, worst of all, its unreal black beard that was nothing more than a patch of black smeared around thin drab lips" (pp. 80–81). As Chavez points out in *But Time and Chance*, it was precisely this snobbish attitude that led to Lamy's campaign to strip village chapels of their *santos*, a campaign carried out with such insulting efficiency that it almost killed the *santero* tradition altogether.

Chavez's acerbic tone, here and elsewhere in the story, stabs deeply into the body of non-Hispanic clergy propagated by Bishop Lamy and his French and Irish successors to wring the "backward," "superstitious," even "immoral" religious practices out of the native people. Bishop Lamy's *pogram* to "modernize" the Church ignored the stabilizing value of a people's religious traditions. Although a clergyman himself, Chavez's resentment of his people's treatment as an "inferior breed of pinto sheep in the Lord's fold" is unrestrained by his collar. In *My Penitente Land*, he amplifies the charge against the de-Mexicanization of the Church:

> Lamy was chosen on the Philistine assumption that French priests, for speaking a language derived from Latin, were ideally suited for a people who spoke a Latin-derived language of their own. This illogic has prevailed ever since, that a smattering of the language will supply for the grasp of a culture upon its native landscape. . . . The clash which occurred between the new and the native clergy was due to radical differences in outlook. . . . The resentment grew stronger when they [the native clergy] felt themselves regarded and treated as dust by the new broom. Chief among them was the famed Padre Martínez of Taos who, unlike his brethren who either left the ministry or exiled themselves to Mexico, stuck to his post and continued the good fight for his people against all abuses, whether civil or ecclesiastical.

It is this bitter knowledge of the Church's abuses and what Chavez calls the French clergy's "insidious feeling of superiority" that informs stories like "The Lean Years," in which a European-born priest, convinced that the village primitives cannot understand "involved allegory," preaches the same sermon every year to the "simple folks who sat wide-eyed . . . like children" (pp. 78–79). Stripped of fellow Hispano clergy like their beloved Padre Martínez, who was summarily excommunicated without due process of canon law by Lamy, it is a wonder Hispanic New Mexicans have remained as steadfastly Catholic as they generally have. In fact, Lamy's "new broom" was so successful at sweeping away the native clergy that not until 1974 was a Hispano, Father Robert Sanchez, installed as Archbishop of Santa Fe—one hundred and twenty-four years of haughty contempt. Such ecclesiastical policies have left scars and lingering distrust, if quiet and brooding.

At the other edge of "The Lean Years" is an increasingly doomed sense that the landscape upon which José and his wife, Soledad, are playing out their drama of human love is straining under the influence of a shattering American social and economic system. The new territorial railroad into Las Vegas brings with it not only the mercantile store, filled with frills people hardly need, but also the saloon and a brothel. At one point, José ventures into Las Vegas to sell his handmade furniture and to "see with his own eyes the strange and unbelievable things" of which he has begun to hear. Once in town, he is drawn into the saloon where he downs more and more sweet-tasting Muscatel and Tokay. Suddenly, two prostitutes, finely dressed and speaking a "strange language," enter the saloon. Drunk by this time, and tempted by these fair women, José stumbles off in the direction of the brothel. Along the way, however, he has a change of heart and decides to return to La Cunita.

Even though this villager has gained a temporary victory over the American plague, the village itself is doomed to extinction. For the people of La Cunita, like people in numerous scattered land grant villages, have been ordered off the land. Soledad's gradual waning and death is a metaphor for the gradual decline of the village and the dissipation of its inhabitants. Chavez, however, does not settle for a symbolic gesture when he can be more direct:

> This past year some tall blond men with jowls like coxcombs had come with long worded papers from Santa Fe, saying that all the prairie around La Cunita now belonged to them. The inhabitants of La Cunita could no longer graze their cattle and sheep on the land. The sheriff of Las Vegas who came with them sheepishly said that they were right, and nothing could be done about it. After getting a pitance for the plots on which their houses stood, the men began taking their families to Las Vegas. They found steady work right away and began replacing the Chinese coolies in the railroad section gangs. (p. 102)

The unmistakable reference to the legal maneuverings of the Santa Fe Ring, with its "long-worded papers" written by shyster lawyers, powerful bankers, and crooked politicians, is strikingly amplified by Chavez's description of the fat flesh hanging from these gringos' clownish faces. Clownish-looking and strange sounding though these strangers may have seemed to the Hispano, they proved to be shrewd and manipulative enough to steal millions of acres in communal and private land holdings. And as always, the victims of this complicity between the Anglo foreigners and the Hispanos in power, represented here by the sheriff from Las Vegas, were the common villagers who, deprived of their grazing rights, were forced to leave their homes for a tenuous existence in larger towns, embryonic cities.

José Vera himself is forced to move to Las Vegas, a booming railroad town in the late nineteenth century. Once there he trades his wood carving tools for a blacksmith's hammer and labors to keep the steam engines moving along the tracks of commerce. José, like most of the dispossessed, endures by strength of will; he even makes a decent living for himself in the city, but life is never really the same. Having been removed from the land, the village folk are cut off from their historical essence, from their cultural lifeblood. The old relationships are broken and people must reconcile their past with an irrevocably altered present.

Even villages that maintained a viable life show the debilitating effects of the Anglo presence. In "The Angel's New Wings" old Nabor remains the lone embodiment of pre-occupation values and mores. A *santero* who is largely reduced to repairing *bultos*, obviously the result of the Church's discouragement of the tradition, Nabor is dumbfounded when told that someone has stolen all of the *santos* from the church. "Who would want to steal them?" he asks the priest; but the answer is only too clear. "There are people in Santa Fe or Taos who buy them for good money" (p. 7). Doubly confounding, Chavez suggests that the same cultural Philistines who, on the one hand, virtually outlaw a people's sacred images, should, on the other, offer "good money" for the "quaint" if "crude" folk art so relished as southwestern decor in their expensive adobe homes.

Yet, Chavez is critical of his own people as well. After all, the children who replace Nabor in setting up the Christmas *nacimiento* carelessly break the herald angel's wing, and on the eve of Christ's birth the villagers are having a raucous dance instead of watching quietly in the church. In fact, Nabor's allegorical, dreamlike wandering through the village in pursuit of the wooden angel that has magically come to life assumes the dimensions of a bewildering journey through a changing era he can little understand. People in the brightly lit dance hall push, make fun, and spin him around—respect for their *ancianos*—their old—clearly diminished. As he proceeds to the mercantile, where tinsel streamers and a mannequin Santa Claus have figuratively replaced the *santos* earlier stolen, it is clear that the shopkeeper, who is "weighing out some sugar with the added pressure of his thumb," is interested only in the flight of silver dollars into his till. However, while this fat shopkeeper is busy making love to his money, his wife lies in the goat-shed making love to another man. Later, of course, all of these characters attend Midnight Mass, but their worship is empty, hypocritical.

While Chavez is careful not to sermonize in this and other stories, his implicit criticism of his own people's failure to watch over their own traditions and values is clear. Nevertheless, the corruptive influences of the American newcomers remain squarely indicted throughout Chavez's fiction that deals with post-1848 New Mexico. If Hispanos too much traded the traditions and rules of the old world for the material superficialities and self-indulgent pleasures of the modern world, it may be because the bright tinsel, coupled with the American profit motive, a motive pictured as based on greed, has been too strong to resist with any sustained effort. Chavez's examination of the Hispano's declining traditions and misdirected values is, to a great extent, seen as an extension of a money economy which diverts the human affections in favor of silver dollars.

In the end, it is apparent that Fray Angelico Chavez's fiction systematically examines the social, cultural, and even moral evolution of Hispano life in New Mexico as it moves from the stable, if troubled, culture of the eighteenth and early nineteenth centuries to a pronounced sense of dislocation as the American presence made itself felt after 1848. Chavez's fiction may be read for its religious themes, since the stories do revolve around a village's religious matrix, but the tensions which test each character's faith are usually generated by events with clear social implications.

There are those who argue that Chavez should have been more pointedly political in his writing; such perspectives, however, like those of many Chicano scholars and critics of this generation, are informed by a period of intense cultural nationalism in which a writer's worth to the Chicano movement is largely determined by the politics of a work. To dismiss Chavez because his writing is not polemic enough is thus wrong. It is like dismissing Charles W. Chesnutt's contribution to Afro-American literature because he wasn't radical enough at a time when he was breaking ground just by getting published in white magazines during the 1890s. Even then, Chesnutt's early fiction, much like Chavez's work a half-decade later, was indeed radical when one scratched that surface of folksy language and characters who edged the common stereotype. Chavez, like Chesnutt, says what he can, given his historical moment, to those discerning enough to understand the subversive uses of allegorical narrative in which a structure of social and political ideas underlies the parabolic actions of simple characters. However restrained Chavez's stories, then, it would be extremely reductive to assume, as some Chicano critics tend, that his fiction is not socio-political in nature, or worse, as do his Anglo reviewers, that he is a churchly hagiographer portraying what P. Albert Duhamel, in a *New York Times Book Review*, once called the "quiet lives of . . . a prayerful people."

MARVIN A. LEWIS

El diablo en Texas: *Structure and Meaning*

Introduction

El diablo en Texas is divided into a prologue and three principal sections:
Presidio 1883, 1942, and 1970—the epilogue. Following techniques of the
new novelists, Aristeo Brito sets forth themes in the prologue which he will
develop in the text. Presidio brings to mind Juan Rulfo's Comala. The town
is somewhere between heaven and hell. Occasionally "ánimas en pena" meet
at an old 17th century fortress to discuss a massacre of Mexicans perpetrated
by Ben Lynch, one of the early barbarians to enter the territory. Presidio is
"far from everywhere" and records the highest daytime temperature in the
United States several times each year. The inhabitants are in a constant
struggle for survival against odds created by both the human and natural
orders. They live a hand-to-mouth existence in agrarian country.

Characters are presented as mere caricatures of humanity, although the
Lynch family, the exploiters, and Francisco Uranga, lawyer and defender of
Mexican rights, are clearly drawn. Principal characters appear in both the
1883 and 1942 segments. The author seems to regard individuals as not that
important, but instead values their collective contributions to the novel's
overall meaning.

Since structure is broadly defined as the "sum of the relationships of
the parts of a literary whole to one another," my purpose is to demonstrate
how these relationships function to make *El diablo en Texas* a coherent whole.
My approach to the novel entails an examination of (1) narrative technique,
(2) imagery and symbolism, and (3) the relationship between form and

From *Contemporary Chicano Fiction: A Critical Survey.* © 1986 by *Bilingual Press/Editorial Bilingüe.*

meaning. It is generally agreed that technique and form are virtually inseparable from theme and world view.

Narrative Technique

Chronological delineation is not one of the author's major concerns, as
readers have to make their own chronology. Action oscillates between two
poles: Ojinaga on the Mexican side of the Río Bravo and Presidio in the
United States. This spatial juxtapositioning accounts for some of the fragmentation in the novel's structure. Through the thoughts and conversations
of the protagonists and occasional straightforward narration the reader is
able to piece together important historical events from the late 19th century
to the present. The conquest and colonization of the Chicano emerge as the
principal preoccupations. In the background one feels the presence of the
omniscient author controlling and manipulating his world.

The principal plot thread winds around several generations of
Urangas: Francisco and his son Reyes; José, son of Reyes; and the unnamed
son of José who is the principal narrator in the 1970 segment. In the 1883
section, which spans the early twentieth century, Francisco Uranga is the
focal point of activity. Through treachery, Ben Lynch is able to buy land that
belongs to Paz, Francisco's wife. Rumor has it that their son Lázaro is
involved in the crooked dealings. The effect of these early manipulations is
seen in the 1942 section, where José and his family, rightful owners of the
land, are forced to survive as field hands. Thus, the plot is constructed in a
manner that shows the cause and effect relationships of exploitation on past,
present, and future generations of Chicanos.

The device of having a fetus address a monologue to the host mother
and relatives is quite thoughtful and effective. To achieve this end, Brito
employs a stream of consciousness technique—interior monologue—that is

> used in fiction for representing the psychic content and process
> of character, partly or entirely unuttered, just as these processes
> exist at various levels of conscious control before they are formu-
> lated for deliberate speech.

In *El diablo en Texas* the unborn baby of Marcela, José's wife, rational-
izes the reasons for his mother's discomfort. "Es que trae cien años de
historia indignada en la panza. Su enfermedad es de palabras que no pueden
salir de aquí, de sus entrañas" (p. 79). Marcela, representing the long-

suffering Mexican mother, bears witness to 100 years of ignoble history. Yet she is unable to articulate her frustrations. The child will be left with the burden of writing the legacy of his people.

Broken chronology, interior monologue, and juxtapositioning of episodes in the narrative all reflect, to a degree, the characters' precarious existence. For the most part, they are unsure and unable to assert themselves in the living hell of Presidio.

Language is another important internal structural device in the novel. Brito's use of Chicano Spanish and portrayal of the actions of his characters is on a level with that of Méndez, Morales, Hinojosa, and Rivera. Mental attitudes and believable reactions are manifested convincingly through popular language. In a work situation, Chale, the crew chief, urges the cotton pickers on in the following manner:

> —Orale ésos, ya oyeron el jefe, ¿qué nel? Así que nada de perra. Aviéntensen o si no, los reporto.
>
> —Uuuu, que zurra el bato, vamos a empelotarlo pa que no se madereye el güey—brincó el Jusito, mientras que las mujeres se enrojecieron y pronto se escurrieron por los zurcos. ¡Chamaco descarado! ¡No tiene pelos en la lengua!
>
> El Chale, al notar el enojo en las caras de los otros, soltó la carcajada.
>
> —Puros mitotes, ésos. ¿A poco me creyeron? Este bato no está lurio ni come lumbre, ésos. ¿Pos quién les dijo que soy amigo del jale? La viuda es corta ésos. Llévensenla suave, al cabo no te dan premios. (p. 59)

The novel is a unique mixture of Chicano Spanish, "standard" Spanish, and English—all used to reflect different realities and levels of awareness. Tours of the fort are conducted in English and Francisco Uranga uses official Spanish. In the above scene there is a combination of comic and serious expression, for the intent is to relieve some of the frustration inherent in the working conditions. Throughout, scene and situations are accurately reflected by language, thereby contributing to the novel's verisimilitude.

Imagery/Symbolism

Two central images dominate the novel: a fort built in 1863 and a 20th-century bridge spanning the river. Both represent divisiveness between the two cultures. The fort remains as a vestige of the early Spanish conquerors and explorers and the bridge symbolizes a general tendency of officialdom to control the movement of Chicanos. An examination of these two symbols reveals that they form an integral part of the novel's structure. The fort, for example grows to nearly mythic proportions within the closed environment of Presidio. It is described in the following manner:

> Allí cerca de Presidio donde llaman la Loma Pelona se levanta el fortín como castillo podrido. Es un castillo de adobe sin puertas que usa el viento como pito de barro. No falta quien pase por allí alguna noche con pelos de puercoespín y diga: el castillo está espantado. Hay espíritus y hay diablos que pasan de cuarto en cuarto botando. Los incrédulos lo niegan diciendo que son mitotes pero lo cierto es que la historia se intuye. Las leyendas de la gente son las páginas de un libro que se arrancaron y se echaron a la hoguera. . . . (p 36)

The existence of the fort gives rise to a set of popular beliefs that equate the fort with evil and the presence of the devil. The spoken word, or oral tradition, forms an important structural element in the novel, as maintained by the assertion that "Las leyendas de la gente son las páginas de un libro que se arrancaron y se echaron a la hoguera. . . ." From a creative standpoint, the combination of fact, fiction, and rumor provides the conceptual basis of *El diablo en Texas*.

The bridge is another unifying image. Two key passages reveal its importance in the narrative.

> El puente son cosas del diablo. (El puente es el arco iris del diablo: dos patas de chivo puestas en dos cementerios.) (p. 9)

> Entonces todos éramos iguales. No es que no séamos, pero ha cambiado desde que pusieron el puente. Qué curioso, Vicke. La gente se siente separada . . . ¿pa qué son esos papeles, Vicke? ¿Por qué los piden esos hombres todo el tiempo? ¿Quiénes son? ¿Y el diablo lo has visto, Vicke? ¿Es cierto que estamos en el infierno? Hace mucho calor aquí pero no es verdá, ¿verdá, Vicke? (p. 19)

Interrelated as internal structural devices are the metaphorical prison and the devil himself: "Presidio, prisión, infierno. Diablo que se carcajea en silencio. Shhh!" (p. 26). These brief excerpts reveal the importance of the bridge, devil, and prison images to the structure and meaning of the novel. Life in Presidio is controlled by both human and natural limitations. That is to say, Presidio inhibits mobility because of a lack of social opportunities. The bridge restricts the free movement of people along the borders. Both the bridge and the fort are viewed as products of the devil himself, whose omnipresence pervades the novel. Hardly an episode takes place which does not concern the bridge, the prison/fort, or the devil.

The snake and the devil—equated with Ben Lynch—appear as evil omens several times, with no apparent effect on the narrative except for representing the evil side of human emotions and behavior. Symbolically, however, they represent the central metaphor in the novel's overall meaning. This revelation comes out in a conversation between two residents: "Pero lo importante es que la víbora era el enemigo de Diosito. Era el mero diablo" (p. 63). In Presidio, too, the proverbial battle between good and evil is being waged. From the opening paragraphs, the víbora/diablo keeps watch over the town and its inhabitants, appearing to derive satisfaction from human suffering.

Conclusion

A noted critic has written that "Time affects every aspect of fiction: the theme, the form and the medium—language." These remarks are certainly applicable to *El diablo en Texas*. The repetition of selected events gives the impression that not much has changed in Presidio for more than a century. That is why actors in the 1883 drama can play roles without difficulty in 1942. Eternal suffering seems to be the Chicano's plight. The novel's temporal fragmentation is due, for the most part, to the direct relationship between past and present in Presidio. The theme of the repression of Chicano culture and values pervades the work. Resistance takes place on an individual basis only.

The novel's message is that over the centuries there has not been much progress in Presidio. Time has been suspended. This point is brought out in the thoughts of José Uranga's son after a hard day's work in the field with his father.

> Así ha ocurrido siempre, padre. Siempre se ha quedado esta tierra maldita con tu sangre, con tu sudor. Y me duele que en cada gota de tu cuerpo vaya parte de tu alma, de una vida que muere para vivir mejor. Yo sé que tus pasos apuntan a un vacío día tras día y

> yo los sigo también. . . . Pero ya me cansé papá, y no te he dicho
> que me voy. Me voy porque estoy seguro de que hay otro
> mundo mejor que Presidio . . . presidio, tejas. Hasta el nombre
> me suena enfermo para haber visto la luz primero, bajo tejas de
> presidio. (p. 96)

The presidio/prison image remains constant throughout the novel. Characters are portrayed as trapped and drained of life-sustaining forces. Escape is the easiest alternative. But in spite of the cyclical and deterministic nature of events, Brito does not deny his characters their humanity. Rather they are imbued with a tremendous capacity for survival and understanding.

José Uranga's son has returned to Presidio for his father's burial. He decides not to leave again but rather "encender la llama, la que murió con el tiempo" (p. 99). Thus the novel ends on a positive note, calling for Chicanos to assess their cultural and historical circumstances in an effort to bring about change. Based on what has happened in the novel, this is not likely to occur. But where there is life, there is hope, and the fragmented, schizophrenic existence reflected in *El diablo en Texas*'s structure will continue until Chicanos control their own destinies.

ALFONSO RODRIGUEZ

Time As a Structural Device in Tomás Rivera's "... y no se lo tragó la tierra!

"
. . . y no se lo tragó la tierra" is one of the first major works of contemporary Chicano fiction to show a marked separation from the traditional
linear narrative of social protest. In the attempt at creating a modern art
form, Rivera elaborates a complex of aesthetic elements; one of these
elements is time, which appears simultaneously as a major theme and as a
structural device. ". . . *y no se lo tragó la tierra*" is structured on three
temporal modalities: present, past, and future, each represented by a cycle.
Furthermore, there are various manifestations of time as a structuring
technique in the novel: circular time, psychological time, a distortion of
linear time by a shuffling of events, and a fusion of separate temporal
sequences through a dislocation of space.

Rivera's treatment of time places him among a rather large group of
contemporary writers whose works exhibit a preoccupation with the relationship between temporal succession and man's search for identity. Rivera structures his novel on the premise that human experience is made up, among other
things, of memory and expectation, both past and future operating in the
present. In this sense, time is inseparable from the concept of the self, for the
quest for existential identity leads to a search of the past and a look into the
future. This is precisely the experience of the protagonist in the novel.

Before we proceed to analyze the text, however, a word about its genre
is in order. Rivera's work is considered a novel by some and rightly so, for it

From *Contemporary Chicano Fiction: A Critical Survey.* © 1986 by *Bilingual Press/Editorial Bilingüe.*

traces the development of the protagonist. Thus, it can be classified as a novel of character. On the other hand, it exhibits the characteristics of a compendium of framework tales, that is, stories within a narrative setting. The introductory story, "The Lost Year," and the concluding one, "Under The House," provide the general setting. The other twelve stories, which form the central column of the work, are stories within the general framework.

The essential meaning of the novel can be arrived at by making a series of associations between the framework and the framework stories, thus detecting the internal logic of the novel. It is worth noting that the diverse settings in the framework stories are part of the protagonist's personal history, pieces of direct and indirect experience that trace the hero's process of individuation. Thus, the three major temporal cycles are manifested as follows: "The Lost Year" represents the present circumstances of the boy-hero, the next twelve stories (which symbolize the months of the year) are his search of the past, and in the concluding story, "Under The House," past and present merge and a new cycle opens up into the future.

Objective or historical time—the time of calendars and watches—is an indispensable convention in practical human affairs. It can be conceived in one of two ways, either as linear or as circular. Rivera treats it as circular. In the first story, "The Lost Year," the protagonist is trapped in the labyrinth of chronological time. He feels the anguish produced by a sense of disorienta-tion. In the very title of this story, Rivera's use of time as a rhetorical device is apparent. The word "year" is repeated seven times until it becomes "the lost year," thus alluding to the circular aspect of objective time and also suggesting the recurrence of the same patterns until the cycle is broken.

The cycle represents a prison in the life of the boy-hero, a no-exit situ-ation. The first sentence in "The Lost Year" is: "That year was lost to him." That is, chronologically, he is one year older, but inwardly he has seen no progress; he feels overwhelmed by present circumstances because of his sense of alienation. However, in order to recuperate the loss, the protagonist must break the cycle in which he is trapped. He can only do so by responding to the voice that keeps calling him. After several unsuccessful attempts, every-thing ends in bewilderment as the cycle continues:

> He would always turn around to see who was calling, always making a complete turn, always ending in the same position and facing the same way. And that was why he could never find out who it was that was calling him, nor the reason why he was being called. (p. 3)

The physical motions of the boy-hero making a complete turn provide a symbol of contemporary man lost in the labyrinth of chronological time. The cycle breaks the moment the protagonist responds to the calling of his inner voice: "Once he stopped himself before completing the turn, and he became afraid. He found out that he had been calling himself. That was the way the lost year began" (p. 3).

In "The Lost Year" the narrator goes beyond the surface; he gazes deeply into the impulses of the unconscious of the boy-hero, who initiates a search into his past through an oneiric process in an attempt to find meaning for his own existence:

> Then he would force himself into thinking that he had never thought anything at all, and that was when everything finally would go blank and he was able to go to sleep. But before falling asleep he would see and hear many things. (p. 3)

At this point, objective (measurable) time comes to a complete stop for the protagonist and subjective (psychological) time takes over. The first cycle ends and the second one begins. The author takes us back to the lost year, which in symbolic terms could represent a whole epoch, as the title of the story suggests and as the narrator implies: "He tried to figure out when it was that he had started to refer to that period as a year" (p. 3).

Objective time, which implies order and direction, is completely distorted in the second cycle. The twelve stories give us twelve different situations as they occurred in the past. But these situations are shuffled around in such a way that they appear as unrelated fragments of the protagonist's direct and indirect experiences. They manifest themselves as a succession of distinct, discontinuous fragments of time due to the disintegration of chronology.

The twelve vignettes are part of what the boy-hero sees and hears in his visions. However, they are presented as independent narrative units, each with its particular structure, rather than as a series of recollections. It is not until the conclusion of the second cycle that the protagonist sorts out in his mind his past experiences and places everything in proper perspective.

A disordering of significant events is the basis for the structure of the second cycle, which as we have indicated is a return to the past. This shattering of chronology is carried even further in individual stories within the cycle. The most evident examples of this technique are seen in such stories as "It Is Painful," "The Night of the Blackout," and "When We Arrive."

Once more, in the title of the concluding story, there is an allusion to circular time. The words "the house" are repeated seven times until they become the title words "Under The House," signifying the conclusion of the second cycle and the consequent return to the present.

In the human psyche, time becomes elastic; it can either be condensed or extended. The introductory story, "The Lost Year," ends as the boy-hero is about to fall asleep. During that night he searches for the lost year, or perhaps for the totality of his life experiences and even beyond. This is entirely possible, which is another way of saying that psychological time is timeless.

The beginning of "Under The House" indicates a return to the historical flow of time (the present). We find the protagonist making an important decision. Rather than attending school that day he chooses to hide under the neighbor's house: "That morning on the way to school he felt the urge not to go" (p. 172). This "urge not to go" is motivated by the dream experiences of the previous night. Now, under the circumstances, he makes a better choice. For him, school is a return to the monotony of practical, everyday affairs, to objective time, from which he tries to flee because it has become oppressive. Thus, he chooses to isolate himself in the dark under the house. The house, in Freudian logic, can be taken as the symbol of the mother's womb, which offers protection and security: "He was lying face down and every time he moved he felt the floor touching his back. This even made him feel secure" (pp. 172–73). It is as though he were escaping to a mythical time, a time of beginnings.

As the boy-hero begins to think in the dark, he resumes his search for identity by reliving the past once again. This time everything is reproduced in his mind in such a way that persons and events appear vested with new significance; what was once a patchwork of pieces without a pattern becomes a meaningful synthesis through psychological time. However, the recapture of time in experience alone is not enough to produce new meanings. In addition to this there has to be the right association of events that happened only once in an individual's life and can never be repeated. The subconscious has a logic of its own. This is why in the protagonist's stream of consciousness, although events flow chaotically, harmony is achieved.

The protagonist's "thoughts returned to the present." His reverie is interrupted by the commotion of the children and the lady of the house, who have discovered his hiding place. When he emerges from the dark he is a new individual because he has found something he never had before. He has gained a new perspective that can never be understood nor appreciated by those who have not gone through a similar experience. The boy hears the woman's remark as he walks away: "Poor family. First the mother, and now him. Maybe he is going crazy. I think he's losing his mind. He has lost his sense of time. He's lost track of the years" (p. 177). But the boy has a different reaction:

> Suddenly he felt very happy because, when he thought about what the lady had said, he realized that he hadn't lost anything. He had discovered something. To discover and to rediscover and to synthesize. To relate this entity with that entity, and that entity with still another, and finally relating everything with everything else. That was what he had to do, that was all. And he became even happier. (p. 177)

This point marks the beginning of the third and last cycle. It is a vision of the future, produced by the boy's hope and optimism. This is expressed through a symbol:

> Later, when he arrived at home, he went to the tree that was in the yard. He climbed it. On the horizon he saw a palm tree and he imagined that someone was on top looking at him. He even raised his arm and waved it back and forth so that the other person could see that he knew that he was there. (p. 177)

The other person is actually the protagonist himself, projected forward in time. What we mean when we assert that the element of time is inextricably fused to the problem of the self can be seen in the experience of the boy-hero in the novel. The anguish caused by an existential vacuum launches him into the past. But the new hope engendered by a deeper sense of self-awareness projects him into the future, which opens up countless possibilities.

HEINER BUS

The Establishment of Community in Zora Neale Hurston's
The Eatonville Anthology (1926) and
Rolando Hinojosa's Estampas del valle (1973)

In his essay "Chicano Literature: The Establishment of Community,'"
Tomás Rivera defined community as "place, values, personal relationships,
and conversation" and subsequently described two short pieces by Rolando
Hinojosa as "attempts to build a community." In the final paragraph he
generalized this observation:

> Up to the present time, one of the most positive things that the
> Chicano writer and Chicano literature have conveyed to our
> people is the development of such a community. We have a
> community today (at least in literature) because of the urge that
> existed and because the writers actually created from a spiritual
> history, a community captured in words and in square objects we
> call books.

The urge to create a community, in and through literature, should be
conceded not only to the Chicanos. To reveal correspondences and diver-
gences in two ethnic literatures, I shall analyze two texts with obvious structural and thematic similarities, Zora Neale Hurston's "The Eatonville
Anthology" published in 1926 and Rolando Hinojosa's "Estampas del valle",
part of his first major work, *Estampas del valle y otras obras* (1973). After the

From *European Perspectives on Hispanic Literature of the United States.* ©1988 by Arte Público Press.

two analytical sections I will compare the two cycles and determine their place in the context of Hurston's and Hinojosa's other works. In the end I very tentatively shall try to distinguish them from mainstream products treating the same theme.

In his *Zora Neale Hurston. A Literary Biography* Robert E. Hemenway highly praises "The Eatonville Anthology":

> It is pure Zora Neale Hurston: part fiction, part folklore, part biography, all told with great economy, an eye for authentic detail, and a perfect ear for dialect . . . It is Hurston's most effective attempt at representing the original tale-telling context . . . the best written representation of her oral art.

"The Eatonville Anthology" consists of fourteen individual pieces. In contrast to Edgar Lee Master's *Spoon River Anthology* (1915) the titles of the sections do not disclose an apparent ordering device, although the combination of place name and "anthology" implies a deeper kinship between the two works, particularly their view of small-town life as a feature of the past.

Most of the fourteen sections open with a statement on the outstanding quality of a character which defines his social status. Whenever this introduction refers to a negative quality, the narrator rushes to the character's help with a modification such as "Coon Taylor never did any stealing" or an extensive explanation like:

> Becky Moore has eleven children of assorted colors and sizes. She has never been married, but that is not her fault. She has never stopped any of the fathers of her children from proposing, so if she has no father for her children it's not her fault. The men round about are entirely to blame.

By this strategy the narrator signals approval of these individual attitudes and the responses of the community: stealing Coon Taylor has to "leave his town for three months" only. In the case of Becky Moore the women of the town isolate her children to prevent contamination. Only the town vamp, Daisy Taylor, eventually leaves for good after overstepping the limits of the townspeople's tolerance. But even here the narrator closes in an ironic and conciliatory tone: "Before the week was up, Daisy moved to Orlando. There in a wider sphere, perhaps, her talents as a vamp were appreciated."

Without deeply probing the psyche or the history of these figures, the narrator and the citizens of Eatonville pragmatically consider even the self-imposed isolation of some of its members constituent for their community. This fact accounts for the static, anti-climactic nature of the place and its portrayal. In hardly any of the stories are the basic situations subject to change. We learn of some unsuccessful efforts in the past to correct obvious iniquities. Generally, however, people just feel amused and entertained like the prospective reader or listener.

The World War, the coming of the railroad, and the departure of individuals occasionally cause physical and spiritual movement depicted as the loosening of morals and the questioning of social rituals. Only when these phenomena endanger institutions guaranteeing the survival of the community do people start reacting: The women e.g. violently defend the family. Normally, the communal self-defense mechanisms are still functioning. Change but complicates matters as the narrator indicates: "Back to the good old days before the World War, things were simple in Eatonville." Continuity is felt or at least pretended within a generation and between the older and younger ones. The general refusal to examine the many dimensions of an individual character perfectly matches with this denial of change by eagerly overrating the stereotypical, the communal rituals. The reader perceives change mainly as a function of biological processes, i.e., the eventual death of the people portrayed.

Though the narrator makes frequent use of irony, he basically shares the attitudes and values of Eatonville. Quite often he adapts his syntax and vocabulary to the plainness of what he is telling. The repetition of words, phrases and situations, the narrator's and his figure's falling back on proverbial wisdom, expose the ritualistic quality of the experience. In the "Village Fiction" sequence the narrator even joins the lying contest with one of the town characters. Nevertheless, his command of various language registers signals detachment. With the exception of the closing formula, Black English is exclusively used whenever the characters are allowed to speak up for themselves. With evident delight in verbalization and in the tasks of the arranger he draws Eatonville as a collection of types permanently re-enacting stereotypical social encounters, thus assigning to this community permanence and continuity, affirming his characters' desire to resist fundamental change.

The selection and positive acknowledgment of repetitive social action as a typical feature of a small Black community is based on a profound respect for individual conduct and a deep trust in the correspondence of human emotions. Hurston closes her "Anthology" with a Brer Rabbit tale explaining why the dog and rabbit hate each other. In contrast to the preceding "crayon enlargements of life," the folk tale displays a firm cause-and-effect relationship. But it refers to a collective, not an individual phenomenon of the animal

world, detached from a specific time and place. It is set "Once way back
yonder before the stars fell." Projecting human behavior into the animal
world signifies a reality-thinking desire, an effort to conjure up imperial
power in a situation of oppression.

These observations should make us see the stabilizing functions of
storytelling as demonstrated in the folk tale and the whole "Anthology". By
closing with a brer Rabbit story, Hurston transfers its strengths and weaknesses to her portrait of a specific community. The formula "Stepped on a
tin, mah story ends" lifts the spell on the folk tale and the whole cycle whose
individual themes and situations were already adapted to the typical features
of the folk tale. The re-construction of Eatonville as a community establishes
a complex interrelation between the narrator and his material and an equally
strong communion between storyteller and his prospective audiences; it is
folklore in the making. Storytelling is as repetitive as the situations re-
enacted and described. Zora Neale Hurston hints at the importance of
cultural identity through ritualization in "Double-Shuffle" where the males
turn the formal dancing into a celebration of the Black musical folk traditions. Before releasing the listener into his own ambiguous world, the
process of selection, verbalization and repetition, affirming and denying the
restrictions of the individual life, of the singular community, of place and
time, has magically fulfilled the basic human need for identification and
permanence and has defeated the notions of isolation and transitoriness.

In a "Preliminary Note" and "A Note of Clarification" Rolando
Hinojosa designates his "Sketches of the Valley" as self-contained and interrelated, claiming their own lives due to the strength of characters and situations. The role of the author is thus restricted from the outset. Consequently,
as in Hurston's "Anthology," the titles of the twenty sketches do not produce
a common denominator.

Looking for framing devices for the obviously heterogeneous materials, we encounter two collective scenes in end position, "Voices from the
barrio" and "Round Table," suggesting an effort to impose order through
atypical and/or functional situation. The search for communication and
orientation reveals itself as a major theme, particularly after studying the first
sketch of the series, "Braulio Tapia": The father of the bride relates his
present situation to his own courting scene. The chain of identification
across the generations ends with his father-in-law, Braulio Tapia, because the
speaker does not possess any further knowledge. His limitations are exposed
in his unanswered final "Whom did don Braulio see at the threshold when
he asked for his wife?" The theme introduced here confirms Hinojosa's
choice of the mode of presentation.

In the third sketch, "Roque Malacara," characters from "Braulio Tapia" recur. Roque Malacara, the former suitor, declares:

> My Tere gets tired and with good reason. We have a son, in addition to my father-in-law, we've also lost three little girls. My father-in-law was a good man. He loved to go fishing and he always found a way to take along his little namesake, Jehú. If people are reborn, I'd say that my son and his granddad are the same person.

Here, the space of time is expanded to the next generation through the basic truths of human life, birth, death and, as in the previous sketch, through memory and identification compensating for loss.

In the two final "estampas" we shall spot this Jehú in a courting scene among the "Voices from the barrio" and in "Round Table" as subject of the conversation of old men. It is significant that they are equally unable to reconstruct history beyond Braulio Tapia. So, the sequence of four generations and the final definition of the place, "Klail City, one of many towns in Belken County, Rio Grande Valley, Texas" circumscribe the margins set for these sketches. Transgression is reserved for some citizens who by this act attain to eminent status, not necessarily for the community, but for individual narrators.

Critics have reflected upon the fragmentation of this restricted world referring mainly to Hinojosa's use of the multiple point-of-view. Articulation and dialogue occur in private situations like marriage, sickness and death requiring ceremony or ritual. The boundaries between the two spheres are not clearly marked as both public and private affairs can miraculously get out of hand and subsequently, provoked misunderstandings and renewed verbalization. Quite frequently the narrators try to show their utter surprise at life's consistencies and inconsistencies. Very seldom do they find reliable stability.

A completely positive picture of human relations is drawn in the sketches dealing with don Víctor and Jehú, and in "Voices from the barrio." In the collective scene the sounds of the younger and older generations are heard. But even there the community is portrayed as an accumulation of separate groups. The appraisal of this night as miraculous, as repetitive and a celebration of the people gives this sketch a superior rank among the many scenes documenting the unreliability of experience. This construction stresses the desire of the people to save themselves some spheres of self-determination in a world closing in on them, also a longing for wholeness and order.

How do the individual narrators and the characters introduced respond to these ambiguities? Like the Blacks in Hurston's "The Eatonville Anthology" many of the Chicanos demonstrate a remarkable pragmatism. They all try to cope with their experience by verbalizing it, by fixing it and making their bewilderment known. Depending on the subject, their degree of personal involvement, their linguistic faculties and education, they develop individual varieties of tone and perspective. But also common attitudes are established: Most of the time they ignore the Anglo and his civilization, seeking their identity and their images in the Chicano world. Some try to relate to the Mexican Revolution or the victories won against the Texas Rangers; others retreat to Chicano folklore, proverbial wisdom and folk medicine. Many insist on family ties and on giving people proper names and nicknames, thus finding orientation in the community, even though these strategies might include some wishful thinking.

Without obvious interference of a superior narrator, the fragments gradually assemble into an expressive mosaic of one major segment of Belken County society. This seemingly self-propellant movement undoubtedly shuts out the nostalgic perspective and maintains the impression of a largely incoherent, unstable but vital reality including various strategies of response, efforts to keep up order and identity. Though the sketches generally evoke an atmosphere of simultaneousness and not of sequence, the younger generation, represented by Jehú and Rafa, slowly but irresistibly moves to the forefront as subject of conversation, as persons pursuing social functions, and as speakers in their own right. Their performances do not promise radical change as both of them seem to tolerate the "static heterogeneity" of this, in many ways, "restricted community."

In my comparison of the two cycles I am going to focus on the individual and the group, continuity and change, and the role of the narrator. Both texts largely define their characters through interpersonal relations. In Hinojosa's "Estampas del valle" the vicarious narrators constitute themselves as a group by their common urge to communicate through the verbalization of their own experience and that of others. Coherence between the individual encounters with reality is established in three collective scenes and through responses to the challenges of life with native strategies of the ethnic group, e.g. language and folklore.

In their actions and speeches the characters express a desire for independence *and* commitment, for individual *and* social identity according to the pressures they feel at the time. The enemy powers are never pinpointed, although we can conclude that the experience of isolation, insecurity, loss and the lack of perspective prompt them to retreat into the group. As they are not able to take advantage of its full potential, e.g. a new historical outlook, the characters do not build up a consistent group identity and very soon fall back into their individual selves. These shortcomings of Hurston's and Hinojosa's figures generate stasis as a predominant condition.

In both texts the group is primarily established in the reader's mind. The characters never consciously define themselves as social beings. Other worlds beyond theirs occasionally forcing them to raise their flag as a community occur only marginally and are generally ignored. Hurston's narrator corrects these failures by cutting the individual encounters to size, to storytelling proportions so that they can become as much part of a communal tradition as the model animal tale. Hinojosa also compensates for his narrators' limitations in "Voices from the barrio," though less visibly and comprehensively than Hurston.

By a process of transformation Hurston retrospectively liberates her characters and their stories from the conditions dominating the individual life, change and eventual death. This procedure asks for the capturing of a phase of small-town life, freezing it, making it disposable exactly as her characters prefer the collective, repetitive, stereotypical phenomena to experience continuity and familiarity. Whenever and wherever change occurs, Hinojosa's characters tend finally to accept it in view of their own ineffectuality. Hurston's figures frequently ignore or deny change in spite of their just-as-remarkable powers of acceptance. "The Eatonville Anthology" deliberately withdraws this place from the temporal process while Hinojosa leaves Belken County open for change and extinction, as his authorial retreat at the beginning implied. Of course, both techniques basically acknowledge the fact that the two traditional societies have been destroyed.

Contrary to this intended invisibility, Hinojosa is present in the selection of his material and, as telling, in his exclusion of many aspects of Chicano life. Hinojosa and Hurston communicate with their audiences through the choice of framing devices, the sequence of the sketches, and the maintenance of the oral folk tone. Hurston seems to have less confidence in her reader, in the self-propellant energies of her characters and stories, in their qualities of endurance and the general cumulative effect of her sketches. Both authors confirm their trust in language as a means of communication, stabilization and preservation.

Both "The Eatonville Anthology" and "Sketches of the Valley" were published in the initial, testing phases of their authors' career. To establish this context, I shall briefly indicate the further development of the themes and techniques described in my analytical and comparative sections.

Zora Neale Hurston returned to the Eatonville setting in various stories, novels, her autobiography, a folklore documentation, a drama, and in some of her essays. Her hometown provides a positive communal mood and morality, source of identification for herself, her characters. and a place where storytelling is practiced. This locality is never exposed to change and development; sometimes even characters and situations recur in later works. The pervasive spirit of the place just receives different status among the structural elements of the texts. Only in *Their Eyes Were Watching God*, in her autobiography, and in *Mules and Men* do we occasionally get contrastive images of other places and social entities. Some texts appear to be mere enlargements of the condensed Eatonville sketches, reversals of the folklore-in-the-making process.

The static quality of the place in the "Anthology" and in all her works seems to contradict Hurston's belief in vitality, in her well-developed sensitivity to contradictions as displayed in her essays and her autobiography. These irritations can be dissipated when we take into consideration that the author assessed the values of Eatonville retrospectively, with a sense of loss, from the distance of her Northern experience. The term "anthology" in the title confirms this perspective. Eatonville is conceived and presented as a reconstructed phase of Black communal life before the distortions through acculturation claimed their toll. For didactic purposes the illusion of permanence has to be established to re-activate the sources of communal ethnic identity. In some of her essays Hurston refused to let the racial question confine her life and art. She rather dedicated her fictional and documentary works to the revitalization and celebration of the heritage, putting it out of the reach of the majority culture.

Rolando Hinojosa's recreation of Chicano small-town life presents itself in a different context. His "Estampas" form part of his first larger work, the first building block of his *Klail City Death Trip Series*, to date comprising seven books. In the subsequent titles the Chicano community loses its static quality as it is included into the historical process. Mobility and confrontation in Belken County cause the eventual destruction of traditional social structures. We already recognized the fragmentary nature of "Estampas" as foreshadowing loss.

In contrast to Hurston's method, Hinojosa chronicles the process of change in detail and does not merely imply it in a saving attempt. Step by step he focuses on more than one reality, various generations, slowly filling a large canvas with scenes of interdependence between individuals and various ethnic groups. In Hinojosa's work in progress the weaknesses and strengths of value systems are tested in a fluid, heterogeneous world producing both despair and endurance as extreme responses. Like human life Hinojosa's individuals and groups are on a permanent death trip. Loss and death compete with vitality and creativity reflecting basic ambiguities of the human condition. This aspect gives the portrayal of the lost society of the "Estampas" struggling for survival a universal meaning. And after all, this world is still stimulating Hinojosa's creative energies as the "recasting and recreation in English" of it in *The Valley* (1983) prove.

Hinojosa imitates the natural expansive mode of social orientation and the sequence of growth, stasis, destruction and reconstruction in the life of a community. Depicting a segment of Belken County society in its earliest memorable period, he invites the reader to reassess the strengths and weaknesses of the traditional Chicano community. This is a procedure honoring the vitality and independence of his characters and readers, more democratic than Hurston's rather prescriptive method. Nevertheless, the two strategies of persuasion are used for the same ends, the establishment of community through the reconstruction and revitalization of the usable past.

Reconstructing small-town life is a theme not quite alien to American mainstream literature. I already mentioned Edgar Lee Masters' *Spoon River Anthology* (1915). The Midwest is also represented by Sherwood Anderson's *Winesburg, Ohio* (1919), the sequel *Poor White* (1920), and Sinclair Lewis' *Main Street* (1920). John Steinbeck contributed *Cannery Row* (1938) and Thornton Wilder built Grover's Corners in *Our Town* (1938). Moving South we could think of William Faulkner's Yoknapatawpha County and Larry McMurtry's Texas novels. Most of these writers described their localities as threatened by change and eventual loss, and the majority of these works were published at a time when these worlds had already been destroyed. And it is also quite obvious that many of the authors wrote against the pervasive ideology among their contemporaries who either let the spirit of these communities fall into oblivion or tried to romanticize and mythologize it. Therefore Anderson, Masters, Lewis, Steinbeck, Wilder, and Faulkner share the intent of reconstruction, documentation, and re-interpretation, of making the past useful. These goals provide many roles for the writers, from historian, teacher, and social worker to outsider and nostalgic dreamer.

Considering these wide areas of correspondence between mainstream and minority, I still believe that themes like language, community, continuity, change and mobility, history, or endurance include special connotations in the works of ethnic writers. The trust in the power of the word as a tool to overcome powerlessness, forced muteness, is a first step towards identity and visibility as a group. For the minority leaving the community does not exclusively mean liberation from the confines of the small town, as for George Willard when he takes the train for Chicago at the end of *Winesburg, Ohio*, but a more ambiguous event, namely abandoning the protection granted by the community and moving into the domain of the enemy. History and community have to be reconstructed and preserved in view of the deliberate denial, uprooting and destruction of alternative concepts as inferior by the majority civilization. This story of debasement forces ethnic writers to start from scratch, at the foundations of the communal building.

From the conserving function of the ethnic writers we should not conclude that they have to restrict themselves to traditional forms of writing. Interpreting the group heritage for a modern audience certainly asks for an innovative spirit who finds appropriate techniques of quote, integration and transformation. And retrieving the Black and Chicano past can be equally revolutionary in a mainstream culture with a shaky conceptional base. In many books a delicate balance between change and continuity is maintained as ethnic writers would not like to affirm an oppressive situation. On the other hand, the urge for stability does not imply a rejection of progress and civilization, a refusal to grow up. Zora Neale Hurston's "The Eatonville Anthology" and Rolando Hinojosa's "Estampas del valle" should be understood in the context of a recurrent trend to think small, to investigate the results of internal colonialism, to stress the varieties of the American and the human experience, and to revalue the sense of community.

ENRIQUE LAMADRID

The Dynamics of Myth in the Creative Vision of Rudolfo Anaya

In the range and breadth of New Mexican literature there is no writer as deeply rooted in the native folkways and regional landscapes as Rudolfo Anaya. Yet, it is his prose that shows the greatest promise of transcending the limitations of narrow regionalism and ethnic literatures. The universal thrust of Anaya's creative vision is based in myth, which he defines impressionistically as "the truth in the heart." In the same discussion of myth he further elaborates his understanding of myth as it relates to harmony and alienation, the archaic and the modern, and the role of the unconscious as link to the universal:

> Our civilizing and socializing influence has made us not as unified, not as harmonious as archaic man. To go back and get in touch, and to become more harmonious, we go back to the unconscious and we bring out all of the symbols and archetypals that are available to all people.

Anaya is a mythmaker, both intuitive and self-conscious, whose raw material is folklore, legends, and what might be termed native metaphysics. A creator rather than a collector, he transforms indigenous materials into a rich synthesis of symbol and archetype, new, yet "true to the heart." As mythmaker, Anaya is at his intuitive best when his conception of myth is guided by his unconscious as in *Bless* Me, *Ultima* (1972), and again in *Tortuga* (1979).

From *Pasó por Aquí: Critical Essays on the New Mexican Literary Tradition, 1542–1988.* © 1989 by the University of New Mexico Press.

151

Heart of Aztlán (1976) is a more deliberate and self-conscious if less effective effort at interweaving myth into a narrative. He uses myth according to archetypal definitions and formulae of Carl Jung, Joseph Campbell, or Mircea Eliade. Critics have been grappling with the dynamics of Anaya's mythopoetics ever since the appearance of *Ultima*. Yet, the critical analyses of myth has been as impressionistic as the author's. Thematic and archetypal analyses of myth have contributed much to elucidate the content of myth, but little to the understanding of its function as a system of cognition and communication. It is this latter aspect of myth that will be emphasized here to understand the achievements as well as the shortcomings of Anaya's mythopoetics.

As the first best seller novel of Chicano literature, it was impossible to dismiss *Ultima's* introduction of compelling mythic themes into the disjunctive context of the combative and polemical ethnic literatures of the late sixties. *Ultima* was serene in the face of this turmoil, full of conflict, yet non combative, a portrait of the developing consciousness of the young protagonist, Antonio. The metaphysics of this emerging consciousness were so convincingly drawn that no reader doubted that the seeds of social conscience were deeply sown if yet untested in the character.

Myth was defined in *Ultima* as a way of knowing and making sense of the world. Myth as praxis, or a way of changing the world, was the next creative challenge Anaya faced in *Heart of Aztlán*. But the search for the juncture of the mythic and the revolutionary became overly self-conscious. The mythmaking flowed much less intuitively from Anaya's pen the more he pursued his stated purpose of "trying to touch the mythological roots." Myth becomes epic archetype and narrative formula rather than a natural dialectical system of knowledge. However, as in *Ultima*, the net of symbols underlying the novel is compelling and coherent: on one side, the same sacred sense of redeeming telluric power that pervaded *Ultima* pitted against a dehumanized industrial capitalism symbolized by the infernal railroad shops with snakes of steel dominated by the SANTA FE tower, "The Holy Faith embedded in a faded cross, a perverted faith in steel" (*HA* 197). What weakens the novel and invalidates it politically speaking for many readers is a neo-classic scheme of mythmaking imposed on it by an author alluding to the classic heroic archetypes outlined by Jung, Campbell, and Eliade: the visionary quest of the hero, the descent into the collective subconscious, the ascent to the mountain, the return. True, the overly familiar quest of Clemente Chávez has its analogues, even in history. A visionary Simón Bolivar climbed the mountain, the Aventine hill outside Rome, to utter his sacred oath vowing to change his world. But this is history mystefied (or "*myth*efied," to use the Spanish equivalent). Leaders emerge and to succeed must project a vision that their people share, but history continues to be forged by the masses. The myth of Aztlán developed in the novel is a collective vision skillfully evoked by Anaya in compelling imagery, the surging river of humanity, the pulsing heart of Aztlán. But it is ultimately incompatible with the deliberate imposition of classical heroic archetypes. Several critics attribute the novel's shortcomings to defects in craftsmanship, that Anaya does not allow his symbols to "accumulate enough power in themselves to exercise power in the text," in the words of Juan Bruce Novoa. It is my contention that the symbolic scheme of Heart of Aztlán is impeccable. The defect lies in the overly scholastic conception and application of myth that obscures the juncture of the mythic and the revolutionary that Anaya was seeking.

Tortuga represents a return to the intuitive mythmaking of *Ultima* with a praxis that operates more in the individual soul than in the collective one. As Anaya has said, " just as the natural end of art is to make us well and to cure our souls, so is our relationship to the earth and its power. . . . I mean that there is an actual healing power which the epiphany of place provides." The protagonist, nicknamed Tortuga is a boy imprisoned in his cast shell by a spinal injury. The disharmony in the boy's universe has physiological rather than social causes. Social institutions, in this case the hospital, are insensitive to the spiritual content of the healing process. The boy has to draw healing power directly from the earth itself in his rehabilitation.

Besides similarities in symbolism and the evocative if sometimes romanticized handling of poetic imagery, Anaya's three novels share an important structural element in mythmaking: the seer or spiritual guide whose role it is to mediate contradictions, the key function in myth as a system of communication. In *Bless Me, Ultima* the chief mediator is Ultima, the curandera, whose message is that conflict and contradiction are not dichotomous but rather dialectical oppositions in the ongoing cycles of the universe. In *Heart of Aztlán*, the seer is the blind Crispín, master of the blue guitar, adviser and guide to Clemente Chávez in his quest for the meaning of Aztlán. In *Tortuga*, the seer is Salomón, Tortuga's fellow patient who shows him the way of hope, "the path of the sun" (T 160). All three seers serve integrative functions, pointing out the oneness and sanctity of the universe and the meaning of human life and the healing power of the human heart.

The mythopoetics of Rudolfo Anaya pervade the entire body of his creative work including his numerous short stories. His most comprehensive insight into the workings and cognitive function of myth as an aspect of popular culture is contained in *Bless Me, Ultima*, the particular focus of this analysis. Anaya strikes a deep chord in portraying two primordial ways of relating to the earth, the pastoral and the agricultural. *Bless Me, Ultima* is not a quaint, ahistorical sketch of rural folkways, but rather a dialectical exploration of the contradictions between lifestyles and cultures. At the novel's heart is the process which generates social and historical consciousness. A Marxist Structuralist perspective defines this process as myth, the collective interpretation and mediation of the contradictions in the historical and ecological experience of a people.

In his account of the relationship between a *curandera* (folk healer) and her young apprentice, Anaya deeply penetrates the mythical conscience of the reader. Despite their enthusiasm for his novel, critics have thus far been unable to define the parameters of this response nor probe the reason for its depth. Contributing elements in the narrative include: the primordial quality of the rivalry of the Luna and Márez clans, the religious conflicts and rich dream life of the boy Antonio Márez, and the power of Ultima herself, which in the end is nothing more nor less than "the magical strength that resides in the human heart" (*BMU* 237). From the first reviews to later articles, an increasing body of vague but glowing commentary points to a rich "mythic" or "magical" dimension that underlies the novel. To those who prioritize the social relevancy of Chicano literature, this psychic plunge seemed disturbing or even reactionary in its irrationality. Despite these claims, there appeared to be something exceptional about the emerging consciousness of the boy. It was mystically harmonious with nature, yet also incorporated a dynamic, even dialectical awareness of historical forces, from the colonization of Hispanic farmers and ranchers to the coming of the Anglos and World War II. These seeming contradictions invite a reexamination of the relation of myth and social consciousness, often defined as antithetical or incompatible categories that erode and undermine each other. Since the novel apparently transcends this impasse, we are obliged to consider a critical model comprehensive enough to explain this achievement. A review of commentary on the novel is the first step in this direction.

Bless Me, Ultima has undergone extensive dream and thematic analyses that include attempts to link its "mythic" elements to precolumbian roots. The preponderance of interest in these "irrational" aspects plus the sometimes supernatural tone of the narrative has lead some politically progressive critics to characterize the novel as ahistorical, having only limited and passing value in depicting the "quaint" folkways of rural New Mexico. Thematic analysis has enumerated various tendencies, especially the folkloric, but is unable to characterize the book as anything more than a local color or *costumbrista* piece. Dream analysis has been more productive because of the consistency and symbolic unity of the many dream sequences. Analysis of the mythic and religious systems, notably the "Legend of the Golden Carp" is unconvincing simply because Anaya's alleged allusions to Aztec or other precolumbian mythologies are not literal enough. True, the idea of successive worlds, intervening apocalypses, and the exile of Gods is common in Native American religions. The suggestion of analogical patterns achieves credibility for the Golden Carp without having to invoke Huitzilopochtli or Quetzalcoatl as other Chicano writers have done. The political analysis, which deems the novel reactionary seems to be based on the assumption that Chicano novels should document only the most relevant social and political struggles. These diverse and fragmentary approaches have fallen short of estimating the overall impact and unity of the work and the structural integrity it has achieved on a number of levels.

Since the "mythic" dimension of *Bless Me, Ultima* is a point of confluence in the above commentaries, a definition of terms is necessary at this point. Thus far, the study of myth in Chicano literature is scholastic. The neoclassic allusions to Aztec and other precolumbian mythological and religious systems is fairly common in Chicano literature, especially in poetry and theatre. Critics have been quick to point this out, elaborating only superficially by tracing the origins of the myths and speculating on how they pertain to the sociocultural identity of the present day Chicano. Freud was able to tap Greek mythology for insight into the European psyche and founded the basis for Western psychology. Inspired by the work of Octavio Paz and Carlos Fuentes on the Mexican national psyche, an analogous process has been initiated in Chicano literature and criticism, although it is doubtful that an institutionalized Chicano psychotherapy would result. The underlying assumption that would prevent this is that these mythic or collective psychological patterns supposedly lie outside time, eternally remanifesting themselves in different epochs. This same danger plagues Chicano cultural studies in general, which often tend to analyze culture and its values as something eternal and independent of history, instead of the dynamic product or actual embodiment of history, conflict, and change.

What I propose is a more dynamic critical approach to myth that goes beyond scholasticism and the tracing of classical mythologies. Myth is here considered to be an ongoing process of interpreting and mediating the contradictions in the everyday historical experience of the people. Such a structuralist approach to myth offers some analytical tools that can be applied in such a way as to avoid the ideological limitations of structuralism while opening the Chicano text to a dialectical analysis potentially much more penetrating and historically relevant than traditional thematic or culturalist approaches.

The reader of *Bless Me, Ultima* recognizes the elderly *curandera* as a kind of repository for the wisdom and knowledge invested in IndoHispanic culture. The novel functions well at this level, for Ultima is indeed in touch with the spirit that moves the land and is intent on conveying this knowledge to Antonio in her indirect and mysterious ways. Yet, the knowledge she commands and the role she plays go far beyond the herbs she knows, the stories she saves for the children, and her dabbling in "white" witchcraft. The crossed pins, the demon hairballs, the rocks falling from the sky, and the fireballs are "colorful" touches that are authentic enough in terms of folk legend. Anaya inserts the "witchery" only after having won the reader's trust in a clever conquest of their disbelief. However, the enumeration of the standard paraphernalia and the usual supernatural feats of a *curandera* are neither the reason for nor a barrier to the novel's success.

There is an ancient system of knowledge that Ultima exercises that in this novel does not happen to be in the herbs she uses. Any anthropologist is aware that taxonomies such as those of ethnobotany actually contain the philosophical roots and perceptual conventions of the culture . However, herbs and related folk knowledge are not the ultimate focus of the novel, although it is understood that UItima is intimately familiar with them. It is her role as a cultural mediator and Antonio's natural inclination towards a similar calling that link them to their real power, which is the ability to recognize and resolve the internal contradictions of their culture. These oppositions are clearly defined in both social and symbolic terms. The rivalry of the Lunas and the Márez, the struggle of good and evil, innocence and experience, Jehovah and the Golden Carp are not simply narrative devices. If they were, then they would be merely pretexts for a combination mystery story, morality play, and Hatfield-McCoy saga with a New Mexican flavor.

Something more profound is at work in *Bless Me, Ultima*, for the oppositions are dialectical, and they are mediated in a way that has counterparts in many different cultures around the earth. In his comparative studies of origin myths, Claude Levi-Strauss extracts the two most basic and primordial ones, which occurred either exclusively or in combination in every culture studied . The "autochthonous" origin myth is exactly as the original meaning of the word implies: "one supposed to have risen or sprung from the ground of the region he inhabits." This version often has a vegetative model: man springs from the earth like a plant. The rival origin myth is more empirically based man is born from woman. Then comes the task of finding the first woman. In *Bless Me, Ultima* the opposition between the agricultural Luna family and the pastoral Márez family has roots that go as deep as the very foundation of human consciousness as it moves from the paleolithic into the neolithic. Each lifestyle and the world view it is based on is as compelling, soul satisfying, and original as the other. The opposition as it occurs in the novel may be schematized as follows:

pastoral economy	agricultural economy
the Márez family	the Luna family
live in Las Pasturas on the open plains	live in El Puerto de la Luna in a fertile valley
people of the sun	people of the moon
descendants of conquistadors and seafarers	descendants of a priest
baptized in the salt water of the sea	baptized in the sweet water of the moon
speak with the wind	speak with their plants and fields
tempestuous, anarchic freethinkers	quiet, introspective pious people
live free upon the earth and roam over it	live tied to the earth and its cycles
the horse is their totem animal	corn is their totem plant

The earthshaking impact of the passage from hunting and gathering (paleolithic) into agricultural (neolithic) economies is recorded in mythologies the world over. The crises and contradictions that history, economic change, and technological innovation bring are the chief motivating factors for the collective cognitive process called myth. The settling down of humankind into the sedentary ways of the neolithic brought with it the emergence of social classes and institutionalized religion and all the economic and social contradictions that accompany the birth of civilization. Likewise, the developments with agriculture of horticulture and animal husbandry are distinct enough to carry with them their own ideologies as evident above. Relating more specifically to the novel in question is the history of the colonization of New Mexico and the tremendous impact of the advent of large scale pastoralism. As grazing became more important, the communal egalitarianism of agrarian society began giving way to an emerging class system based on the partidario grazing system and the rise of *patrones* (bosses). However, such developments are not evident in the novel, perhaps because its locale, eastern New Mexico, was the last area to be settled before American annexation. The anarchic freedom enjoyed by the Márez clan was ephemeral, the basic historical irony of the story. The coming of the Texas ranchers, the railroad, and the barbed wire destroyed the freedom of the plains. As the popular saying goes, "Cuando vino el alambre, vino el hambre" (When the barbed wire came, so did hunger). When an economic system is threatened, so is its ideology which starts filling with nostalgia as its dreams are broken.

These historical pressures intensified the oppositions listed above and made the birth of the boy Antonio Márez Luna especially portentious for both clans whose blood coursed through his veins. Each felt the importance of having their values dominate in the boy and both vied to establish their influence at the dream scene of Antonio's birth:

> This one will be a Luna, the old man said, he will be a farmer and keep our customs and traditions. Perhaps God will bless our family and make the baby a priest.
>
> And to show their hope they rubbed the dark earth of the river valley on the baby's forehead, and they surrounded the bed with the fruits of their harvest so the small room smelled of fresh green chile and corn, ripe apples and peaches, pumpkins and green beans.
>
> Then the silence was shattered with the thunder of hoof-beats; vaqueros surrounded the small house with shouts and gunshots, and when they entered the room they were laughing and singing and drinking.
>
> Gabriel, they shouted, you have a fine son! He will make a fine vaquero! And they smashed the fruits and vegetables that surrounded the bed and replaced them with a saddle, horse blankets, bottles of whiskey, a new rope, bridles, chapas, and an old guitar. And they rubbed the stain of earth from the baby's forehead because man was not to be tied to the earth but free upon it. (BMU, 5)

The disposal of the baby's umbilical cord and placenta was also a point of contention. The Lunas wanted it buried in their fields to add to their fertility and the Márez wanted it burned to scatter the ashes to the winds of the *llano* (plain). The intervention of Ultima to settle the feud illustrates her role of mediator and demonstrates the basic mechanism of myth. As in all cultures the thrust of mythical thought progresses from the awareness of oppositions towards their resolution Thus the importance in the mythic process of the mediator, which in many cultures assumes the form of powerful tricksters like coyote and raven in Native American mythology. In *Bless Me, Ultima,* both the *curandera* and the boy serve as mediators between the oppositions within their culture. Their intermediary functions can be traced throughout the text.

The middle ground that Ultima and Antonio occupy is evident even in special and geographic terms. Ultima has lived on the plain and in the valley, in Las Pasturas as well as El Puerto de la Luna, gaining the respect of the people in both places. Antonio's family lives in Guadalupe in a compromise location at mid point between Las Pasturas and El Puerto. Through the father's insistence, the house is built at the edge of the valley where the plain begins. Antonio mediates between father and mother, trying to please the latter by scraping a garden out of the rocky hillside:

> Every day I reclaimed from the rocky soil of the hill a few more feet of earth to cultivate. The land of the llano was not good for farming, the good land was along the river. But my mother wanted a garden and I worked to make her happy (BMU, 9)

Even within the town Antonio occupies a centralized neutral position: "Since I was not from across the tracks or from town, I was caught in the middle." (BMU, 212). This positioning made it impossible to take sides in the territorial groupings of his peers.

Anaya explains the power of the *curandera* as the power of the human heart, but in fact demonstrates that it is derived from the knowledge of mythic thought processes, the awareness and resolution of contradictions within the culture. People turn to Ultima and Antonio at crucial moments in their lives because they are instinctively aware that mediators (*curanderos* and tricksters) possess an overview or power of synthesis that can help them resolve their problems. The multiple episodes of Antonio playing the role of priest are especially significant in this light. It is his mother's and her family's dream for Antonio to become a Luna priest and man of knowledge. In fact he performs the role seriously, administering last rights to Lupito, a war-crazed murderer and Narciso, an ally of Ultima and Antonio's family. The blessings he bestows on his brothers and his friends are real and invested with a power they never fully realize as they taunt him. In his spiritual searching, Antonio discovers the contradictions in Christianity and realizes that the scope of his mediations would include the "pagan", animistic forces implicit in the very landscape he inhabited. In his musings to himself, he feels the new synthesis that he will be a part of: "'Take the llano and the river valley, the moon and the sea, God and the golden carp—and make something new.' . . . That is what Ultima meant by building strength from life" (BMU, 236).

The dynamism of mythic thought and its power of synthesis is poigni-antly expressed in Antonio's description of the feelings and emotions that are aroused by contact with Ultima:

> She took my hand and I felt the power of a whirlwind sweep around me. Her eyes swept the surrounding hills and through them I saw for the first time the wild beauty of our hills and the magic of the green river. My nostrils quivered as I felt the song of the mockingbirds and the drone of the grasshoppers mingle with the pulse of the earth. The four directions of the llano met in me, and the white sun shone on my soul. The granules of sand at my feet and the sun and sky above me seemed to dissolve into one strange, complete being. (BMU, 11)

The power invested in the mythical process is the knowledge derived from seeing the world as a totality and understanding its contradictions in a dialec-tical manner. There are other characters in the novel who demonstrate differing degrees of awareness of this totality, proving that it is indeed a mechanism of popular culture rather than a mystery reserved for a privi-leged, visionary few. A good example is Narciso, a powerful man of the *llano* who nevertheless lives in the valley, having discovered its secrets. Ample evidence of this is his exuberant, drunken garden, the likes of which not many *llaneros* (plainsmen) could foster (BMW, 101).

In perhaps the most global or cosmic synthesis of the novel, Ultima in a dream reveals to Antonio the totality which subsumes the oppositions contained in his culture at the moment they seemed about to split into a dichotomy and create another apocalypse:

> Cease! she cried to the raging powers, and the power from the heavens and the power from the earth obeyed her. The storm abated.
>
> Stand, Antonio, she commanded, and I stood. You both know, she spoke to my father and my mother, that the sweet water of the moon which falls as rain is the same water that gathers into rivers and flows to fill the seas. Without the waters of the moon to replenish the oceans there would be no oceans. And the same salt waters of the oceans are drawn by the sun to the heavens, and in turn become again the waters of the moon. Without the sun there would be no waters formed to slake the dark earth's thirst.

> The waters are one, Antonio. I looked into her bright, clear
> eyes and understood her truth.
> You have been seeing only parts, she finished, and not
> looking beyond into the great cycle that binds us all. (BMU, 113)

The implied definition of apocalypse in this system of thought is the destructive result of changes that are not assimilated, of oppositions that are not mediated. The awareness of the characters of the apocalyptic threat of the atomic bomb, first tested just to the southwest of their fertile valley, demonstrates a real and historical dimension of apocalypse. They sense the previous balance has been disturbed. The bomb seems to have changed the weather just as surely as World War II had twisted the souls of the men from the area who had fought. The need for a new synthesis is as urgent as ever in this new time of crisis. Ultima immediately involved herself in the healing of men who were suffering war sickness and it would be up to Antonio to continue the tradition of mediating contradictions both old and new.

In one sense the knowledge of Ultima may seem mystical because of the way it incorporates nature as well as culture, but when applied to society and history it is just as penetratingly comprehensive and its value just as valid. With Ultima's eventual death, her knowledge continues in Antonio and the reader feels sure that whatever his fate will be, he possesses the conceptual tools to continue to benefit his people and culture with their internal conflicts as well as with the oncoming struggle with a whole new set of oppositions stemming from the fast approaching and aggressive proximity of the Anglo culture and way of life.

In portraying power as the ability to think and understand in a dialectical way, Anaya demonstrates in *Bless Me, Ultima* the ancient collective cognitive process of mythical thought in Chicano culture and the importance of those individuals who take on the role of mediators (*curanderos*, tricksters, or activists) in pointing out and moving towards the resolution of the contradictions generated by human history and new technology. It is this dialectical conception of myth which underlies Anaya's most powerful and moving creative work. Only with the self-conscious application of heroic archetypes and a scholastic conception of myth can he be accused of mystifying his political and social concerns. In the former vision the magical qualities of Anaya's work become a form of knowledge while in the latter they run the risk of becoming little more than a quaint distraction or worse, an obfuscation of clear political thought.

ERLINDA GONZALES-BERRY

Two Texts for a New Canon: Vicente Bernal's Las Primicias *and Felipe Maximiliano Chacón's* Poesía y prosa

This long over-due project, Recovering the U. S. Hispanic Literary Heritage, by its very nature places us in the rather uncomfortable position of creating a literary canon, that is to say, in the position not only of codifying an ethnic literary identity, but also of assigning a standard of value to a corpus of texts. We must begin by recognizing that we are engaging in an act of political interpretation, and that interpretive acts, as Elizabeth Meese reminds us, "inevitably install us in a matrix of difference and differential relations, an (ex)tended field of tensions which are reduced to or contained only with limited success as pure 'identity'" (33). Fifteen or twenty years ago the task might have been easier. At that time many of us here would have agreed that it was possible to create a monolithic Chicano identity. We were perhaps mistaken but more certain then, than we are now, of what configurations that identity might assume. Today we hear Chicano scholars like Ramón Gutiérrez admitting that Chicano scholarship of the early years "defined the Chicano community as more homogeneous and unified that it really was." Gutiérrez adds that "emerging paradigms have forced Chicanos to explore the way factors like race, class, gender, sexual preference and geographic location alter Chicano identity" (1990). I believe that these factors obtain not only for the present but also for past centuries and that they cannot be ignored when assessing literary texts of earlier epochs.

From *Recovering the U.S. Hispanic Literary Heritage.* © 1993 by Arte Público Press.

If the development of this recovery project is indeed governed by an awareness of a "matrix of difference," my apprehension diminishes somewhat, for I can then envision the creation of what Meese calls a canon of abundance rather than one of scarcity (31). There is still the problem, however, of value. How do we assign value to the texts we recommend? Do we approach them with the notion that they possess some "intrinsic" or "universal" value? If so, how do we arrive at a consensus regarding what exactly constitutes such elusive qualities? Is it our objective to select texts that show life as it "really was," that is, are we seeking historical accuracy and authenticity? If so, how do we, from our present position, judge how life really was in the past? Are we committed to publishing works with a specific ideology?

We must base our judgments on the understanding "that the value of the text is contingent on how well it may perform certain desired/able functions for one set of subjects" (Hernstein Smith 30). We must understand, of course, that we are merely one set of subjects with specific desires. And even then, we may not all be motivated by the same desires nor by shared responses to the corpus of texts under consideration. The best that I can do at this moment is attempt to clarify my own subject position—expose my own criteria for assigning contingent value.

To begin with, I part from the position assumed by Genaro Padilla, that "what interests me is not so much to [affix] a degree of historical truth-value to [these] testimonies or [to argue] the merits of their representativeness of Hispano Mexicano culture . . . [but rather] to recover the voices and stories of these ghosts" (93). However, since I am certain that limited funds will force us to be selective with regard to the actual number of ghostly voices we can resurrect, a guideline for me in the selection of pre-twentieth century texts, would reside in the response to the following question: "To what extent does the text stand as a discourse of contestation?" This criteria would allow me to privilege all texts that were written in Spanish regardless of the author's class interest. The very use of Spanish by authors who were literate in English (e.g. Felipe M. Chacón, Miguel C. de Baca) was an act of contestation to the mainstream canon. I would not, however, exclude texts written in English merely because they were written in the dominant language, so long as they clearly demonstrate an attempt to contest texts that privileged hegemonic practices. I think specifically of María Amparo Ruiz Burton's *The Squatter and the Don*, a novel riddled with ambivalence that clearly points toward the desirability of assimilation for the *rico* class, yet protests loudly against the machinations and chicanery by which this class was stripped of its landholdings in California. Her posture toward *las clases populares* is offensive, to be sure, yet therein lies her position in the matrix of "difference."

In keeping with my criteria of contestation, I recommend the publication of as many texts written/or narrated by women as possible, for these narratives lead us to conclude that voices uttered from a male subject position, tainted by the biases of patriarchal phallocentric discourse, can be either limited in scope or misdirected in their interpretations of the *mexicana* experience. The narratives of María Inocenta Pico, Eulelia Pérez, Dorotea Valdez and Felipa Osuna de Marrón in the Bancroft Library chronicle the coming of the *americanos* and the reactions of the *mexicanos* in California to their disposession and marginalization. These narratives also call attention, in a most compelling way, to the responses of Californio women to historical change. The publication of as many of these texts as possible would go a long way in eschewing a canon of scarcity, openly recognizing gender difference as an important and inexorable component of the broader hispano/mexicano experience.

A nineteenth century text to which I assign a high level of contingent value is the anonymously penned drama *Los tejanos* (The Texans). This well-documented play lies hidden away in the pages of a 1944 issue of the journal Hispania (Espinosa and Espinosa). *Los tejanos* is a historically important text that stands out like a beacon in an era of literary scarcity. That the author of this play may well have been the Spaniard who appears as Capitán Ramírez playing one of the two main roles in the play should not discourage its inclusion in our project. Regardless of whom the writer may have been he explicitly supported self-determination for *el pueblo Nuevomexicano* (New Mexican people).

Los tejanos should be printed along with various versions of another inaccessible New Mexican drama, *Los Comanches* (A. Espinosa 1907). This late eighteenth century text is important but because it demonstrates that, despite the geographical isolation of the New Mexican colony, there was a sense of belonging to a broader culture, of affiliation with a literary tradition whose threads can be traced back to the epic verses of Pérez de Villagrá, *La Historia de la Nueva México* (1610), and Ercilla de Zúñiga's *La Araucana* (1569)—an epic on the attempted conquest of the Araucanos (Chile)—, and to the Iberian medieval dramatic tradition.

This tradition had a colonial agenda about which we must be very honest. It is important that we attempt to clarify if there are links which allow us to understand how the colonial subject was transformed into the colonized subject of Chicano literature. How do we bind together into a single tradition works whose authors must be situated in two very distinct positions: those bearing testimony to a Spanish colonial project and those writing from a position of colonized "otherness." While it is not my intent to resolve this aporia here, I will point out some possible links.

The soldiers who wrote about northern New Spain, some of them barely literate, attempted to justify a project which, failing to deliver the new Tenochtitlan, was suspect at best, illegitimate at worst. It was their duty to convince their superiors that their labor was not in vain. The inscription of self as agents of a precarious enterprise was as often riddled with exaggeration as with disillusion. Much of the literature written by the *mexicano* population of the Southwest after the Mexican American War bears testimony to a similar disillusion. Those who hoped the new regime would bring the progress promised but unrealized by Mexican rule, inscribed their disillusion in their own chronicles of despair. Mariano Vallejo, for example, registered the following: "What a difference between the present time and those that preceded the usurpation by the Americans. If the Californians could all gather together to breathe a lament, it would reach Heaven as a moving sigh which would cause fear and consternation to the Universe. What misery!" (Paredes 48).

The distance of Spain's colonial soldiers from their cultural and political centers also produced in their writing a sense of rupture and discontinuity. Their dependence on those centers led them to produce chronicles that communicated their experiences in unknown territories. An examination of the literature produced by *mexicanos* after 1848 in the occupied American Southwest likewise reveals a strong sense of rupture and discontinuity. These writers, faced with the traumatic separation which the annexation of Mexican territory to the United States brought them, attempted through the written word to bridge this political rupture and to remain linked to a cultural tradition by recording their experiences in the unknown cultural territories imposed upon them.

Nuevomexicano literature of the nineteenth century offers some interesting examples of works that bear a strong sense of grief and disillusion of the sort than can be found in colonial texts. The prolonged battle for statehood and the accompanying defamation campaign, which was nurtured by a flagrant discourse of domination, placed the Nuevomexicano population in a defensive position, the very position held by the frustrated seekers of the New Tenochtitlan. This position accounts in part for the sometimes ambivalent tone of the literature of this period. The need to sustain and to remain identified with a cultural tradition whose future was threatened by political rupture inspired a bounteous corpus of Spanish-language texts in all genres. As I stated elsewhere, "One senses from a reading of the extant material that the motivating force was to affirm cultural identity by a positing of the

Spanish-language word as an amulet against imminent displacement" (5). We must also acknowledge that the desire to validate the image of Nuevomexicanos vis-à-vis Anglo Americans, who would issue judgment regarding their fitness for statehood, lent itself to an exaggerated rhetoric of patriotism not unlike the exaggerated rhetoric of Fray Marcos de Niza who attempted to convince the viceroy of the worthiness of his enterprise. Despite this ambivalence, the majority of the texts produced during the territorial period by Nuevomexicano writers bear witness, some in a veiled manner, others blatantly, to a spirit of resistance to forces of assimilation that threatened cultural survival and continuity.

Returning to the selection of texts for this historical recovery project, I would urge strongly the publication of the two novellas of Eusebio Chacón *Hijo de la tempestad* (Son of the Storm) and *Tras la tormenta la calma* (After the Storm the Calm). These brief texts were produced by a journalist and newspaper editor who rallied with force against the displacement of Nuevomexicanos. Although published in 1893 in Las Vegas, New Mexico, they have long been ignored. When Francisco Lomelí and Donald Urioste found the slim volume that contains both novellas ensconced in the special collections section of the University of New Mexico Library in the early 1970s, they rejoiced at having found the "first Chicano novel." Since then, earlier works have been discovered. Nonetheless these two novellas continue to be important testimonies to the awareness by Nuevomexicanos of the aesthetic and literary currents of the rest of the Spanish-speaking world and of their desire to form a part of its literary tradition despite the reality of political rupture and of pressures to abandon *that* cultural identity in favor of "Americanization." *Hijo de la tempestad* is perhaps the quintessential example of *sturm und drang* Romanticism in the literature of Aztlán. As such, it makes for interesting analysis at the aesthetic level. My agreement with Lomelí's response to the work as an allegory of protest and resistance would lead me also to assign this text a high value on the scale of contestation.

A text of special interest to me is Manuel Salazar's *Aurora y Gervasio, o sea, la historia de un caminante* (Aurora y Gervasio, or rather, the Traveler's Story). One of the first novels of Aztlán, it remains an obscure unpublished text. The original, dated 1881 and beautifully penned on the pages of a business ledger, is currently in the hands of Anselmo Arellano who was given the text by Salazar's family. The story bears the marks of the French neoclassical, neopastoral genre. It also contains resonances of Peninsular neopastoral narratives of the period. Despite what to a modern reader might seem to be a mere treatment of frivolous love triangles, this text stands in competition with the dime novels of the period penned by writers of the dominant culture which contributed creation of the Mexican-as-barbarian stereotype. The main characters in *Aurora y Gervasio* are a far cry from the greasers that populated the discourses of the dominant culture of that period and of Hollywood films in the twentieth century. The males in Salazar's novel are well-bred gentlemen, though not all of them landed gentry—Gervasio is, in fact, the son of peasants—motivated by idealized love and an equally idealized code of honor. The women are coquettes upon whose individual virtue depends the intricacies of the Hispanic code of honor. And though honor and female virtue may appear trivial to us today, we must recognize that it was an important code that for centuries, as Ramón Gutiérrez affirms, governed social relations in the Spanish/Mexican borderlands. Salazar's text sheds light on an important cultural phenomenon that has received little attention beyond Gutiérrez's seminal study.

Two texts written by Miguel C. de Baca also merit republication. *Vicente Silva y sus cuarenta bandidos* (Vicente Silva and His Forty Bandits, 1896), is fairly well known and accessible through translations. The other, a serialized narrative about Las Gorras Blancas (The White Caps), which appeared in an 1892 newspaper, *El Sol de Mayo* (The May Sun), owned by C. de Baca, is more obscure. This latter text, apocaliptically titled *Noches tenebrosas en el Condado de San Miguel* (Spooky Nights in San Miguel County), will not elicit a favorable response from a contemporary Chicano reading audience who has come to view Las Gorras Blancas as folk heroes for their acts of guerilla resistance in late nineteenth-century New Mexico. C. de Baca, from his position as a member of the conservative elite, treats Los Gorras Blancas with the same scorn he reserved for the bandido Vicente Silva. Their leader, *El Gran Capitán*, is portrayed as an opportunist who dupes the obreros (workers) "*ignorantes*" and leads them on rampages, which include fence cutting, barn burnings, the beating of non-collaborative widows, and the rape of their young daughters. Its value, and thus its relationship to Ruiz Burton's novel, lies in what it can teach us about the attitudes of New Mexico's *rico* class toward accommodation with the dominant Anglo political order.

Two Texts for a Canon

The remainder of this essay focuses on the work of two Nuevomexicano writers whose lives spanned the territorial and early statehood periods in New Mexico and the nineteenth and twentieth centuries: Vicente Bernal and Felipe Maximiliano Chacón. Bernal's poetry of exile is perhaps more interesting for what it does not express than for what it does. His apparently neutral stance toward the political events of his time does not necessarily reflect acquiescence. But neither does his work fall explicitly within a discourse of resistance that was gradually being written by those who found themselves marginalized from mainstream society. Perhaps his ambivalent stance was the only one afforded Nuevomexicanos at a time when they were trying to prove their worth as bona fide American citizens, yet were not completely oblivious to the machinations that denied them legitimacy. Chacón also grapples with this issue as he extolled the patriotic virtues of his fellow Nuevomexicanos, urging them to be model citizens. There is, nonetheless, an awareness in his work of the damaging effects of the discourse of domination. Contrary to more blatant countertexts, Chacón makes much of the fact that having endured and survived that discourse is precisely what, in the long run, will make Nuevomexicanos more worthy of a place in the new order afforded by statehood.

The contingent value of these texts for me lies in the fact that both of these writers continued to inscribe in their work the Spanish language literary tradition introduced to the region in the sixteenth century, despite the fact that they were products of an English language education, and that they did not view assimilation with a jaundiced eye. My desire is to create a space for these authors in our new canon lest they be forgotten forever.

Vicente Bernal, 1888-1915

Born in 1888 and spending the early part of his life with his grandparents in Costilla, New Mexico, Vicente Bernal, like many New Mexicans of his generation, worked tending sheep and farming. His education began at the Presbyterian Mission School in Costilla and in 1907 he transferred to the Menaul Presbyterian School in Albuquerque. In 1910 he was admitted to Dubuque College in Iowa and would have attended Dubuque Seminary had he not died on April 28, 1915, of a brain hemorrhage. His single collection of poetry and ten brief pieces of prose and oratory were published posthumously by the Telegraph-Herald of Dubuque in 1916. This work demonstrates mastery of a classic American education and of the language of that culture. He does not, however, ignore his mother tongue as half of his collection is written in Spanish. Those who commented on his life and work praised young Bernal for "his diligent and conscientious spirit of getting the best from his tasks." Robert McLean who with Vicente's brother, Luis Bernal, gathered and edited *Las Primicias* (First Fruits), comments further in his brief prologue to the text that Bernal "was quiet and unassuming but with a beauty of character that remains to this day strong in the memories of his classmates and teachers" (7). W. O. Rouston, Dean of the College, in an introduction to the text, adds to the minimal sketch we have of Bernal that "in his association with men, the boy showed ready wit, which made him an acceptable companion. . . . Indeed humor was one of his chief intellectual qualities and enabled him always to keep a cheerful outlook" (10).

Las Primicias: The Fruits of Assimilation or Sublimation?

Bernal's early experiences in rural New Mexico left a deeply imprinted love and appreciation of nature that surfaced again and again in his poetry. In fact, nature is often a source of comfort and revelation, a mediator between the secular poetic voice and the divine:

> Two birds I spied on [a] verdant hill;
> Their heads were near, their breasts more near;
> I heard no warbling, heard no trill,
> But was inflamed by God's own love.
>   ("To Miss Self and Jimmy," 24)

In addition to religiously inspired verse of this nature, there are examples in *Las Primicias* of metaphysical musings. A poem bearing the noncommital title "To _____," reveals a contemplative posture and a highly lyrical sense of the precarious nature of human existence:

> But why should I desire to scan
> More thorny hills, if life's a breath
> Which seeks an ampler sphere!
> A flickering flame, the life of man
> Extinguished by the breath of death
> Which lurks forever near. (28)

This is but one of several poems with allusions or direct references to death and one wonders if Bernal had a premonition of his own premature death. If, in fact, he did, he does not pine away but, rather, exalts in his love of life: "Oh let me kiss thy brow and locks, / And draw thee to my side, my life" (28).

There are a number of occasional poems, some expressing admiration for unnamed young women, others dedicated to classmates. Three of the twenty-four English language poems are songs dedicated to the college, one of which was set to music and accepted as the alma mater of Dubuque College. Bernal's sense of humor is apparent in his poetry, though it is not always goodwilled. It occasionally takes on a biting edge, thus allowing him to satirize behavior that he finds objectionable. The following lines from a poem called "A Teacher," clearly demonstrate this side of Bernal's wit:

> But years brought greater needs
> and greater needs more money.
> Till mother lived on weeds,
> while he was saying "Honey." (25)

Humor quickly turns to satire in this poem, as Bernal chastises selfish young men who live the good life while their parents sacrifice.

An intriguing question regarding this pioneer New Mexican poet is one upon which we can only speculate for there are no answers in his creative production. Given the times in which Bernal lived, given his ethnic and class background, given the spiritual rootedness, the *querencia* of Nuevomexicanos for their land, one wonders whether Vicente Bernal felt alienated during his tenure at Dubuque. Bernal lived in a period in which Hispanics were feeling the increasing pressure of displacement. Beyond their social and economic marginalization, New Mexican mexicanos were severely maligned during the statehood battle. The unflattering portraits initiated as a result of early contacts by Josiah Gregg, William W. Davis, Susan Shelby Magoffin, Lewis Garrard, Phillip St. George Cook, and others, became in the 1880s and 1890s full-fledged caricatures in Eastern newspapers.

Surely Bernal's teachers and classmates were not ignorant of the political fracas between Washington D.C. and New Mexico nor of the stigmatized images of Nuevomexicanos produced by the conflict. But if Bernal indeed felt like a foreigner upon his arrival in Iowa in the fall of 1910, or during any part of his six-year tenure at Dubuque College, his English language texts leave no clues regarding social alienation. Dubuque was a mission school dedicated to the education of foreigners. Its primary objective was to teach "so many of strange tongue the syllables of liberty and brotherhood, guiding their first steps to higher planes of usefullness" (editor's dedicatory note of *Las Primicias* to Dubuque College). This attitude may well have discouraged explicit expression of feelings of culture shock or of ethnic and cultural differences.

Instead of giving vent to feelings of alienation, Bernal's poetry demonstrates a high level of assimilation to the new cultural experiences offered by

Dubuque College. The fruits of his immersion in his secular studies are apparent in his frequent intertextual dialogs with poets and writers of the English Language. "Rubyat," "To Tennyson," "To Byron," "Elvira by the Stream," "To Miss Self and Jimmy," are examples of the homage he paid to those who inspired his own muses. Bernal's response to the historical reality of his times, with a serious commitment to education, was not out of context. Doris Meyer in her investigation of New Mexican newspapers of the territorial period observes: The newspapers reveal a three-part reaction by Mexican Americans to negative stereotyping—first, an awareness of being rejected on the grounds of inferiority and unfitness, especially regarding the agonizing quest for statehood; second, a strong defensive reaction critical of unfounded negative stereotyping; and third, a campaign to transform the image of Mexican Americans through education" (77).

Did Bernal indeed write this poetry to prove his worth as an American citizen? We will never know, yet early readers of his poetry must have been convinced that this young man "from the hills of New Mexico" (*Las Primicias* 7), unequivocally had mastered the rules of the game and thus had become a fit candidate for acceptance to the club.

Putting aside the political issues, we turn now to examine a more personal question. Bernal was immersed in a foreign milieu far removed from his home. Judging from his poetry, Bernal's exile was not of the sort that sharpens the vision of the homeland or engenders nostalgia for the familiar. It was rather an exile that appears to have obliterated his past. The allusions to the landscapes of New Mexico are few. One lone dark-haired girl, a poem to his mother, a short poem prompted "by a postal received from home bearing a picture of a house and the word *Bonita*" (Editor's note 18), scant generic references to the mountain and desert landscapes of the West exhaust the inventory. There is one short story that suggests Hispanic trappings. In "The Wedding Feast," the names of the characters are Estrella, Porfirio, and Bernardo. And though a specific setting is not indicated, the description of the wedding feast and mysterious apparitions conjure the voices of New Mexico villagers spinning folk yarns of *brujería* (witchcraft) and the like. Beyond this short sketch, however, we find no other traces of New Mexican custom or tradition in Bernal's English-language prose or poetry.

There remains one very clear indication that Bernal did not totally negate his Hispanic ancestry, though he indeed seems to gloss over his cultural roots. About half of the poems included in the collection are written in Spanish. It is in these poems that we find some, though not persistent, expression of longing for home. The frequent mention of letters is perhaps a projection of his *tristeza*. In one poem called "Parte de una carta," (Part of a Letter) nostalgia forms the central motif of the poem. In the following lines he focuses on the strangeness of a typical Midwestern repast:

¡O! de papas no te decía
Pues esas nunca faltan.
Las tengo tres veces al día
Si supieras, ya me hartan (69)

(O! Had I mentioned potatoes
Well there are plenty of those.
I eat them three times daily
If only you knew how fed up I am)

The final expression of being "fed up" might just be figurative as well as literal, in which case a sense of alienation may lie between the lines. The fact that the theme is handled humorously is perhaps an indication of a need to sublimate explicit negative evaluations regarding his experiences in the Midwest and his status at Dubuque College.

The inclusion of Greenleaf Whitter's poem "The Barefoot Boy," in translation, is an interesting choice. In this poem the simple education of a barefoot youth under the tutelage of nature suggests Bernal's own upbringing. In fact, explicit identification of the poetic voice with the addressee of the poem occurs in the final line of the first verse: "Parabienes jovencito / Yo también fui descalcito" (Best wishes barefoot boy / For I too was one of you, 55). This poem together with one in which Bernal calls attention to his duties as a dishwasher and with the poem in which he chastises his spendthrift classmates suggest that Bernal was not unaware of his underprivileged position at Dubuque College. Rouston, upon calling attention to the fact that Bernal spent his vacations working in local establishments, suggests that Bernal's situation did not represent the norm for Dubuque students. As such, we might conclude that the young poet experienced a double dose of marginalization. Yet he was apparently more willing to call attention to his class status than to his ethnicity. In fact, the latter would have been lost to future readers had he not written some verse in his mother tongue.

Bernal's Spanish language poems do not equal, neither in rich intertextuality nor in the treatment of universal themes, those written in English. And though Rouston assures us that Bernal studied both English and Spanish literatures, his Spanish language poetry tends to be uninspired and characterized by facile rhyme. Nonetheless, these poems stand as testimony to

Bernal's pride in being bilingual and to his willingness to call attention to the very aspect that for so long marked his people as unfit for citizenship in the United States.

Vicente Bernal intended to return to New Mexico as an ordained minister. He hoped also to write a history of the region based on his grandfather's recollections. Unfortunately, this was not to be, for he lived only twenty-eight years. "Written on notebooks, and upon odd-sized pieces of papers" (*Las Primicias* 14), his poetry left notice of his life and of a gift which, in the words of Dean Rouston, was "finely literary" (14). His "first fruits" moreover stand as one more link in New Mexico's long and rich Hispanic literary tradition.

Felipe Maximiliano Chacón, 1873-1948

The work of Felipe Maximiliano Chacón virtually has gone unrecognized. The poetry and short prose pieces collected under the title *Obras de Felipe Maximiliano Chacón, "El Cantor Neomexicano": Poesía y prosa, 1924* (The Works of Felipe Maximiliano Chacón, "The New Mexican Singer: Poetry and Prose), come from the pen of a man with a sharp sense of the past and its relation to his time, and a profoundly reflective and poetic sensibility. The little that we know of Chacón's life is included in the prologue of the collection written by historian and statesman Benjamin Read. Read is generous in his praise of "the New Mexican Bard" and impressed that he wrote in a language for which there were few opportunities for formal training. Read's praise of Chacón as the first "to call attention to his country in the beautiful language of Cervantes" (5), demonstrates that the literary achievements of earlier Nuevomexicano writers (Eusebio Chacón, Manuel C. De Baca, Vicente Bernal) were either ignored or embedded in oblivion. Whether or not Chacón's published collection received attention or acclaim in its time is not known. We do know that the collection was not mentioned in any of the early Southwestern or New Mexican literary bibliographies. Yet Chacón was somewhat of a public figure. Like his father Urbano Chacón, who served as the public school superintendent for Santa Fe County in the 1880s, Felipe was involved in journalism. He edited such varied Spanish language newspapers as *La Voz del Pueblo* (The People's Voice), *La Bandera Americana* (The American Flag), *El Eco del Norte* (North Echo), and *El Faro del Río Grande* (The Lighthouse of the Río Grande).

Given Chacón's work in the newspaper industry, he very likely used this medium as an outlet for his poetry prior to publication of *Poesía y prosa*. Read affirms that Chacón's verse, which he began to write at the age of fourteen, was celebrated extensively in New Mexico, but he does not indicate the medium through which it reached the public. Further research may divulge that some of the anonymous satirical ditties printed in the late 1880s in *La Aurora*, a newspaper edited by Don Urbano, belong to Felipe. These bear a distinct similarity to the "Saeta política" and the "Nocturno a . . ." included in the 1924 collection. However, Anselmo Arellano's collection of New Mexican Spanish-language periodical poetry includes only samples from Chacón's published collection. If Chacón did indeed print some of his poetry anonymously, this gives all the more reason to believe Read's opinion regarding Chacón's modesty: "Another characteristic of Chacón is his aversion to publicity, his dislike for appearing important . . . . Chacón is a genius, and like all geniuses, he does not know how to esteem himself" (10-11, translations mine).

Read mentions that Chacón attended public primary schools and later studied at St. Michael's College, which at that time provided only secondary training. He dropped out in order to help support the family when his father died, but he continued to educate himself on his own. That his education went beyond what he might have achieved in high school is apparent in the frequent and extensive classical and historical references in his poetry. Likewise, seven translations of poets such as Byron, Longfellow, and Dresden, included in the prologue of *Poesía y prosa*, as well as references to Latin American poets, demonstrates the breadth of his exposure, in two languages, to the humanities. That he may have flaunted his knowledge is suggested by the fact that Casimiro Varela maliciously refers to Chacón as "el catedrático" (the professor; see note 6).

Matters of the Heart, the Soul and the Body Politic

A reader familiar with Latin American literature will be struck by occasional resonances of Spanish-American Modernism in Chacón's work. Especially in his more abstract poems, Chacón in true Modernist style, avoids commonplace vocabulary and prosaic expression, deliberately stringing his lines in such a way as to capture the musicality of Modernist verse. Though he is not as adept as a Leopoldo Lugones or Rubén Darío, he does create original, well-wrought strophes such as the following:

Y continuando ufana su carrera
Vino la noche y la metió en desvelo

Y ya en casa, en su ambición y celo
Tomó el candil por flor en primavera ("La vida" 46)

(As she pursued her haughty flight
Night arrived and cast its spell
And once at home in greed and zeal
For a flower she mistook the flame)

Chacón parts ways with the Modernist aesthetic in that he does not cultivate the "ivory tower" pose of the majority of Modernists. In fact, he proves himself to be solidly grounded in the concrete events of his time and not above imitating folk humor through the exploitation of oral verse forms. His stylistic eclecticism is observed in the neoclassical trappings of his heroic odes and the romantic embellishments of his novella, "Eustacio y Carlota," and of a poem called "Nocturno a . . . ." In this poem Chacón demonstrates that he was familiar with at least one Latin American poet, the Mexican Manuel Acuña, whose famous romantic verse he imitates to ridicule a political figure whom obviously he disdained. The disparity between his topic and the form and language chosen to express his sentiments renders an acerbic yet humorous attack. The subject of the poem is identified as one Oñate, though a footnote clarified that the name is fictitious. Further probing in historical annals may reveal that the object of his barb is territorial governor Miguel Otero. What is impressive about this poem is Chacón's fidelity in syllabication and rhyme—on occasion he copies lines verbatim from Acuña's poem only to add an unexpected humorous twist—to the original model. This sort of discipline, demonstrated throughout his verse making, tells us that Chacón took poetry seriously and was indeed a master of his craft.

Chacón's *Poesía y prosa* is divided into three sections: "Cantos patrios y miscelánea" (Patriotic Verse and Miscellaneous), "Cantos del Hogar y traducciones" (Family Verse and Translations), "Saetas políticas y prosa" (Political Barbs and Prose). The first part is the most extensive and also the most interesting because of its variety. The forty-five Spanish-language poems in this section of the book can be placed in six broad categories: love, personal misfortune, philosophical musings, patriotism and homage, commemoration of special occasions and humor. The poems of personal misfortune, together with those of philosophical bent and his domestic poems, demonstrate his Modernist tendencies. In his poems of misfortune, the specific sources of the vicissitudes endured remain unnamed, though the poems of death, unrequited love and betrayal by friends certainly must be taken as evidence of misfortune. We know, for example, that Chacón's family was touched by death on several occasions. In addition to the death of two children mentioned in the domestic poems, the nostalgic poem entitled "Santa Fe" alludes to the death of his mother and some brothers. In the poem "Al enviudar mi madre" (Upon the Widowing of my Mother), he takes the death of his father—according to Read, Chacón was thirteen years old at the time—as the point of departure. But, rather than focusing on the father's attributes or on his own sentiments on the death of Don Urbano, Chacón calls attention to the mother's pain, as the poetic voice assumes the mother's persona:

Sola, sola lloré,
Y al tenderme la noche sus crespones,
Mi llanto con un suspiro agoté. (89)

(Alone, alone I cried,
and as night cast her darkness upon me,
I spent my tears with sighs.)

A poem of equal lyrical quality is the sonnet "Devoción." Here the poet speaks of a lost love to whom he remains devoted and whose resting place he frequently visits. As in all the poems dedicated to his children, the garden is the key metaphor:

¡Oh, cielo!, que tesoro me ha costado
Ese albergue de un polvo tan querido
Ese sitio de flores nacarado
Su cadaver precioso está dormido
Bajo esa bóveda que yo he regado
Con lágrimas del alma que he vertido (74)

(Oh! Heaven, how dear has been the price
paid for that niche of dust I so deeply love
For that nectar bed of flowers
The precious cadaver sleeps
Under that dome that I have showered
With tears wrenched from my soul)

There is no indication whatsoever who this loved one might be. It is tempting to speculate that it is a wife. Of the ten poems dedicated to family members, not a single one mentions a mate as the object of love. Two poems speak in passing of a mother and a father, and the first person plural verbs allude to both parents, but never by name or by epithet is the wife referred to here or elsewhere. Could it be that the absence is deliberate and perhaps linked to the personal tribulations alluded to, not only in several poems but also in a conversation attributed to Chacón by Read: "I have suffered great strokes of bad luck on various occasions in my life . . . but I have not known a pain that I have not been able to conquer. I have faced my fortune, acerbic tribulations, reminding myself that they could be worse, and in that manner triumphed vis-à-vis adversity" (10). The poetry itself reveals only passing allusions to misfortune, and the tenor is one of acceptance rather than of self-pity. Related to the poems of this category are those whose theme is unrequited love. Once again the tone is not one of intense emotion but rather one of resignation. Of course, it is possible that the poems of this ilk were written in adolescence and not linked in any way to misfortune in his adult life.

Chacón's sense of acceptance in the face of adversity tends to be expressed in a number of poems in which he stirs the ashes of the most ancient and perplexing of riddles. It is not, however, twentieth-century horror of the abyss that Chacón expresses but rather tempered sorrow in view of the ephemeral nature of life. These pale sentiments of angst are further overcome by the conviction that it is through action that humans give meaning to life and inscribe themselves in immortality:

> Porque sólo el hombre que lucha cada hora
> Transmite su nombre perene a la Historia
> ¡Jamás su memoria se aleja y se va!

> (For only he who acts each hour
> Transmits forever his name to History
> And never his memory will time devour!)

This conviction is the motivating force behind his many poems dedicated to persons whom he admired and events he held in awe. "A La Señora Adelina Otero Warren" (To Mrs. Adelina Otero Warren), "Al explorador del Oeste" (To the Explorer of the West), "A los legisladores" (To the Lawmakers), and a poem in honor of Octaviano Larrázolo, reveal a poet who admired men and women of action. Together with his patriotic poems, these homages are particularly interesting for what they reveal of Chacón's attitudes toward the sociopolitical events of his time. They also allow us to glimpse the beginning of an ideology that allowed middle class Nuevomexicanos to balance their precarious position in a rapidly changing society and to maintain a foothold in the political arena.

Taken as a lot these poems reveal the tenor of Chacón's thought in two directions. The first is a didactic appeal to Hispanic New Mexicans to take pride in their ancestral culture. The lesson is replete with examples of the deeds of honorable and heroic fellow Nuevomexicanos and with warnings against the evils inherent in being mislead by "others." Additional incentives are offered when he calls attention to the racial prejudice and injustices suffered by Nuevomexicanos particularly in the long battle for statehood. And while he speaks of burying the past and creating a new slate filled with honorable acts, in "A Nuevo Mexico" he nonetheless feels compelled to inscribe past injustices, thereby calling attention to his people's mettle. Despite decades of ignominious acts by outsiders, they have endured and survived with their integrity intact, prepared to be outstanding citizens. They must not, however, forsake their origins is his message in "A los legisladores."

The second tendency in these poems is an insistence on bearing witness to personal and collective patriotism. As proof of loyalty to the United States, Chacón recalls the participation of Nuevomexicanos in the Civil and Spanish American Wars. In a long panegyric dedicated to Nuevomexicanos who fought in World War I, Chacón attempts to set the record straight once and for all. It is not enough, however, to state merely that they fought bravely; it is the *Americanness* of their acts that ennobles the soldiers and completes the encomium. How burdened Hispanics of this period must have been with the suspicion of disloyalty!

The high point of Chacón's patriotic rhetoric is reached with a poem written in 1918, commemorating the Declaration of Independence of the United States. Six years have passed since New Mexico joined the Union and citizen Chacón has weathered the storm of change. Gone are all allusions to injustice and gone the insecurity embedded in the defensive testimonies of collective loyalty of other poems. Instead, we hear in "A la patria" (To My Country) a self-assured poet claim filial ties to his forefathers Washington, Adams and Jefferson as he unabashedly appropriates for himself the myths of their (now his) country:

> Mas al pensar bendigo yo la estrella
> Que dirije en la tierra mi destino [sic]
> Y que guía mis pasos con su huella
> de cívica igualdad por el camino
> Bajo el pendón augusto que descuella
> Sobre tu altar cual símbolo divino
> Do Wáshington trazó con letras de oro

"La Libertad", el sin igual tesoro. (24)
(Reason leads me to bless the star
That leads my destiny upon the earth
And in its wake with civic equality
It guides my steps upon that path
'Neath the august banner wrapped
As a divine symbol round your altar
Where Washington wrote with golden letters
"Liberty," the unequalled treasure)

In exchange for the privilege of filiation, the poet offers his unyielding patriotism: "Recibe por tanto, Patria mía / Las notes de mi ardiente patriotismo" (Receive therefore sweet land of mine / the notes of my fervent patriotism).

At first glance Chacón's patriotic discourse would seem to indicate that he was under extreme pressure to demonstrate, display, or otherwise prove his loyalty and that he seizes the pen to do so. Nonetheless, we cannot ignore the fact that his verse is written in Spanish and therefore intended for a Spanish rather than an English reading public. Did his public need be reminded of its own loyalty and patriotism? Probably not. How then can we reconcile Chacón's ambivalent rhetoric which, on the one hand, calls for loyalty to and pride in ancestral culture and, on the other, pledges uncompromising patriotism to the "new way" in a language that bears testimony to his commitment to the former? It is unlikely that Chacón was openly advocating official cultural pluralism. The struggle for statehood had proven, in a most profound manner, that cultural difference was not viewed favorably by the dominant culture. Thus, to assume a position of advocacy when the events were still within the reach of memory might have been dangerous. Perhaps herein lies a clue to Chacón's use of Spanish. He could do, in that language, what he dared not do in English. And, yet, there remains a blatant contradiction. If Chacón's demonstration of patriotism deflates somehow what appears to be a radical and potentially dangerous call to cultural preservation, as I believe it does, why did he bother with this push-me-pull-me pose in the first place? Is it possible that his rhetoric on the importance of cultural identity was more symbolic than radical? The appeal to ethnic identity has long been a universal ploy of the ethnic middle class to consolidate power within boundaries of dominant sociopolitical networks. Since this has been and continues to be a political *modus operandi* in New Mexico, what we have in Chacón's creative work is evidence of the early stages of this strategy. When Chacón exclaims in his homage to Larrázolo that it is not only the Democratic party that stood behind him, but *the people*, we can almost detect the message implicit in his verse: "Together we elect one of our own; / divided [into two parties] we loose out to the bulls of the world" (To the Lawmakers). Save face but maintain (political) space is what Chacón's ambivalent rhetoric advises. The achievement of the task he laid out before himself involved a certain amount of skill and a good dosage of veiled manipulation. There is no doubt that Chacón the editor (the political persona) hid behind Chacón the poet to inspire poetry that covertly testifies to a deeply entrenched Nuevomexicano political ploy that for decades has nurtured cultural survival and simultaneously ensured participation in the political machine of the dominant society.

F. M. Chacón's three narrative pieces complement, each in its own way, the poetry. The first piece, "Un baile de caretas" ("A Masked Ball") is a humorous sketch that tells the story of the deception of a fatuous young man by his buddies who set him up to fall for a mysterious stranger at a masquerade ball. Upon unmasking herself, Carmen Hinojosa turns out to be José Olivas. The smitten lover takes the next train out of town and does not return for many years. The highbrow style of what turns out to be a rather mundane tale places the story squarely in the Modernist vein, recalling the narrative of Rubén Darío.

"Don Julio Berengara" tells the sad tale of a sheepherder who splurges his money on a saloon girl with whom he falls in love. Crushed when he discovers that she has abandoned him for an americano, he takes solace in the memory of the night he met her, the night that "he was king." The final note expressed in this sketch is very much in keeping with Chacón's attitude of accepting one's lot as doled out by destiny.

The modern reader of the third prose piece entitled simply "Eustacio y Carlota" might be tempted to read it as a parody, inasmuch as Chacón resuscitates the trappings of the by then worn-out Byzantine novel that has as its theme separation, mistaken identity, and subsequent recognition of two loved ones. However, since no motive for parody is apparent, the second choice is to dismiss the piece as a product of Chacón's romantic temperament. There are some interesting details in the story which suggest an allegorical reading. The two Quintanilla orphans, after the death of their mother in a tenement in New York City, are adopted by Anglo parents and given Anglo names. The young boy makes a name for himself in the Rough Riders batallion during the Spanish American War. The sister is educated by a wealthy family in Colorado. As fate would have it, they meet in California, fall in love, and marry, only to discover as they undress on their wedding night, the identical medals given to them by their dying mother. And just to make sure, the young girl bears the proverbial identifying birthmark. The marriage is annulled and Amanda marries her brother's childhood friend, Orlando. The two children born of this union are given the original names of the orphan siblings: Carlota and Eustacio. Despite the melodramatic tone of this romance, might it be possible to read it as a parable for the *rico* class of New Mexico? Such a reading is suggested by the loss of natural parents (Mexico); "legal" adoption by Anglo parents (United States) and subsequent assimilation; discovery and acceptance of true identities; affirmation and reappropriation of ancestral roots by restoring original names and bequeathing them to the new generation. There is, furthermore, a character named Melitón Gonzales, a native New Mexican who like Henry fought bravely in the Spanish American War. His popular speech sets him apart, identifies him as a member of the non-elite group. He is not fond of women (symbol of marriage, the machinery that most rapidly sets the assimilation process in motion). In the end Melitón succumbs to the inexorable hand of destiny. He marries a distinguished woman from San Bernardino, ever acting with "nobility of heart, sanity, common sense," and fidelity to duty. Is that duty the duty of husband to wife, or the duty of citizen to country? (The same patriotic duty displayed by Melitón's participation in the Spanish American War?) Patriotic duty oils the wheels of assimilation. If this reading is considered, the message of Chacón's ideology, hidden beneath an ambivalent rhetoric of assimilation and of ethnic preservation, draws to a neat closure.

The lives of Felipe Maximiliano Chacón and Vicente Bernal spanned two centuries and two cultures. Like their fellow Nuevomexicanos they had begun to assimilate those aspects of the dominant culture that would ensure them participation in the mainstream social order. They did not, however, deem it necessary to abandon their own cultural values and traditions but rasher struggled to achieve a state of biculturalism whereby they could remain faithful to the ways of their ancestors, yet enjoy the promise offered by their new political status. Their work reveals, in one case overtly and in the other more subtly, an ambivalent double-edged discourse of resistance and assimilation from which we can glean some insight into the process of inscribing colonial subjectivity.

ALVINA E. QUINTANA

Ana Castillo's The Mixquiahuala Letters: *The Novelist as Ethnographer*

In recent years the academy has been shaken by a significant shift in scholarly concerns which raises provocative questions regarding the politics of representation. By addressing problems in the Western intellectual tradition, cultural critics have uncovered what has come to be thought of as a crisis in representation. Giving rise to such subjects as the objectification of women and other minorities, their debates challenged theories of interpretation. Mary Louise Pratt's quote resonates with a self-critical mode characteristic of the present moment in history, a moment in which dominant ideas and assumptions are problematized because of their ideological implications. While illustrating how questions raised in this time of reassessment have been appropriated by modern anthropological discourse, Pratt also reveals how some anthropologists have begun to question their own practices. She is, in fact with her treatise, deconstructing the ethnographic process, as she sharpens her focus on the concept of ethnographic authority, questioning the notion of objectivity. When we consider Pratt's assertions concerning personal narrative and formal ethnographic description, it becomes evident that we must also reevaluate the authority of personal experience. For in classical anthropological terms:

> Ethnography is a research process in which the anthropologist closely observes, records, and engages in the daily life of another culture—an experience labeled as the fieldwork method—and

From *Criticism in the Borderlands: Studies in Chicano Literature, Culture, and Ideology.* © 1991 by Duke University Press.

> then writes accounts of this culture, emphasizing descriptive
> detail. These accounts are the primary form in which fieldwork
> procedures, the other culture, and the ethnographer's personal
> and theoretical reflections are accessible to professionals and
> other readerships. (Marcus and Fischer 1986, 18)

Pratt's voice is but one of many which have begun to question ethnographic authority, reflecting on the relationship between personal narrative and "formal ethnographic description." We can view her approach as one which developed in dialectical relationship to a re-envisioning process that was initiated by Clifford Geertz's *The Interpretation of Cultures* (1973). What Geertz called for in his text was a reassessment of the ethnographic fieldwork process—a process he still thinks of as objective, though symbolic and interpretive in nature. Pratt, on the other hand, suggests that the representation of culture involves a creative and interpretive mode of writing which reflects the subjective experiences of the ethnographer.

Although Geertz and Pratt connect the symbolic and interpretive quality of ethnographic writing, it is Pratt who implies that ethnographies are never simply ethnographies but rather "ethnographies for," written in the interest of the dominant culture. But as dominant culture is a value-laden term which signifies a point of view that has been traditionally dominated by a male perspective, as both the tradition of novel writing by men and traditional ethnography have functioned to systematically marginalize or "other" women, we begin to see the ideological limitations of both of these narrative forms. And once we apprehend that ethnographies are merely interpretations, we must determine the extent to which these interpretations or detailed descriptions can qualify as factual and objective documentations. Following this line of inquiry brings forth an interesting paradox concerning the creative, interpretive process. Is it possible to develop a discourse that is both interpretive and objective? Because the relationship between interpretation and subjectivity is a blurred one, it would seem that the anthropologist's method for observing and documenting the "daily life of another culture" could easily be viewed as subjective literary production. In George Marcus's and Michael Fischer's terms (1986) ethnography becomes a personal and imaginative vehicle by which anthropologists provide cultural critiques rather than objective representations.

What becomes evident at this point in our inquiry is the relationship between imaginary writing and ethnography as a written product. Both forms of writing reflect limited ways of seeing the world; both are influenced by social conditions and the ideology of a particular historical moment. In this light it is interesting to think about feminist writers of fiction, who, much like an anthropologist, might focus on microcosms within a culture, unpacking rituals in the context of traditional symbolic and social structures of subjugation. Yet unlike both the conventional anthropologist and the classical Chicano writer of fiction, the Chicana feminist is also interested in scrutinizing the assumptions that root her own cultural influences, unpacking so-called tradition and political institutions that shape patriarchal ways of seeing. Even though the Chicano narrative has always had some cultural context, focusing on the ethnic identification process by redefining past traditions as the work of Tomás Rivera, Américo Paredes, and Oscar Zeta Acosta illustrates, it has for the most part overlooked issues that revolve around female gender identification.

The Mixquiahuala Letters (1986) is a postmodernist, Chicana feminist novel that reflects the historical forces of the eighties, as well as an incredible diversity of concerns, literary and otherwise, from what has been previously recognized and legitimized by canonical structures. What I want to explore is not so much the pervasive ramifications of an American literary canon, which serves to reify social injustice and inequality as it suppresses the nature and development of the experiences of people of color, but rather how a close reading of *The Mixquiahuala Letters* reveals Ana Castillo's attempt to retaliate, by striking out against the limitations created by canonical structures. Castillo's novel functions as an oppositional feminist discourse that challenges the limitations inherent in both Anglo-American and Mexican culture. Certainly, feminist literary criticism has helped to expose the limitations of a canon which fails to equitably represent the nature and development of "white" women in America. But when we consider how mainstream feminist theory has likewise, because of its failure to appraise race and class oppression, helped to perpetuate white middle-class values, it seems to me that we can deem Chicana feminist creative writings as emancipatory cultural formations, that are either in alternative or oppositional relationship to Anglo-American feminist discourse.

Chicano culture draws on two external forces and has been labelled by anthropologists as a "creole culture" because it is one which draws on two or more origins: (1) a long-standing culture one is born into, and (2) a culture in terms of its social and political forces in the immediate environment. Both of these points of origin are limiting for Chicanas in that neither addresses gender issues. The Chicana writer is thus engaged in mediating and negotiating between two cultural systems, constructing a cultural and feminist identity as she works to deconstruct the predominantly male cultural paradigms that have worked to suppress a female perspective. Following this train of thought, Chicana literature functions as a bold cultural intervention, which ironically enough resembles what we have come to respect as interpretive or experimental ethnography. I want to begin my study by juxtaposing the words of two cultural critics, Clifford Geertz and Ana Castillo:

> There is no such thing as human nature independent of culture. {Geertz 1973)

> There was a definite call to find a place to satisfy my yearning spirit, the Indian in me that had begun to cure the ails of humble folk distrustful of modem medicine; a need for the sapling woman for the fertile earth that nurtured her growth. (Castillo 1986)

Geertz and Castillo, though utilizing different discourses directed to different audiences, raise similar issues concerning culture and human nature. Geertz's comments are drawn from his rather elaborate discussion on culture in chapter 1 of *The Interpretation of Cultures*. He contends that humans are like animals suspended in the "webs of significance" they themselves have spun. An analysis of these webs should not be viewed as an experimental science in search of law but rather as an interpretative search for meaning. If humans are suspended within cultural webs, it seems obvious that "there can be no such thing as human nature independent of culture." Geertz's ideas, taken out of their anthropological context, seem innocent enough, but we must remember that he is speaking as an ethnographer, speaking in terms of "the Other" and so-called "primitive culture." If we consciously avoid the subtle trappings of this hierarchical way of seeing, his metaphor can also be used to describe the self-fashioning process marginal ethnic groups undertake in the United States, as they attempt to create an existence, drawing from not one but two distinct cultural systems. It is important to note that Geertz's views on culture and his notion of interpretive analysis (thick description as he calls it) have been appropriated by many feminist scholars, since the feminist analysis of women's culture also involves decoding and interpreting many of the same systems with which traditional anthropologists are concerned (i.e., gender relations, kinship, sexuality, taboos, etc.).

Castillo's words are different than Geertz's in that they are taken from a work of fiction—*The Mixquiahuala Letters*. She makes no claims of factualism, but states rather explicitly early on that her text is fiction, and that "Any resemblance it may have to actual persons or incidents is coincidental" (Introduction, n.p.). Even so, it is clear in the above passage that as a creative writer, she, like Geertz, is grappling with the influence of an elusive, but powerful, cultural force. It becomes clear to Castillo's readers that her protagonist's existential well-being is dependent on culture. When we carry forward Geertz's semiotic concept of culture and evaluate the ethnographic writings of traditional anthropologists as representations based on individual interpretations, it becomes difficult to qualify them as objective, factual accounts of reality. Once we admit that these cultural representations should also be viewed as a mixture of descriptive and interpretive modes of discourse, the gap between imaginary and ethnographic writing shrinks before our eyes as both forms of writing are reduced to a particular way of seeing the world. And as such, we can see that Castillo, like Geertz, is involved in the process of describing and interpreting culture.

But aside from what appears to be a somewhat natural affinity, these two quotes are also interesting because on a broader level, they illustrate the vast difference in objective and subjective writing. Geertz, in the straightforward language of an "authority," states that all human nature is influenced by culture. In contrast, Castillo's language, more personal in tone, elaborates on Geertz's comments regarding the significance of culture. As they bring to life a rather academic yet direct observation, her words seem to embroider Geertz's by illustrating why or how his thoughts might be applied in the real world of subjective experiences. With her words she has in effect grounded his theory in practice. In the final analysis it is evident that each quote seems to grow in insight when juxtaposed to the other. This grounding of theory with practice becomes relevant when we begin to consider the rather abstract subject: the Chicana writers' quest for self-definition.

Put simply, the process of fashioning any kind of marginal identity (whether it be Chicana, feminist, or hyphenated American) involves a series of negotiations and mediations between the past and the future—a past and a future which for the Chicana is culturally explosive in terms of women's experiences and historical implications because, at this point in history, she attempts to define herself as she maneuvers between two opposing realities that fail to acknowledge her existence. Chicanas are not represented, but instead fall into the category of structured absences in both Chicano and Anglo feminist ideologies. Because of the Chicana's positioning between the Chicano and Anglo feminist postures, she is faced with the task of formulating an ideology, an identity out of two plans: the nostalgic plan of the past and the stereotypical Anglo feminist plan for the future. The nostalgic past refers to the idealization of old customs, largely a patriarchal interpretation of Mexican cultural traditions and history. The limitations of this plan are obvious when compared to the barriers created by an Anglo-American feminist movement which has, for the most part, failed to acknowledge female differences based on culture and ethnicity. It is because of this movement's failure to acknowledge differences that Anglo-American feminist theory has provided Chicanas with more of a mirage than a vehicle for understanding or change. *The Mixquiahuala Letters* illustrates Chicanas caught between these two polarities, moving closer to self-discovery by drawing and synthesizing usable aspects from both Anglo and Mexican cultures, weaving a complicated present out of the past and future options. The novel centers on the marginal experiences of two friends, Teresa and Alicia, as they live and travel through Mexico and the United States. By representing the daily activities of these two women, Castillo is able to reveal exactly what is at risk when an invisible entity attempts to define itself out of the structured omissions of two oppositional ideologies.

Stephen Greenblatt's *Renaissance Self-Fashioning* (1980) is useful for conceptualizing the Chicana's self-definition process. Although his discussion focuses on self-fashioning in Renaissance literature, it provides a workable method for analyzing the Chicana's struggle for self-identification. It is because of the clear distinctions he makes between self-fashioning in upper and marginal classes that his approach becomes useful to our inquiry. He states that for marginal classes:

> Self-fashioning is achieved in relation to something perceived as alien, strange, or hostile . . .; self-fashioning always involves some experience of threat some effacement or undermining, some loss of self . . .; we may say that self-fashioning occurs at the point of encounter between an authority and an alien, that what is produced in this encounter partakes of both the authority and the alien that is marked for attack, and hence that way achieved identity always contains within itself the signs of its own subversion or loss. (1980, 9)

Greenblatt's discourse emphasizes the issues involved when marginals ("aliens" as he calls them) seek to obtain an autonomous status created by self-identification. When we consider Greenblatt's analysis, we can see how the Chicanas' self-fashioning "always involves some experience of threat" or "some loss of self." Castillo's protagonist, Teresa, speaks of such a loss when she reflects on her relationship to Mexico in letter number nineteen: "Mexico. Melancholy, profoundly right and wrong, it embraces as it strangulates. Destiny is not a metaphysical confrontation with one's self rather, society has knit its pattern so tight that a confrontation with it is inevitable"

(59). Teresa's words reveal that she understands that her destiny as a woman is not determined through a confrontation with herself, but rather through a confrontation with a society that holds the very real threat of restricting, silencing, and marginalizing women. In letter number thirteen, Teresa refers to another threat, while at the same time revealing her attitudes about Anglo women. She writes to Alicia:

> why i hated white women and sometimes didn't like you:
> Society had made them above all possessions
> the most desired. And they believed it.
> My husband admitted feeling inferior to them. . . .
> i hated
> white women who took black pimps
> everyone knows savages have bestial members
> i hated
> white women who preferred Latins and Mediterraneans because
> of the fusion of hot and cold blood running through the very core
> of their erections and nineteenth-century romanticism that makes
> going to bed with them much more challenging than with WASP
> men who are only good for making money and marrying. (43)

Teresa's thoughts communicate how she, as an individual, perceives white women as a threat. But when we consider this letter as a symbolic representation of cultural attitudes, it tells us something basic about the Chicana woman's experience. Yet her reference to her husband's admission of feeling inferior to them illustrates how the threat created by white women moves beyond gender distinctions. With this letter Castillo has unmasked one of the ideological limitations of Anglo feminist theory, a feminism with little concern for issues of race, class, or culture. It becomes apparent in Teresa's letter that the subordination and control of "women of color" is further complicated when white women are elevated to the status of "most desirable": as a backlash to this white privilege, women of color, regardless of their gender, are relegated to a subordinate position with respect to white women, simply because the standards for desirability are based on light skin beauty. And once we consider the structured absences in feminist theory, Chicana autonomy becomes a critical issue that cannot be overlooked.

For Greenblatt autonomy, though important, does not represent the central issue. What is crucial here is the power one has to impose a shape upon oneself, a power to control one's identity. He, like Geertz and, for that matter, many Chicano writers, argues that the interplay between

external forces is what determines self-fashioning. His discussion reinforces the need to understand the external forces that will ultimately affect
the Chicana's self-fashioning process. If we are to carry this discussion
further, then we must consider these "external forces" and the implications
involved whenever Chicanas attempt to define themselves in cultural and
feminist terms. The issues I wish to address, therefore, focus specifically on
how *The Mixquiahuala Letters* negotiates and mediates between the external
forces which encompass time and space as well as the past and future.

Chicana critic Norma Alarcón conceives of Chicana poets as "umpires"
mediating between a past Chicano patriarchal interpretation of culture,
which holds the potential for locking them into "crippling traditional stereotypes," and a future that can be equally limiting within an "Anglo-American
feminist promise" (1985). In *The Mixquiahuala Letters*, Ana Castillo has
moved beyond her role as poet "umpire" into the position of modern (experimental) ethnographer, as she has produced a personal narrative which mediates between objective and subjective narratives, thereby overcoming what
James Clifford has identified as anthropology's "impossible attempt to fuse
objective and subjective practices" (1986, 109). The significance of Clifford's
point becomes clearer when we consider Eric Wolf's thoughts on fieldwork
in *Europe and the People Without History* (1982):

> Fieldwork—direct communication with people and participant
> observation of their on-going activities . . . became a hallmark of
> anthropological method. Fieldwork has proved enormously
> fruitful in laying bare and correcting false assumptions and erro-
> neous descriptions. It has also revealed hitherto unsuspected
> connections among sets of social activities and cultural forms. Yet
> the very success of the method lulled its users into a false confi-
> dence. It became easy for them to convert merely heuristic
> considerations of method into theoretical postulates about
> society and culture. (13)

Indeed, if we consider *The Mixquiahuala Letters* as a personal narrative that
mediates between objective and subjective practices, we can envision—as I
have argued elsewhere (1988)—examining the social sciences and literature
together to set the stage for a more inclusive type of theorizing. In other
words, once we make one minor adjustment and move toward an interdis-
ciplinary approach, anthropology's impossibilities appear to become possibilities. Likewise, when we consider Castillo's text as a mediation between
objective and subjective practices, the imaginary, fictive content of this

novel seems to transcend its form. Once we are able to make this leap in consciousness, opening rather than closing our respective discourses, the limitations created by our fragmented visions quickly begin to dissipate.

Because Castillo's epistolary novel consists of letters that systematically observe, record and describe experiences that take place in the daily life of Mexican and American culture—a process we have previously described as the fieldwork method—we can read it as a parody of modern ethnographic and travel writing. It is interesting to note that Castillo's process of textual production is somewhat suggestive of Linda Hutcheon's *A Theory of Parody* (1985). Drawing from the double etymology of the prefix *para* she concludes: "on a pragmatic level parody was not limited to producing a ridiculous effect [para as 'counter' or against], but that the equally strong suggestion of complicity and accord [para as 'beside'] allowed for an opening up of the range of parody. This distinction between prefix meaning, has been used to argue for the existence of both comic and serious types of parody" (53).

As a parody of modem ethnography, Castillo's text becomes an enterprise that provides the voices and experiences involved in growing up Chicana, revealing in Wolf's words "unsuspected connections among sets of social activities and cultural forms." Like an ethnographer, Castillo uses the voice of her informant, Teresa, to focus on what is at risk when a Chicana attempts to fashion an identity in response to two opposing cultures. In letter number four, Teresa foregrounds the Catholic church's enormous influence on young women as the institution molds individual Mexican/Chicana identity into a cultural model that promotes women's passivity and guilt. She writes:

Alicia,
Do you know the *smell* of a church? Not a storefront, praise the Lord, hallelujah church, or a modest frame building with a simple steeple projecting to the all heavens, but a CATHEDRAL, with doors the height of two very tall men and so heavy that when you pull one open to enter you feel as small as you are destined.
You were never led by the hand as a little girl by a godmother, or tugged by the ear by a nun whose dogmatic instruction initiated you into humility which is quite different from baptism when you were anointed with water as a squirming baby in the event that you should die and never see God face-to-face because you had not been cleansed of the sin of your parents' copulation.
It smells of incense, hot oils, the wax of constant burning candles, melting at a vigilant pace, the plaster of an army of saints

watching with fixed glass eyes, revered in exchange for being mediators and delivering your feeble prayers. It smells of flowers and palms that precede Easter. It smells of death. The last time i went to CHURCH, genuflecting my way to the confessional, i was eighteen years old.

i was a virgin, technically speaking, a decent girl, having been conditioned to put my self-respect before curiosity. This did not satisfy the priest, or should i say, stimulate his stagnant duty in that dark closet of anonymity and appointed judgement.

He began to probe. When that got him no titillating results, he suggested, or more precisely, led an interrogation founded on gestapo technique. When i didn't waiver under the torment, although feeling my knees raw, air spare, he accused outright: *"Are you going to tell me you haven't wanted to be with a man? You must have let one do more than. . . than what?*

i ran out of the booth in tears and in a rage, left the CHURCH without waiting to hear my penance for absolution of my unforgivable sins. (24–25)

Her emotional narrative describes religious rituals that have limited the development of a feminist political consciousness. Her thoughts on religion also resonate with the powerful words of Chicana feminist and social activist Cherrie Moraga:

> Women of color have always known, although we have not always wanted to look at it, that our sexuality is not merely a physical response or drive, but holds a crucial relationship to our entire spiritual capacity. Patriarchal religions—whether brought to us by the colonizer's cross and gun or emerging from our own people— have always known this. Why else would the female body be so associated with sin and disobedience? Simply put, if the spirit and sex have been linked in our oppression, then they must also be linked in the strategy toward our liberation. (1983, 132)

Castillo uses the epistolary form as a vehicle, enabling her to move freely from one issue to another, from one country to another as she describes the relationship between the sexes. But more importantly, it is the epistolary form which gives her the flexibility to describe the differences between the way women are viewed in the United States and Mexico. In an entry devoted to recollections about her experiences in Veracruz, Teresa recalls a conversation she had with Ponce, a Mexican engineer:

> He began, "I think you are a 'liberal woman.' Am I correct?"
> His expression meant to persuade me that it didn't matter what
> I replied. In the end he would win. He would systematically
> strip away all my pretexts, reservations, and defenses, and end
> up in bed with me.
>
> In that country, the term "liberated woman" meant some-
> thing other than what we had strived for back in the United
> States. In this case it simply meant a woman who would sleep
> nondiscriminately with any man who came along. I inhaled
> deeply from the strong cigarette he had given me and released
> the smoke in the direction of his face which diminished the
> sarcastic expression. (73)

In postmodernist fashion Castillo provides her readers with a pastiche
of what has been a nearly invisible section of Chicano culture. Her fragmented approach is a powerful tool that enables her to negotiate and mediate
as she probes the female psyche. Her style reflects the influence and power
of many of Latin America's greatest writers. And because of this it comes as
no surprise that she dedicates her novel "in memory of the master of the
game, Julio Cortázar" (Introduction, n. p.).

Following Cortázar, Castillo is also a mistress of play, an author who
seems to intuitively understand the issues at stake when providing a puzzle-
like narrative. The text comes to life as a series of games revolving around
courtship, wit, and women. In the opening letter to the reader, Castillo play-
fully suggests three proposed readings of her novel: "It is the author's duty to
alert the reader that this is not a book to be read in the usual sequence. All
letters are numbered to aid in following any one of the author's proposed
options: For the Conformist; For the Cynic; For the Quixotic" ("Dear
Reader," n. p.). She closes by including a message "For the reader committed
to nothing but short fiction, all the letters read as separate entities. Good
luck whichever journey you choose!" Castillo forces her readers to select a
sequence; the interpretation of an itinerary through her text is in fact left
open to them. By taking this step she has managed to release her readers
from what could be referred to as her personal biases or subjective interpretations. Castillo's narrative strategy aimed at releasing her readers from a
prescribed reading, encourages them to become active participants in her
text. Umberto Eco's concept of the "open work" is reminiscent of Castillo's
process of textual production.

[i] "open works," insofar as they are in movement, are characterized by the invitation to make the work together with the author
and [ii] on a wider level [as a subgenus in the species "work in
movement"] there exist works, which though organically
completed, are "open" to a continuous generation of internal
relations which the addressee must uncover and select in his act
of perceiving the totality of incoming stimuli. [iii] Every work
of art, even though it is produced by following an explicit
poetics of necessity, is effectively open to a virtually unlimited
range of possible readings, each of which causes the work to
acquire a new vitality in terms of one particular taste, or
perspective, or personal performance. (1979, 63)

Castillo's use of the "open work" structure allows her to become an active
participant in her own novel. She is in this way not only mediating between
"personal narrative" and "objective description," but also between her role as
author and her role as reader. It is through this mediation process, as an aside
to the reader, that she raises questions regarding the issue of authority and
interpretation, an issue which has become problematic in the disciplines of
history and anthropology. We could very easily think of Castillo's text as
meta-ethnography.

    Thus Castillo's novel functions as a linguistic artifact that does more to
inform readers about the Chicana's struggle for self-definition than many of
the contemporary theoretical efforts, which because of their failure to consider
race, ethnicity, and class as variables have produced ineffective, one-dimen-
sional paradigms. In *The Mixquiahuala Letters* Castillo attempts to retaliate
against social injustice and inequality by documenting what is at risk when the
Chicana defies authority in order to break away from the stagnant traditions
and ideals that smother and suppress female desire. She explores the female
psyche—the unspeakable, unveiling secrets and taboos in language that are
profound and whimsical, perverse and waggish. Ultimately, the text can be read
as a revolt against order, which eloquently illustrates why it is essential for
feminists to expose and thereby destroy the power of any outside or foreign
"authority" by creating a space for themselves. The novel reveals how subjective experiences provide relevant strands of information, which are essential to
creating a space that is fundamental to the Chicana's self-definition process. In
this way Castillo's epistolary novel (like mainstream feminist theory) is effective in simultaneously marking out women as special selves and claiming, in
Marilyn Strathern's words, "that knowledge of the self as such can come only
from acknowledging this special nature" (1984, 22).

MONIKA KAUP

Crossing Borders: An Aesthetic Practice in Writings by Gloria Anzaldúa

"I am a border woman. I grew up between two cultures, the Mexican (with a heavy Indian influence) and the Anglo (as a member of a colonized people in our own territory)." This is how Gloria Anzaldúa, a Chicana lesbian-feminist poet and critic, introduces herself to her readers in the preface to her book *Borderlands/La Frontera: The New Mestiza*. Yet even before she presents herself, in a book that is nourished by the autobiographical experience of "life on the borders," she introduces the border region after which the book has been named:

> The actual physical borderland that I'm dealing with in this book is the Texas-U.S. Southwest/Mexican border. The psychological borderlands, the sexual borderlands and the spiritual borderlands are not particular to the Southwest. In fact, the Borderlands are physically present wherever two or more cultures edge each other, where people of different races occupy the same territory, where under, lower, middle, and upper classes touch, where the space between two individuals shrinks with intimacy. (*Borderlands*, Preface)

Borderlands is a book about the culture of the Chicana-*mestiza*, straddling one national border and multiple racial and sexual borders. In this sense it is a paradigmatic text that recreates the world of "women of color"

From *Cultural Difference & the Literary Text: Pluralism & the Limits of Authenticity in North American Literatures.* © 1996 by the University of Iowa Press.

in writing while avoiding a totalizing identity. I would like to situate *Borderlands* in the context of two anthologies of writings by women of color to which Anzaldúa has significantly contributed and whose publication dates at the beginning of the 1980s and the 1990s provide a neat general frame around Anzaldúa's 1987 Chicana case study. It is a frame that I propose to read as a history of imagined identities with a beginning, then subsequent developments in whose course Anzaldúa invents a new style of imagined communities, a border-crossing imagination that then shapes the form of the later anthology. This anthology, edited by herself alone, is entitled *Making Face, Making Soul/Haciendo Caras: Creative and Critical Perspectives by Women of Color.* The earlier anthology I am referring to is the well-known *This Bridge Called My Back: Writings by Radical Women of Color,* which Anzaldúa coedited with Cherríe Moraga. Even though *This Bridge,* as the title implies, focuses on the notion of crossing borderlines as essential to the writing of women from nonwhite ethnic groups and as the main strategy for an overarching community of "women of color," my argument is that Anzaldúa carries this much further. She places borderlands, border-crossing, and in-between languages and states of mind center stage and makes crossbreed thinking a definite stylistic paradigm for imagining color in the multicultural plural.

The style in which communities are imagined, as Benedict Anderson puts it, changes with culture (6). This is not a question of true or false: all communities larger than villages of face-to-face contact are imagined or invented. The "deep, horizontal comradeship" (Anderson 16) of religion or nation and, if we extend Anderson's argument, race, ethnicity, and class has been created through acts of political imagination on the part of its members. The world of a modern culture is a world of plurals, constituted by anonymous but representative detail. Social space coheres through its typical elements; difference easily counts as deviation and thus as nonessential to the definition of communal identity.

Before we ever heard of the category "women of color," white feminists invented a much larger common denominator, the generic notion of "women"—across nationality, class, race, and time. In both cases, texts as diverse as theory, autobiography, poetry, fiction, letters, ethnology, and historiography contributed to drawing the borders of the cultural territory or plural to which it refers. About a decade after the beginning of the women's movement women of color protested against the racism of white women. Activities sometimes called "saming" and "othering," exposed by women in male-authored writing, were also exposed in white feminist texts. Not only at the root of sexism, but also of racism, the logic of the universal includes some individuals, events, and real or symbolic objects in the plural "us" and excludes other individuals, events, and objects in the plural "them/not us." The space between is the border.

Although the community of women of color, according to this logic, uses the attribute of color to exclude whites, making skin color the watershed to divide "us" from "not us," my point is that it is the slipperiness of the concept of color that has caused this community to be "written" in a style that resists the common meaning of cultural borderlines. Color is a key metaphor that unites disparate lifeworlds and histories that even today, despite television, do not intersect. Brown, yellow, or black have no natural relation—as the category of color might suggest—because white racism is the common problem that they share. Racism is not a substantive bond, it is a negative force directed from white culture against every marginal minority by itself. If the struggle against racism is to be unified, not separatist, its participants must first create that bond. Furthermore, women writers of color who identify as more than black, Chicana, Native American, or Asian must first fill the space outlined by the concept "of color." There are certain culture-specific conditions of style for imagining this community: Organic unity through blood and self-sameness are unfit models, but the slippery unity of colors in the plural suggests frames with permeable borders.

In *Borderlands* Anzaldúa wrests the voice and the experience of the Chicana-mestiza from her previous silence and invisibility. This half-theoretical, half-poetic study of her own culture gives voice to and is shaped by the conflicts resulting from life on the borders between cultures. The struggle for a mestiza voice culminates in the final chapter of the first, theoretical part, where Anzaldúa describes how the identity of the mestiza crosses over "towards a new consciousness."

The new *mestiza* copes by developing a tolerance for contradictions, a tolerance for ambiguity. She learns to be an Indian in Mexican culture, to be Mexican from an Anglo point of view. She learns to juggle cultures. She has a plural personality, she operates in a pluralistic mode. . . .

As a *mestiza* I have no country, my homeland cast me out. . . . (As a lesbian I have no race, my own people disclaim me; but I am all races because there is the queer of me in all races.) I am cultureless because, as a feminist, I challenge the collective cultural/religious male-derived beliefs of Indo-Hispanics and Anglos. (79-80)

Anzaldúa has cast the concrete experience of the mestiza lesbian at the intersection of cultures, the experience of her own life, in a model sufficiently abstract and fluent in the language of Western academia to count as acceptable theory, yet she has not canceled the viewpoint of the experiencing self which is here signaled, for example, by sensuous detail. Anzaldúa's model of collective "identity formation" is one from which white feminists can learn about a "colored" style of negotiating the polarities of "identity" and "difference" that have haunted their own theories. While white feminists have resorted to combining an increasing number of concepts from Freudian psychoanalysis, French deconstruction, semiotics, or British socialist thought and have crossed the boundaries of European and white American knowledge, they have not been able to break out of their white frame of reference. Adding color to the psychoanalytic concept of the split self, for example, does not work. By contrast, locating one's identity on the borderline between cultures, crossing the line between ethnic and academic language, changes the meaning of the border from "division" to "bridge," a stage for a new generation of "multicultural" women writers. As Anzaldúa writes, defining the identity of the mestiza-Chicana: "This is my home/this thin edge of/barbwire" (3).

The concepts of the reassuring opposition of the self to its other and its upsetting counterpart, "The other in me. I am an other," are also elements of Western thought. However, the latter subject condition, subversive of a coherent and centered self, has been a condition of the existence of minorities in a majority culture. As Sneja Gunew puts it, "minorities seem always to have been within the condition of post-modernism" (22). This is especially true for ethnic minorities like the Chicanos, Mexican Americans in the United States, who set a paradigm for a hybrid culture. Racially mixed, of both Indian and Hispanic European ancestry, their mestizo race came into existence with the first union of a European father and an Indian mother in the Spanish conquerer Cortés and his Indian translator and mistress La Malinche. A majority in their home country, Mexico, Mexicans of northern Mexico became U.S. citizens and a minority in the United States with the annexation of the territory that is now the American Southwest in the Treaty of Guadalupe Hidalgo in 1848.

The most ancient of cultural layers in the Southwest is Aztlán, the mythic homeland of the Aztecs before their southern migration to the valley of Mexico hundreds of years before Cortés. The Indian has returned north as the mestizo Mexican. In several waves of migration they came as farmworkers and railroad builders, on postwar U.S. government programs and as refugees from the Mexican revolution, legally and illegally. Mexicans have named Chicanos *pochos*, traitors disloyal to their home country (*pocho* means bleached of their color); Americans have discriminated against them as Mexicans. Among Chicanos, as they renamed themselves in their civil rights movement in the 1960s, with reference to their Indian heritage, there is group pressure not to be too *agringado*, assimilated to the white Anglo culture. Despite some migration into the big cities of the Northeast, the geographical homeland of the Chicanos still is the so-called American *border-lands*, including California, Arizona, New Mexico, the southern part of Colorado, and Texas, especially southern Texas. Chicano culture is still geographically located alongside what they perceive as an artificial national border dividing an old Hispanic-Indian space. Academic publications in English about the area use the term *borderlands* to refer to a "zone of influ-ence" stretching inland into Mexico and the United States on both sides of the thin national borderline. Border crossers both in terms of blood and home, Chicanos are also experts in survival between a Third World and a First World culture.

Chicano history is the subject of the introductory chapter in *Borderlands*. As subjects change, so do narrative voices. Although written by a single author, *Borderlands* is a story told by many voices and reflecting diverse centers of consciousness—both poetic and academic—and mythic and scientific sources of knowledge. *Borderlands* represents its subject, the nonteleological history and marginal position of Chicano culture and the Chicana's place in it, in a nonlinear and heterogeneous narrative. The book is bilingual, written in English interspersed with Spanish phrases that the English reader will understand from the context. Anzaldúa explains: "The switching of 'codes' in this book from English to Castillian Spanish to the North Mexican dialect to Tex-Mex to a sprinkling of Nahuatl to a mixture of all these, reflects my language, a new language—the language of the Borderlands. There, at the juncture of cultures, languages cross-pollinate and are revitalized; they die and are born" (Preface). *Borderlands* is also in two parts, the first consisting of cultural description, the second poetry, the first concerned with fact, the second with fiction.

In the first part, entitled *"Atravesando Fronteras/*Crossing Borders," Anzaldúa employs the discourse of disciplines such as historiography, auto-biography, ethnography, mythography, and social linguistics and the different language of utopian vision to explore the diverse aspects of her cultural heritage. In order to reverse the hierarchy between Western and native sources of knowledge, the general pattern of part one is to juxtapose academic information on a subject with either autobiographical or mythic native knowledge on the same subject. Anzaldúa then uses the meaning of linear sequence—"narrative time" in academic texts—which commonly signifies an advance in learning, to raise the status of native Chicano sources. For example, chapter 3 introduces Mexican and Aztec deities in the voice of the Western ethnographer. Writing on a level of academic reflection that one usually expects in anthropological studies, she explains the significance of Coatlalopeuh, the serpent:

> She is the central deity connecting us to our Indian ancestry. *Coatlalopeuh* is descended from, or is an aspect of, earlier Mesoamerican fertility and Earth goddesses. . . . The male-domi-nated Azteca-Mexica culture drove the powerful female deities underground by giving them monstrous attributes and by substi-tuting male deities in their place. . . . *Tonantsi*—split from her dark guises, *Coatlicue, Tlazolteotl,* and *Cihuacoatl*—became the good mother. (27)

In the following chapter, entitled "The *Coatlicue* State," the voice of the Indian visionary and mystic takes over to make the most profound meaning out of the subject, Coatlicue: "I've always been aware that there is a greater power than the conscious I. That power is my inner self, the entity that is the sum total of all my reincarnations, the godwoman in me . . . *Coatlicue-Cihnacoatl-Tlazolteotl-Tonantzin-Coatlalopeuh-Guadalupe*—they are one" (50).

The general pattern of the seven chapters of part one is to move from a rational voice to a voice both visionary and theoretical, from a recovery of the buried past and the Indian, female, and lesbian heritage to a look into the future. Anzaldúa thus avoids committing herself to one single authoritative stance of academic objectivity in narrating her own culture, a task previously performed in this manner mainly by white ethnologists. Herself a member of the culture she writes about, Anzaldúa dons the masks of diverse white acad-emic narrators and nonacademic Chicano storytellers in the attempt to represent the crossbreed character of her culture. Her narrative strategy is to combine and entangle subject and object positions in cultural narration, a style that does away with closed-off, bordered positions of neutral knowers and of cultural actors. In terms of the cultural field described, this mirrors the mixed-breed version of authentic Chicano experience—not wholeness and well-defined identity but divided loyalties: "The struggle is inner: Chicano, *indio*, American Indian, *mojado* [wetback], mexicano, immigrant Latino, Anglo in power . . . our psyches resemble the bordertowns and are populated by the same people" (87). Anzaldúa's book about the *mestiza*, mixed-race product of colonizer and colonized, translates the racial process of what the Mexicans call *mestizaje*, the mixing of colored with white blood, into a *mestizaje* text. It is in this sense that the attribute "of color" defines the form of her text. Blood is employed as a leading metaphor but to subversive ends. The notions of color and of the cultural space outlined by Anzaldúa are shape shifters, properties of a community imagined to go through states of emergence and change. The vision outlined in the final chapter, entitled "The Mestiza Way," is an injunction for the Chicana to "deconstruct, construct" her heritage and act as a mediator, a translator "going between" its conflicting aspects. (82)

The path for this open form is prepared in chapter 1, entitled "The Homeland, Aztlán" and told in the voice of the historiographer. Its subject is the border dividing Mexico from the United States:

> The U.S.-Mexican border *es una herida abierta* where the Third World grates against the first and bleeds. And before a scab forms it hemorrhages again, the lifeblood of two worlds merging to form a third country—a border culture. Borders are set up to define the places that are safe and unsafe, to distinguish *us* from *them*. A border is a dividing line, a narrow strip along a steep edge. A borderland is a vague and undetermined place created by the emotional residue of an unnatural boundary. It is in a constant state of transition. The prohibited and forbidden are its inhabitants. (3)

In these first sentences of the book (if we leave aside an introductory poem), we learn about two types of border: a natural and acceptable type of border and an unnatural boundary, an artificial human construct needing to be broken down. The Rio Grande, whose course marks half of the present U.S.-Mexican border, is an example of a natural border turned artificial: Today the Rio Grande has become national boundary first and river second. The racial memory of a long past of migrations dating back to the original southern migration of the Aztecs to what is today Mexico City reopens the thin barbed wire line. The right to migrate to Atzlán, "homeland without boundaries," overrules the law of modern bordered nation-states. As a result, the borderline expands into a wider space of a bridge culture, a stage for the "new mestiza."

In keeping with the principle of internalizing cultural conflict within the mestiza self, in its composite parts or masks/faces, the body acquires a prominent place in Anzaldúa's aesthetics of the border. Especially in part two, the poetry, but also in her description of the process of writing, Anzaldúa performs an aesthetics of the grotesque, playing with the boundaries of the body, changing its shape. According to Bakhtin, in the art of the grotesque the borders between the body and the world and between individual bodies take forms different from those represented in classical art: In contrast to the finished, bordered, individualized body, the grotesque body is a pre- or postindividual body, a body in the process of becoming (Rabelais 310–317). To Anzaldúa, writing is an endless process of inflicting pain on the body and relieving it, penetrating the borders of her body and thus metaphorically changing the shape of her self:

> Living in a state of psychic unrest, in a Borderland, is what makes poets write and artists create. It is like a cactus needle embedded in the flesh. It worries itself deeper and deeper, and I keep aggravating it by poking at it. . . . the fingers pressing, making the pain worse before it can get better. . . . That's what writing is for me, an endless cycle of making it worse, making it better, but always making meaning out of the experience. . . . It feels like I'm creating my own face, my own heart—a Nahuatl concept. My soul makes itself through the creative act. It is constantly remaking and giving birth to itself through my body. (*Borderlands* 73)

Her play with corporeal borders and individual identity is at its most radical in the poems in part two. In the poems "Poets have strange eating habits" and "The Cannibal's *Canción*," the union of lovers metamorphoses into cannibalism: "Her body caves into itself/through the hole/my mouth" (140). Wounds inflicted are the places of healing: "Wounding is a deeper healing" (140). The speaker is being consumed by the universe and vice versa: "I burrow deep into myself/pull the emptiness in" (141); "dark windowless no moon glides/across the nightsky/the maw opens wide I slip inside" (141). "Letting Go," a poem that deals with acts of ritual disemboweling that cleanse or liberate the body from containing other parts of creation —small animals, corn—winds up in a scene of inverted evolution, where the female speaker regresses into a primitive creature:

> And soon, again, you return
> to your element and
> like a fish in the air
> you come to the open
> only between breathings.
> But already gills
> grow on your breasts. (165–166)

The aesthetics of permeable borders and the metamorphosis of the mestiza self, as I pointed out in the beginning, also shapes Anzaldúa's editorial design of her anthology *Making Face, Making Soul/Haciendo Caras*. The Nahuatl concept of creating one's own face and heart has found its way into the title and is expanded into Anzaldúa's editorial story of how women of color construct individual and communal identity. In her introduction Anzaldúa juxtaposes the many faces and masks women of color wear as a result of their position at the intersection of cultures with a new term, *interface*, which refers to the seams stitched to hold those conflicting identity fragments together:

> "Face" is the surface of the body that is most noticeably inscribed by social structures, marked with instructions on how to be *mujer*, *macho*, working class, Chicana. As mestizas—biologically and/or culturally mixed—we have different surfaces of each aspect of identity. . . . We are "written" all over, or should I say, carved and tattooed with the sharp needles of experience. . . . In sewing terms, "interfacing" means sewing a piece of material between two pieces of fabric to provide support and stability. . . . Between the masks we've internalized, one on top of another, are our interfaces. The masks are already steeped with self-hatred and other internalized oppressions. . . . In this anthology and in our daily lives, we women of color strip off the *máscaras* others have imposed on us. . . . We rip out the stitches, expose the multilayered "inner faces.". . . We begin to acquire the agency of making our own *caras*. You are the shaper of your flesh as well as of your soul. (*Making Face* xv-xvi)

> We transform the . . . apertures, . . . *abismos* that we are forced to speak from. Only then can we make a home out of the cracks. (*Making Face* xxv)

In keeping with this notion of speaking and creating from the borders is her call for "*mestizaje* theories": "Theorists of Color are in the process of trying to formulate 'marginal' theories that are partially outside and partially inside the Western frame of reference, . . . theories that overlap many worlds" (*Making Face* xxvi). "Doing Theory" is the final section of the anthology's seven sections. In the following, I quote section titles at length to recreate the sense of a continuing story of women of color moving toward a more hopeful situation. This forward-looking design contrasts with the static "drawing the balance" approach of earlier anthologies. *Making Face, Making*

Soul begins with two sections on racism—"Still Trembles Our Rage in the Face of Racism" and "Denial and Betrayal"—the common cause to found the basis of unity of people of color. These are followed by a section on hopes and visions—"(De)Colonized Selves: Finding Hope through Horror"—in turn followed by two sections on the emergence from silence into writing— "In Silence, Giving Tongue" and "Political Arts, Subversive Acts." The sixth section discusses how to form alliances with whites and other women of color—"If You Would Be My Ally: In Alliance, In Solidarity." While *Making Face, Making Soul* ends with theory, the earlier anthology *This Bridge Called My Back* ends with a section on visions of a Third World feminist future— "El Mundo Zurdo: The Vision"—the subject of a middle section in *Making Face*. A characteristic of both anthologies that distinguishes them from other anthologies of writings by women of color (like Dexter Fisher's *The Third Woman* or Janice Mirikitani's *Time to Greez!*) is that their sections are arranged thematically, instead of each section being devoted to but one ethnic group. For example, in *The Third Woman* writings by American Indian women are followed by writings by black women, and so forth. Arranged in a sequence, the sections of Anzaldúa's anthologies constitute something like a communal narrative across the different shades of color, a narrative that arches over the disparate voices and pieces of writing. In terms of the concept of editorship, this is reminiscent of the rise of the novel from earlier genres of short narrative: the editors have begun to make a common story out of scattered writings, giving titles to each new chapter in the adventures of the heroines of color. Still, in Anzaldúa's *Making Face* there is a significant change in the style of imagining the plural: Toni Cade Bambara's foreword to *This Bridge* is characterized by the rainbow coalition style of adding up the contributing voices. Additions, however, cannot penetrate and change the integrity of the individual voices. It is not by chance that the title metaphor of the anthology is the bridge connecting what are seen as separate ethnic groups: "Blackfoot amiga Nisei hermana Down Home Up Souf Sistuh sister el Barrio suburbia Korean The Bronx Lakota Menominee Cubana Chinese Puertoriqueña reservation Chicana" (vi). By shifting the site of the struggle between identity and difference from communities to the conflict within the individual, Anzaldúa's model makes significant progress in dissolving boundaries that are, as many of the contributors confirm, the foundation of racism.

Chronology

1874   *Reminiscences of Dorotea Valdez*, recorded by Henry Cerruti.

1878   *Memoirs of Felipa Osuna de Marron*, recorded by Thomas Savage.

1881   *Aurora y Gervasio*, unpublished novel by Manuel Salazar.

1892   *Noches tenebrosas en el Condado de San Miguel / Spooky Nights in San Miguel County*, serialized narrative by Miguel C. De Baca.

1893   *Hijo de la Tempestad / Son of the Storm* and *Tras las Tormenta la Calma / After the Storm the Calm*, novellas by Eusebio Chacón.

1896   *Vicente Silva y sus cuarenta Bandidos / Vicente Silva and His Forty Bandits*, narrative by Miguel C. De Baca.

1916   *Las Primicias / First Fruits*, poems by Vicente Bernal.

1924   *Obras de Felipe Maximiliano Chacón, "El Cantor Neomexicano:" Poesía y prosa / The Works of Felipe Maximiliano Chacón, "The New Mexican Singer: Poetry and Prose*, by Felipe Maximiliano Chacón.

1935   *My Life on the Frontier, 1864-1882*, by Miguel Antonio Otero.

1940   *New Mexico Triptych*, short stories by Fray Angelico Chavez.

1941   *Shadows of the Past*, folklore narrative by Cleofas Martínez-Jaramillo.

1945   *Eleven Lady-Lyrics and Other Poems*, by Fray Angelico Chavez.

1948   *The Single Rose: Poems of Divine Love*, by Fray Angelico Chavez.

1954   *We Fed Them Cactus*, novel by Fabiola Cabeza de Baca.

1955   *Romance of a Little Village Girl*, autobiography by Cleofas Martínez-Jaramillo.

1956   *Spiks*, short stories by Pedro Juan Soto.

1957   *From an Altar Screen: Tales from New Mexico*, short stories by Fray Angelico Chavez.

1958   *With a Pistol in His Hand: A Border Ballad and Its Hero*, by Américo Paredes.

1959   *Pocho*, novel by José Antonio Villarreal.
        Usmail, novel by Pedro Juan Soto.
        The Virgin of Port Lligat, poems by Fray Angelico Chavez.

1962   *Autobiography of Jose Clemente Orozco*, translated by Robert C. Stephenson.

1969   *The Plum Plum Pickers*, novel by Raymond Barrio.

1970   *Chicano*, novel by Richard Vásquez.

1971   *"Y no se lo tragó la tierra"/ "And the Earth Did Not Part,"* novel by Tomás Rivera.
        Barrio Boy, autobiography by Ernesto Galarza.

1972   *Bless Me, Ultima*, novel by Rudolfo A. Anaya.
        The Autobiography of Brown Buffalo, novel by Oscar Zeta Acosta.
        Schwammenauel Dam, novel by Arturo Garcia.

1973   *Estampas Del Valle*, novel by Rolando Hinojosa.
         Hot Land, Cold Season, novel by Pedro Juan Soto.
         The Revolt of the Cockroach People, novel by Oscar Zeta Acosta.
         Sabor a mi, poems by Cecilia Vicuna.
         Always and Other Poems, by Tomás Rivera.

1974   *Two Ranges*, novel by Roberto C. Medina.

1975   *The Road To Tamazunchale*, novel by Ron Arias.
         Puppet: A Chicano Novella, by Margarita Cota-Cardenas.
         Rain of Scorpions and Other Writings, by Estela Portillo
         Trambley.

1976   *Nambé—Year One*, autobiographical novel by Orlando Romero.
         El Diablo en Texas, novel by Aristeo Brito.
         Below the Summit, novel by Joseph Torres Metzgar.
         The Castle, novel by Ron Arias.

1977   *Memories of the Alhambra* and *Inheritance of Strangers*, novels by
         Nash Candelaria.
         Poems: Third Chicano Literary Prize and *Bloodroot*, poems by
         Alma Luz Villanueva.

1978   *Mother, May I?* poems by Alma Luz Villanueva.

1979   *Tortuga*, novel by Rudolfo A. Anaya.

1981   *Emplumada*, poems by Lorna Dee Cervantes.

1982   *Hunger of Memory*, novel by Richard Rodriquez.
         The Legend of La Llorona: A Short Novel, by Rudolfo A. Anaya.
         Not By the Sword, novel by Nash Candelaria.

1983   *Our House in the Last World*, novel by Oscar Hijuelos.
         Precario / Precarious, poems by Cecilia Vicuna.

1984   *Clemente Chacon: A Novel* by José Antonio Villarreal.
         The Iguana Killer: Twelve Stories of the Heart, by Alberto Rios.
         The Rain God: A Desert Tale, novel by Arturo Islas.
         The Iguana Killer, short stories by Alberto Alvaro Rios.

1985   *The Migrant Earth*, novel by Tomás Rivera.
        Inheritance of Strangers, novel by Nash Candelaria.
        The House on Mango Street, novel by Sandra Cisneros.
        Partners In Crime and *Dear Rafe*, novels by Rolando Hinojosa.
        Life Span, poems by Alma Luz Villanueva.
        The Moths and Other Stories, short stories by Helena Maria
        Viramontes.
        Rituals of Survival: A Woman's Portfolio, short stories by
        Nicholasa Mohr.

1986   *Trini*, novel by Estela Portillo Trambley.
        A Chicano in China, travel journal by Rudolfo A. Anaya.
        The Last of the Menu Girls, novel by Denise Chavez.
        The Mixquiahuala Letters, novel by Ana Castillo.
        Giving Up the Ghost: Teatro in Two Acts, by Cherrie Moraga.

1987   *Home Again*, novel by Jose Yglesias.

1988   *The Ultraviolet Sky*, novel by Alma Luz Villanueva.
        Tortuga, novel by Rudolfo A. Anaya.
        The Harvest: Short Stories, by Tomás Rivera.
        The Day the Cisco Kid Shot John Wayne, novel by Nash Candelaria.
        The Brick People and *Death of an Anglo*, novels by Alejandro
        Morales.

1989   *The Mambo Kings Play Songs of Love*, novel by Oscar Hijuelos.
        The Wedding, novel by Mary Helen Ponce.
        The Line of the Sun, novel by Judith Ortiz Cofer.
        Latin Jazz, novel by Virgil Suarez.
        Five Against the Sea: A True Story of Courage and Survival, biog-
        raphy by Ron Arias.

1990   *The Mambo Kings Play Songs of Love* wins 1990 Pulitzer Prize.
        Sapagonia: An Anti-Romance in 3/8 Meter, novel by Ana Castillo.
        La Wik'una, poems by Cecilia Vicuna.
        Migrant Souls, novel by Arturo Islas.
        The Searchers: Collected Poetry, by Tomás Rivera.
        A Summer Life, reminiscences by Gary Soto.
        Fire and Rain, novel by Oswald Rivera.
        Diablo en Texas / The Devil in Texas, novel by Aristeo Brito.

1991   *From the Cables of Genocide: Poems of Love and Hunger,* by
Lorna Dee Cervantes.
The Rag Doll Plagues, novel by Alejandro Morales.
The Cutter, novel by Virgil Suarez.
The Doorman, novel by Reinaldo Arenas.
Leonor Park, novel by Nash Candelaria.

1992   *How the Garcia Girls Lost Their Accents,* novel by Julia Alvarez.
Albuquerque, novel by Rudolfo A. Anaya.
Unraveling Words and the Weaving of Water, poems by Cecilia
Vicuna.
Mrs. Vargas and the Dead Naturalist, short stories by Kathleen
Alcala.
Dreaming In Cuban, novel by Christina Garcia.
The Hidden Law, novel by Michael Nava.
The Boy Without a Flag: Tales of the South Bronx, short stories by
Abraham Rodriguez, Jr.

1993   *Remembering to Say Mouth or Face,* short stories by Omar S.
Castaneda, wins 1993 Nilon Award for Excellence in Minority
Fiction.
Hoyt Street: An Autobiography, by Mary Helen Ponce.

1994   *Loose Woman,* poems by Sandra Cisneros.
Releasing Serpents, poems by Bernice Zamora.
Weeping Woman / La Llorona and Other Stories, short stories by
Alma Luz Villanueva.
So Far From God, novel by Ana Castillo.

1995   *My Father Was a Toltec and Selected Poems,* by Ana Castillo.

1996   *El Milagro and Other Stories,* by Patricia Preciado Martin.
Loverboys: Stories, by Ana Castillo.

Contributors

HAROLD BLOOM is Sterling Professor of Humanities at Yale University and Professor of English at New York University. In 1987–88 he was Charles Eliot Norton Professor of Poetry at Harvard University. He is the author of *The Anxiety of Influence, Poetry and Repression,* and many other volumes of literary criticism. His forthcoming study, *Freud: Transference and Authority,* considers all of Freud's major writings. A MacArthur Prize Fellow, Professor Bloom is general editor of five series of literary criticism published by Chelsea House.

JANE ROGERS is the author of a novel, *Promised Lands.* Her essays on Hispanic fiction have appeared in the *Latin American Literary Review* and the *Hispanic Review.*

ELIUD MARTINEZ is the author of *The Art of Mariano Azuela: Modernism in La Malhora, El Desquite, and La Luciernaga* and *Voice-Haunted Journey.*

NORMAN D. SMITH, critic of Hispanic American fiction, received a Ph.D. from Oklahoma State University.

LUTHER S. LUEDTKE is editor of *Making America: The Society and Culture of the United States, The Study of . . . American Culture: Contemporary Conflicts,* and *Nathaniel Hawthorne and the Romance of the Orient.*

NASARIO GARCIA is the author of *Tata: A Voice From the Rio Puerco* and *Comradres: Hispanic Women of the Rio Puerco Valley.* He is editor of *Abuelitos: Stories of the Rio Puerco Valley.*

EDUARDO SEDA BONILLA is a scholar of Puerto Rican migration to the United States. He is the author of *Social Change and Personality, Requiem por una Cultura* and *Cultural Construction of Reality Among Puerto Ricans*.

VERNON E. LATTIN is editor of *Contemporary Chicano Fiction: A Critical Survey* and coeditor, with Rolando Hinojosa and Gary D. Keller, of *Tomás Rivera, 1935–1984: The Man and His Work*.

MARVIN A. LEWIS is the author of *Introduction to the Chicano Novel, Afro-Argentine Discourse: Another Dimension of the Black Diaspora*, and *Afro-Hispanic Poetry 1940–1980: From Slavery to Negritude in South American Verse*.

MARTA E. SANCHEZ is the author of *Contemporary Chicana Poetry: A Critical Approach to an Emerging Literature*.

EDWARD ELIAS has written frequently on Hispanic prose and poetry. His articles include "Carlos Fuentes and Movie Stars: Intertextuality in a Mexican Drama" and "Entrevista: Ernesto Cardenal."

TOMAS RIVERA was a professor of literature and a Chancellor of the University of California, Riverside. His works include literary criticism, novels, short stories, and poetry.

GENARO M. PADILLA is assistant professor of English at the University of California, Berkeley. He is editor of *The Stories of Fray Angelico Chavez* and completing a book on Chicano autobiography.

ALFONSO RODRIGUEZ, poet and critic, has published articles and essays on Chicano artists and writers, including Manuel Unzueta, Tony Lopez, Estella Portillo, Samuel Ramos, and Tomás Rivera. His poems have appeared in *Confluencia*.

HEINER BUS has published studies on Chicano literature and poetry, and on the works of Washington Irving and Jean Toomer.

ENRIQUE LAMADRID is a professor in the Department of Modern and Classical Languages at the University of New Mexico. His published works include articles on Chicano literature and New Mexican folklore.

ERLINDA GONZALES-BERRY is Chair of the Department of Spanish and Portuguese at the University of New Mexico. She is coeditor of *Las Mujeres Hablan: An Anthology of Nuevo Mexicana Writers*, editor of *Pasó por Aquí: Critical Essays on the New Mexico Literary Tradition*, and author of a novel, *Paletitas de Guayaba*.

ALVINA E. QUINTANA is assistant professor of English and Women's Studies at the University of Delaware. She has published essays in several journals and books of criticism and is the author of *Home Girls: Chicana Literary Voices*.

MONIKA KAUP received a Ph.D. from Ruhr University, Bochum, Germany. She is the author of *Mad Intertextuality: Madness in Twentieth-Century Women's Writing* and is currently preparing for publication *Rewriting North American Borders in Canadian and Mexican American Literature*.

Bibliography

Acosta, Oscar Zeta. *The Autobiography of a Brown Buffalo*. San Francisco: Straight Arrow Books, 1972.

———. *The Revolt of the Cockroach People*. New York: Bantam, 1974.

Acosta-Belen, Edna, editor. *The Puerto Rican Woman: Perspectives on Culture, History and Society*. New York: Praeger, 1986.

Alurista, Alberto. "Cultural Nationalism and Chicano Literature During the Decade of 1965–1975," *MELUS: The Journal of the Society for the Study of the Multi-Ethnic Literature of the United States*, 8:2 (Summer 1981): 22–34.

Anaya, Rudolfo A. "An American Chicano in King Arthur's Court," *Old Southwest, New Southwest: Essays on a Region and its Literature*. Ed. Judy Nolte Lensink. Tucson, Arizona: The Tucson Public Library, 1987.

———. *Bless Me, Ultima*. Berkeley, California: Quinto Sol Publications, 1972.

———. *A Chicano in China*. Albuquerque, New Mexico: University of New Mexico Press, 1986.

———. *Heart of Aztlán*. Albuquerque: University of New Mexico Press, 1988.

———. "Iliana of the Pleasure Dreams," *ZYZZYVA* I:4 (Winter 1985): 50–61.

———. "In Search of Epifano," *Voces/Voices*. Ed. Rudolfo Anaya. Albuquerque: University of New Mexico Press, 1988.

———. *Lord of the Dawn, the Legend of Quetzalcoatl*. Albuquerque: University of New Mexico Press, 1987.

———. *Silence of Llano, Short Stories*. Berkeley: Tonatiuh-Quinto Sol International Publishers, 1982.

———. *The Adventures of Juan Chicaspatas*. Houston: Arte Público Press, 1984.

———. *The Legend of La Llorona: A Short Novel*. Berkeley: Tonatiuh-Quinto Sol International Publishers, 1984.

———. *Tortuga*. Albuquerque: University of New Mexico Press, 1988.

———, editor. *Voces/Voices: An Anthology of Nuevo Mexicano Writers*. Albuquerque: University of New Mexico Press, 1988.

——— and Antonio Marques, editors. *Cuentos Chicanos*. Albuquerque: *New America*, Department of American Studies, University of New Mexico, 1980. Revised edition, University of New Mexico Press, 1984.

————— and Simon Ortiz, editors. *Ceremony of Brotherhood, 1680–1980.* Albuquerque: Academia Publications, 1981.

Anzaldúa, Gloria. *Borderlands/La Frontera: The New Mestiza.* San Francisco: Aunt Lute Books, 1987.

—————, editor. *Making Face, Making Soul/Haciendo Caras: Creative and Critical Perspectives by Women of Color.* San Francisco: Aunt Lute Books, 1990.

—————. *Prietita Has A Friend/Prietita tiene un Amigo.* Children's Book Press, 1991.

Arias, Ron. *Five Against the Sea: A True Story of Courage and Survival.* New York: New American Library, 1989.

—————. *The Road to Tamazunchale.* Reno, Nevada: West Coast Poetry Review, 1975.

—————. *The Castle.* Jamaica, New York: Bilingual Press, 1976.

Barrio, Raymond. *The Plum Plum Pickers.* Guerneville, California: Ventura Press, 1969.

Bauder, Thomas A. "The Triumph of White Magic in Rudolfo Anaya's *Bless Me, Ultima,*" *Mester* 14:1 (Spring 1985): 41–54.

Bernal, Vicente. *Las Primicias.* Dubuque, Iowa: Telegraph-Herald, 1916.

Brito, Aristeo. *Diablo en Texas / The Devil in Texas.* Tempe, Arizona: Bilingual Press, 1990.

Bruce-Novoa, Juan. *Chicano Authors: Inquiry by Interview.* Austin: University of Texas Press, 1980.

—————. *RetroSpace: Collected Essays on Chicano Literature, Theory and History.* Houston: Arte Público Press, 1990.

Calderón, Héctor. "At the Crossroads of History, on the Borders of Change: Chicano Literary Studies Past, Present, and Future," *Left Politics and the Literary Profession,* editors Lennard J. Davis and M. Bella Mirabella. New York: Columbia University Press, `990. 211–35.

—————. "To Read Chicano Narrative: Commentary and Metacommentary," *Mester* 11:2 (1983): 3–14.

————— and Jose David Saldivar, editors. *Criticism in the Borderlands: Studies in Chicano Literature, Culture and Ideology.* Durham, North Carolina: Duke University Press, 1991.

Candelaria, Cordelia. *Chicano Poetry: A Critical Introduction.* Westport, Connecticut: Greenwood Press, 1986.

Candelaria, Nash. *Memories of the Alhambra.* Ypsilanti: Bilingual Press, 1977.

—————. *Not By the Sword.* Ypsilanti, Michigan: Bilingual Press, 1982.

—————. *The Day the Cisco Kid Shot John Wayne.* Tempe, Arizona: Bilingual Press, 1988.

—————. *Inheritance of Strangers.* Ypsilanti: Bilingual Press, 1977.

—————. *Leonor Park.* Tempe: Bilingual Press, 1991.

Castillo, Ana. *Loverboys: Stories.* New York: W.W. Norton, 1996.

—————. *Massacre of the Dreamers: Essays on Xicanisma.* New York: Plume, 1995.

—————. *The Invitation.* USA: A. Castillo, 1979.

—————. *Sapagonia: An Anti-Romance in 3/8 Meter.* New York: Anchor Books, 1990.

—————. *My Father Was a Toltec and Selected Poems.* New York: W.W. Norton, 1995.

—————. *So Far From God.* New York: Plume, 1994.

Chabran, Angie and Rosalinda Fregoso, editors. *Chicana/o Cultural Representations: Reframing Critical Discourses.* Special issue of *Critical Studies* 4:3 (1990).

Chacón, Felipe Maximiliano. *Obras de Felipe Maximiliano Chacón."El Cantor Neomexicano," Poesía y prosa.* Albuquerque: F.M. Chacón, 1924.

Chavez, Fray Angelico. *The Virgin of Port Lligat.* Fresno, California: Academy

Literary Guild, 1959.

———. *Clothed With the Sun*. Santa Fe, New Mexico: Writer's Editions, 1939.

———. *Eleven Lady Lyrics and Other Poems*. Paterson: St. Anthony Guild, 1945.

———. *Selected Poems with an Apologia*. Santa Fe: Press of the Territorian, 1969.

———. *New Mexico Triptych*. Paterson, New Jersey: St. Anthony Guild, 1940.

———. *From an Altar Screen: Tales from New Mexico*. New York: Farrar, Straus & Cudahy, 1957.

———. *The Lady from Toledo*. Fresno: Academy Guild Press, 1960.

Chavez, John R. *The Lost Land: The Chicano Image of the Southwest*. Albuquerque: University of New Mexico Press, 1984.

Cisneros, Sandra. "Cactus Flowers: In Search of Tejana Feminist Poetry," *Third Woman* 3:1–2 (1986): 73–80.

Cordova, Teresa, Norma Cantu, Gilberto Cardenas, Juan Garcia and Christine M. Sierra., editors. *Chicana Voices: Intersections of Class, Race, and Gender.* Austin, Texas: Center for Mexican American Studies, 1986. (Proceedings of the National Association of Chicano Studies Annual Meeting, Austin, Texas, 1984)

Cota-Cardenas, Margarita. "The Chicana in the City as Seen in Her Literature," *Frontiers: A Journal of Woman Studies* 6:1–2 (Spring-Summer 1981): 13–18.

Elizondo, Sergio D. "A Question of Origins and Presence in Chicano Literature," *Latin American Literary Review* 11:21 (Fall-Winter 1982): 39–43.

Grajeda, Rafael. "The Pachuco in Chicano Poetry: The Process of Legend-Creation," *Revista-Chicano-Riquena* 8:4 (1988): 45–59.

Herrera-Sobek, Maria, editor. *Beyond Stereotypes: the Critical Analysis of Chicana Literature*. Binghamton, New York: Bilingual Press, 1985.

——— and Helena Maria Viramontes. *Chicana Creativity and Criticism: Charting New Frontiers in American Literature*. Houston: Arte Público Press, 1988.

Hinojosa, Rolando. *Claros Varones de Belken / Fair Gentlemen of Belken County*. Tempe, Arizona: Editorial Bilingüe, 1986.

———. *El Condado de Belken—Klail City*. Tempe: Editorial Bilingüe, 1994.

———. *Crossing the Line: The Construction of a Poem*. Milwaukee: University of Wisconsin-Milwaukee, College of Letters and Science, Spanish Speaking Outreach Institute, 1981.

———. *Dear Rafe*. Houston: Arte Público Press, 1985.

———. *Estampas del Valle*. Tempe: Editorial Bilingüe, 1994.

———. *Estampas del Valle y Otras Obras = Sketches of the Valley and Other Works*. Berkeley: Quinto Sol, 1973; Editorial Justa, 1977, 1980.

———. *Generaciones, Notas, y Brechas = Generations, Notes, and Trails*. San Francisco: Casa Editorial, 1978.

———. *Klail City: a Novel*. Houston: Arte Público Press, 1987.

———. *Partners in Crime: A Rafe Buenrostro Mystery*. Houston: Arte Público Press, 1985.

———. *Rites and Witnesses: A Comedy*. Houston: Arte Público Press, 1982.

———. *The Useless Servants*. Houston: Arte Público Press, 1993.

———, Vernon E. Lattin, and Gary D. Keller, editors. *Tomás Rivera, 1935–1984: The Man and His Work*. Tempe: Bilingual Review/Press, 1988.

Horno-Delgado, Asuncion, Eliana Ortega, Nina M. Scott and Nancy Saporta-Sternbach, editors. *Breaking Boundaries: Latina Writings and Critical Readings*. Amherst: University of Massachusetts Press, 1989.

Jimenez, Francisco, editor. *The Identification and Analysis of Chicano Literature*. New York: Bilingual Review Press, 1979.

Márquez, Antonio C. "Richard Rodriguez' *Hunger of Memory* and the Poetics of

Experience," *Arizona Quarterly* 40:2 (Summer 1984): 130–41.

Miller, Beth, editor. *Women in Hispanic Literature: Icons and Fallen Idols.* Berkeley: University of California Press, 1983.

Moraga, Cherrie, and Gloria Anzaldúa, editors. *This Bridge Called My Back: Writings by Radical Women of Color.* New York: Kitchen Table / Women of Color Press, 1983.

Morales, Alejandro. *The Brick People.* Houston: Arte Público Press, 1988.

———. *The Rag Doll Plagues: A Novel.* Houston: Arte Público Press, 1991.

———. *The Death of an Anglo.* Tempe, Arizona: Bilingual Press, 1988.

Olivares, Julian, editor. *International Studies in Honor of Tomás Rivera.* Houston: Arte Público Press, 1985.

Ordóñez, Elizabeth. "The Concept of Cultural Identity in Chicana Poetry," *Third Women* 2:1 (1984): 75–82.

Padilla, Genaro M. "The Recovery of Nineteenth-Century Chicano Autobiography: 'tis not vengeance, it is regaining a loss,'" *American Quarterly* 40:3 (1988): 286–307.

Rivera, Tomás. *Always and Other Poems.* Sisterdale, Texas: Sisterdale Press, 1973.

———. *". . . y no se lo tragó la tierra."* Berkeley: Quinto Sol Publications, 1971.

———. *The Harvest: Short Stories.* Houston: Arte Público Press, 1988.

———. *The Searchers: Collected Poetry.* Houston: Arte Público Press, 1990.

———. *The Migrant Earth.* Houston: Arte Público Press, 1985.

Romero, Orlando. *Nambé—Year One.* Berkeley: Tonatiuh International, 1976.

Romo, Ricardo, editor. *Chicana Voices: Intersections of Class, Race and Gender.* Austin: Center for Mexican American Studies Publications, 1986.

Saldivar, Jose David, editor. *The Rolando Hinojosa Reader: Essays Historical and Critical.* Houston: Arte Público Press, 1985.

———. "The Ideological and the Utopian in Tomás Rivera's *. . . y no se lo tragó la tierra* and Ron Arias' *The Road to Tamazunchale,*" *Missions in Conflict: Essays on U.S.-Mexican Relations and Chicano Culture.* Renate von Bardeleben et al., editors. Tubingen: Narr, 1986. 203–14.

———. "Towards a Chicano Poetics: The Making of the Chicano-Chicana Subject, 1969–1982," *Confluencia: Revista Hispanica de Cultura y Literatura* I:2 (Spring 1986): 10–17.

Saldívar, Ramón. *Chicano Narrative: The Dialectics of Difference.* Madison: University of Wisconsin Press, 1990.

Sánchez, Marta Sánchez. *Contemporary Chicana Poetry: A Critical Approach to An Emerging Literature.* Berkeley: University of California Press, 1985.

Sanchez, Rosaura. *Chicano Discourse: Socio-Historic Perspectives.* Rowley, Massachusetts: Newbury House, 1983.

———. "Postmodernism and Chicano Literature," *Aztlán* 18:2 (Fall 1987): 1–14.

Sommers, Joseph, and Tomas Ybarra-Frausto, editors. *Modern Chicano Writers: A Collection of Critical Essays.* Englewood Cliffs, New Jersey: Prentice-Hall, 1979.

Soto, Pedro Juan. *Usmail.* Puerto Rico: Club del Libro, 1959.

———. *Spiks, Short Stories.* Mexico: Los Presentes, 1956.

———. *Hot Land / Cold Season.* New York: Dell, 1973.

———. *Palabras ad Vuelo.* Havana, Cuba: Casa de las Americas, 1990.

———. *Memoria de mi Amnesia.* Puerto Rico: Editorial Cultural, 1981.

Vásquez, Richard. *Chicano.* New York: Avon, 1970.

Villarreal, Jose Antonio. *Pocho.* Garden City, New York: Doubleday, 1959.

Zamora, Bernice. *Releasing Serpents.* Tempe, Arizona: Bilingual Press, 1994.

———. *Restless Serpents.* Menlo Park: Disenos Literarios, 1976.

Acknowledgments

"The Function of the La Llorona Motif in Anaya's *Bless Me, Ultima*" by Jane Rogers *Latin American Literary Review* Vol. V, No. 10 (Spring-Summer 1977). Reprinted in *Contemporary Chicano Fiction: A Critical Survey*, edited by Vernon E. Lattin. Copyright © 1986 by *Bilingual Press / Editorial Bilingüe*.

"Ron Arias' *The Road to Tamazunchale*: A Chicano Novel of the New Reality" by Eliud Martínez from *Latin American Literary Review* Vol. V, No. 10 (Spring-Summer 1977). Reprinted in *Contemporary Chicano Fiction: A Critical Survey*, edited by Vernon E. Lattin. Copyright © 1986 by *Bilingual Press / Editorial Bilingüe*.

"Buffaloes and Cockroaches: Acosta's Siege of Aztlán" by Norman D. Smith from *Latin American Literary Review*, Vol. V, No. 10 (Spring-Summer 1977). Copyright © 1977 by the *Latin American Literary Review*.

"*Pocho* and the American Dream" by Luther S. Luedtke from *Minority Voices* Vol. 1, No. 2 (Fall 1977). Reprinted in *Contemporary Chicano Fiction: A Critical Survey*, edited by Vernon E. Lattin. Copyright © 1986 by *Bilingual Press / Editorial Bilingüe*.

"The Concept of Time in *Nambé—Year One*" by Nasario García from *Latin American Literary Review* Vol. 7, No. 13 (Fall-Winter 1978). Reprinted in *Contemporary Chicano Fiction: A Critical Survey*, edited by Vernon E. Lattin. Copyright © 1986 by *Bilingual Press / Editorial Bilingüe*.

"On the Vicissitudes of Being 'Puerto Rican': An Exploration of Pedro Juan Soto's *Hot Land, Cold Season*" by Eduardo Seda Bonilla from *MELUS: The Journal of the Society for the Study of the Multi-Ethnic Literature of the United States*, Vol. 6, No. 3 (Fall 1979). Copyright © 1979 by the University of Southern California.

Index